Stand By Me

Daily, Sabbath and Festival Prayers

ISRA€L365

Stand By Me

*Daily, Sabbath
and Festival Prayers*

VOLUME 2

Edited by Shira Schechter and Rabbi Tuly Weisz

Table of Contents

Shira Schechter

ND IT WILL be, if you hearken to My commandments that I command you this day to love the Lord, your God, and to serve Him with all your heart and with all your soul" (Deuteronomy 11:13).

The great sage Maimonides (1204–1138) interprets the command to serve God with all your heart as a reference to prayer. Thus, prayer is often called 'worship of the heart.' But what does this mean?

Rabbi Samson Raphael Hirsch explains that the Hebrew word that means "to pray," (*lehitpalel*), is a reflexive form of the word *palel*, and means "to judge yourself." When we pray, we are not trying to change God's mind about what we do and do not deserve. Prayer is a form of self-reflection and transformation, a way to change ourselves so that we deserve the things that we are asking for.

But prayer is more than just making requests of God. The sages teach us that after the Temple in Jerusalem was destroyed in 70 CE, prayer replaced the daily offerings and animal sacrifices. This is based on the verse in Hosea 14:3, "Instead of bulls we will pay [the offering of] our lips." The Hebrew word for offering is *korban* (קרבן), which derives from the Hebrew word *karov* (קרוב), meaning "close." The purpose of bringing offerings in the Temple was to draw us closer to God. Similarly, through our prayers, we forge a deeper and closer relationship with the Almighty. In essence, prayer serves as a means of self-improvement and a way to connect more intimately with God.

When God created the world, He left the final step unfinished: "When no shrub of the field was yet on earth and no grasses of the field had yet sprouted, because the Lord God had not sent rain upon the earth and there was no man to till the soil" (Genesis 2:5). According to the medieval commentator known as Rashi (1040-1105), the world was missing a human being to recognize the need for rain and to pray for it. Since God desires a relationship with each and every one of us, He built the need for prayer into the natural order of the world.

"Worship of the heart" signifies this profound act of connecting with God through prayer. It is an internal process of self-judgment and transformation, aimed at aligning ourselves, our desires and our actions, with His will. Through heartfelt prayer, we not only change ourselves and ask God for help but also cultivate a closer, more intimate relationship with our Father in heaven. By going through this process, we fulfill the command to serve the Lord with all our heart and soul.

In *Stand By Me: Daily, Sabbath and Festival Prayers*, we present a selection of daily prayers and prayers said on holidays and special occasions. These prayers provide a framework for self-reflection on a daily basis, helping us to continually nurture and strengthen our relationship with the Almighty. This volume also includes prayers for the Sabbath and other sacred holidays, helping us draw closer to God through the unique spirit of these holy days.

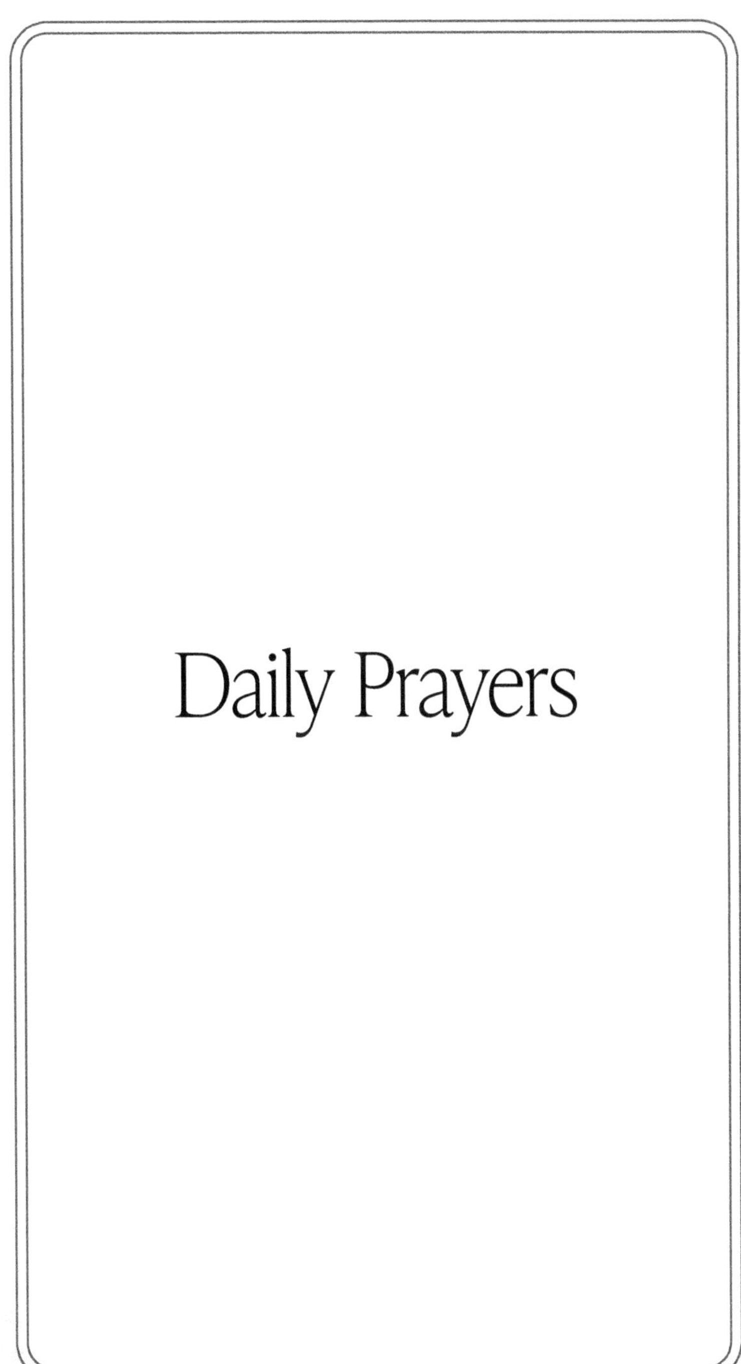

Daily Prayers

I Give Thanks

MODEH ANI, WHICH means "I give thanks," is a Jewish prayer recited daily upon waking up in the morning. We begin our day by thanking God for restoring our souls each morning.

Modeh ani lefanecha melech

chai vekayyam shehechezarta

bi nishmati bechemlah, rabbah

emunatecha.

מוֹדֶה אֲנִי לְפָנֶיךָ מֶלֶךְ

חַי וְקַיָּם שֶׁהֶחֱזַרְתָּ

בִּי נִשְׁמָתִי בְּחֶמְלָה, רַבָּה

אֱמוּנָתֶךָ.

I give thanks to You living and everlasting King for You have restored my soul with mercy. Great is Your faithfulness.

Notes

____

____

____

____

____

____

____

____

My Soul is Pure

R ECITED EVERY MORNING, this prayer expresses gratitude for the gift of our souls. It ends with a mention of the rresurrection, connecting our daily awakening to the future restoration at the time of redemption. The prayer also acknowledges that the souls God gives us are pure, and any of our defects or imperfections are the result of our own mistakes and shortcomings.

Elohai neshamah shennatatta
bi tehorah hi attah veratah attah
yetzartah attah nefachtah bi
ve'attah meshammerah bekirbi
ve'attah atid littelah mimmenni
ulehachazirah bi le'atid lavo,
kol zeman shehanneshamah
bekirbi modeh ani lefanecha
adonai elohai veilohei avotai
ribbon kol hamma'asim adon
kol hanneshamot: baruch attah
adonai hammachazir neshamot
lifgarim meitim.

אֱלֹהַי נְשָׁמָה שֶׁנָּתַתָּ
בִּי טְהוֹרָה הִיא אַתָּה בְרָאתָהּ אַתָּה
יְצַרְתָּהּ אַתָּה נְפַחְתָּהּ בִּי
וְאַתָּה מְשַׁמְּרָהּ בְּקִרְבִּי
וְאַתָּה עָתִיד לִטְּלָהּ מִמֶּנִּי
וּלְהַחֲזִירָהּ בִּי לֶעָתִיד לָבֹא,
כָּל זְמַן שֶׁהַנְּשָׁמָה
בְּקִרְבִּי מוֹדֶה אֲנִי לְפָנֶיךָ
יְהֹוָה אֱלֹהַי וֵאלֹהֵי אֲבוֹתַי
רִבּוֹן כָּל הַמַּעֲשִׂים אֲדוֹן
כָּל הַנְּשָׁמוֹת: בָּרוּךְ אַתָּה
יְהֹוָה הַמַּחֲזִיר נְשָׁמוֹת
לִפְגָרִים מֵתִים.

My God! The soul which You bestowed in me is pure; You created it, You formed it, You breathed it into me and You preserve it within me. You will eventually take it from me, and restore it in me in the time to come. So long as the soul is within me I give thanks to You, the Lord my God, and God of my fathers, Lord of all creatures, Master of all souls. Blessed are You, the Lord, Who restores souls to dead bodies.

Master of the Universe

Adon Olam, Master of the Universe, is a poem recited at the beginning of the morning prayers. It speaks of the greatness of God and declares our faith in His eternal sovereignty and His unwavering protection. In this prayer, God is referred to as an *Adon*, Master, as opposed to a *Melech*, King. The difference between a "King" and a "Master" lies in their levels of involvement in the lives of individuals. A king typically remains distant from the daily lives of the average citizen, whereas a master is deeply engaged in the lives of each of his servants. God is not only our King, but also our Master—intimately involved in every aspect of our lives.

Adon olam asher malach,	אֲדוֹן עוֹלָם אֲשֶׁר מָלַךְ,
beterem kol yetzir nivra.	בְּטֶרֶם כָּל יְצִיר נִבְרָא.
le'eit na'asah vecheftzo kol,	לְעֵת נַעֲשָׂה בְחֶפְצוֹ כֹּל,
azai melech shemo nikra.	אֲזַי מֶלֶךְ שְׁמוֹ נִקְרָא.
ve'acharei kichlot hakkol,	וְאַחֲרֵי כִּכְלוֹת הַכֹּל,
levaddo yimloch nora.	לְבַדּוֹ יִמְלֹךְ נוֹרָא.
vehu hayah vehu hoveh,	וְהוּא הָיָה וְהוּא הֹוֶה,
vehu yihyeh betif'arah.	וְהוּא יִהְיֶה בְּתִפְאָרָה.
vehu echad ve'ein sheini,	וְהוּא אֶחָד וְאֵין שֵׁנִי,
lehamshil lo lehachbirah.	לְהַמְשִׁיל לוֹ לְהַחְבִּירָה.
beli reshit beli tachlit,	בְּלִי רֵאשִׁית בְּלִי תַכְלִית,
velo ha'oz vehammisrah.	וְלוֹ הָעֹז וְהַמִּשְׂרָה.
vehu eili vechai go'ali,	וְהוּא אֵלִי וְחַי גּוֹאֲלִי,
vetzur chevli be'eit tzarah.	וְצוּר חֶבְלִי בְּעֵת צָרָה.
vehu nissi umanos li,	וְהוּא נִסִּי וּמָנוֹס לִי,
menat kosi beyom ekra.	מְנָת כּוֹסִי בְּיוֹם אֶקְרָא.
beyado afkid ruchi,	בְּיָדוֹ אַפְקִיד רוּחִי,

be'et ishan ve'a'irah.

ve'im ruchi geviyyati,

adonai li velo ira.

בְּעֵת אִישַׁן וְאָעִירָה.

וְעִם רוּחִי גְּוִיָּתִי,

יְהֹוָה לִי וְלֹא אִירָא.

Master of the Universe Who reigned before any creature was created. At the time when all was made by His will, then was His Name proclaimed King. And after all things shall cease to be, the Awesome One will reign alone. He was, He is, and He shall be in glory. He is One, and there is no second to compare to Him, to associate [with Him]. Without beginning, without end, power and dominion are His. He is my God and my ever-living Redeemer, the Rock of my destiny on the day of distress. He is my flag and my refuge; He is the portion of my cup on the day I call. Into His hand I entrust my spirit [both] when I sleep and when I awaken. And with my spirit my body [too], the Lord is with me, I shall not fear.

Notes

Exalted be the Living God

THE *YIGDAL* PRAYER presents Maimonides' thirteen princi-
ples of faith' in poetic form. It is recited at the beginning
of the morning service and often sung at the conclusion of
the evening service on the Sabbath and on holidays.

Yigdal elohim chai veyishtabbach,	יִגְדַּל אֱלֹהִים חַי וְיִשְׁתַּבַּח,
nimtza ve'ein eit el metzi'uto.	נִמְצָא וְאֵין עֵת אֶל מְצִיאוּתוֹ.
Echad ve'ein yachid keyichudo,	אֶחָד וְאֵין יָחִיד כְּיִחוּדוֹ,
ne'lam vegam ein sof le'achduto.	נֶעְלָם וְגַם אֵין סוֹף לְאַחְדוּתוֹ.
Ein lo demut hagguf ve'eino	אֵין לוֹ דְמוּת הַגּוּף וְאֵינוֹ
guf, lo na'aroch eilav kedushato.	גוּף, לֹא נַעֲרֹךְ אֵלָיו קְדֻשָּׁתוֹ.
Kadmon lechol davar asher nivra,	קַדְמוֹן לְכָל דָּבָר אֲשֶׁר נִבְרָא,
rishon ve'ein reishit lereishito.	רִאשׁוֹן וְאֵין רֵאשִׁית לְרֵאשִׁיתוֹ.
Hinno adon olam lechol notzar,	הִנּוֹ אֲדוֹן עוֹלָם לְכָל נוֹצָר,
yoreh gedullato umalchuto.	יוֹרֶה גְדֻלָּתוֹ וּמַלְכוּתוֹ.
shefa nevu'ato netano, el anshei	שֶׁפַע נְבוּאָתוֹ נְתָנוֹ, אֶל אַנְשֵׁי
segullato vetif'arto. Lo kam	סְגֻלָּתוֹ וְתִפְאַרְתּוֹ. לֹא קָם
beyisra'el kemosheh od, navi	בְּיִשְׂרָאֵל כְּמשֶׁה עוֹד, נָבִיא
umabbit et temunato. Torat emet	וּמַבִּיט אֶת תְּמוּנָתוֹ. תּוֹרַת אֱמֶת
natan le'ammo el, al yad nevi'o	נָתַן לְעַמּוֹ אֵל, עַל יַד נְבִיאוֹ
ne'eman beito. Lo yachalif ha'el	נֶאֱמַן בֵּיתוֹ. לֹא יַחֲלִיף הָאֵל
v'lo yamir dato, le'olamim lezulato.	וְלֹא יָמִיר דָּתוֹ, לְעוֹלָמִים לְזוּלָתוֹ.
Tzofeh ve'yodei'a setareinu,	צוֹפֶה וְיוֹדֵעַ סְתָרֵינוּ,
mabbit lesof davar bekadmato.	מַבִּיט לְסוֹף דָּבָר בְּקַדְמָתוֹ.
Gomel le'ish chesed kemif'alo,	גּוֹמֵל לְאִישׁ חֶסֶד כְּמִפְעָלוֹ,
notein lerasha ra kerish'ato.	נוֹתֵן לְרָשָׁע רַע כְּרִשְׁעָתוֹ.
Yishlach lekeitz hayyamin	יִשְׁלַח לְקֵץ הַיָּמִין
meshicheinu, lifdot mechakkei	מְשִׁיחֵנוּ, לִפְדוֹת מְחַכֵּי
keitz yeshu'ato. Meitim yechayyeh	קֵץ יְשׁוּעָתוֹ. מֵתִים יְחַיֶּה

el berov chasdo, baruch adei ad

sheim tehillato.

אֵל בְּרֹב חַסְדּוֹ, בָּרוּךְ עֲדֵי עַד שֵׁם תְּהִלָּתוֹ.

Exalted be the living God and praised, He exists unbounded by time. He is One, and there is no unity like His, He is inconceivable and His oneness is infinite. He has no physical form and is not corporeal, His holiness is beyond comparison. He preceded everything that was created, He is the First, and nothing existed before Him. He is the Master of the world and all that it contains, He shows His greatness and sovereignty. He granted the flow of prophecy to His treasured and glorious people. There has not arisen in Israel another prophet like Moses, who beheld His image. He gave the true Bible to His people through His prophet, His trusted house. God will never alter or change His law for eternity. He watches and knows our hidden secrets, He sees the end of a thing at its beginning. He recompenses man with kindness according to his deeds, He gives the wicked evil according to their wickedness. He will send, at the end of days, our Messiah, to redeem those who await His final salvation. God will revive the dead with His abundant mercy, Blessed is His glorious name forever.

Notes

Morning Blessings of Gratitude

Every day, at the beginning of the morning prayers, we recite a number of blessings in which we thank God for the good that He bestows upon us but which we so often take for granted. We express appreciation for all of the things that help us function in the world. Here are some of these morning blessings:

Baruch attah adonai eloheinu
melech ha'olam pokei'ach ivrim.

בָּרוּךְ אַתָּה יְהֹוָה אֱלֹהֵינוּ
מֶלֶךְ הָעוֹלָם פּוֹקֵחַ עִוְרִים.

Baruch attah adonai eloheinu
melech ha'olam malbish arummim.

בָּרוּךְ אַתָּה יְהֹוָה אֱלֹהֵינוּ
מֶלֶךְ הָעוֹלָם מַלְבִּישׁ עֲרֻמִּים.

Baruch attah adonai eloheinu
melech ha'olam mattir asurim.

בָּרוּךְ אַתָּה יְהֹוָה אֱלֹהֵינוּ
מֶלֶךְ הָעוֹלָם מַתִּיר אֲסוּרִים.

Baruch attah adonai eloheinu
melech ha'olam zokeif kefufim.

בָּרוּךְ אַתָּה יְהֹוָה אֱלֹהֵינוּ
מֶלֶךְ הָעוֹלָם זוֹקֵף כְּפוּפִים.

Baruch attah adonai eloheinu
melech ha'olam roka ha'aretz al
hammayim.

בָּרוּךְ אַתָּה יְהֹוָה אֱלֹהֵינוּ
מֶלֶךְ הָעוֹלָם רוֹקַע הָאָרֶץ עַל
הַמָּיִם.

Baruch attah adonai eloheinu
melech ha'olam she'asah li kol-
tzareki.

בָּרוּךְ אַתָּה יְהֹוָה אֱלֹהֵינוּ
מֶלֶךְ הָעוֹלָם שֶׁעָשָׂה לִי כָּל־
צָרְכִּי.

Baruch attah adonai eloheinu
melech ha'olam hammeichin

בָּרוּךְ אַתָּה יְהֹוָה אֱלֹהֵינוּ
מֶלֶךְ הָעוֹלָם הַמֵּכִין

mitz'adei gaver.

מִצְעֲדֵי גָבֶר.

Baruch attah adonai eloheinu
melech ha'olam ozeir yisra'el
bigvurah.

בָּרוּךְ אַתָּה יְהֹוָה אֱלֹהֵינוּ
מֶלֶךְ הָעוֹלָם אוֹזֵר יִשְׂרָאֵל
בִּגְבוּרָה.

Baruch attah adonai eloheinu
melech ha'olam oteir yisra'el
betif'arah.

בָּרוּךְ אַתָּה יְהֹוָה אֱלֹהֵינוּ
מֶלֶךְ הָעוֹלָם עוֹטֵר יִשְׂרָאֵל
בְּתִפְאָרָה.

Baruch attah adonai eloheinu
melech ha'olam hannotein
layya'eif koach.

בָּרוּךְ אַתָּה יְהֹוָה אֱלֹהֵינוּ
מֶלֶךְ הָעוֹלָם הַנּוֹתֵן
לַיָּעֵף כֹּחַ.

Baruch attah adonai eloheinu
melech ha'olam hamma'avir
shenah me'einai utenumah
me'af'appai.

בָּרוּךְ אַתָּה יְהֹוָה אֱלֹהֵינוּ
מֶלֶךְ הָעוֹלָם הַמַּעֲבִיר
שֵׁנָה מֵעֵינָי וּתְנוּמָה
מֵעַפְעַפָּי.

Blessed are You, the Lord our God, King of the Universe,
Who gives sight to the blind.
Blessed are You, the Lord our God, King of the Universe,
Who clothes the naked.
Blessed are You, the Lord our God, King of the Universe,
Who releases the imprisoned.
Blessed are You, the Lord our God, King of the Universe,
Who straightens the bent.
Blessed are You, the Lord our God, King of the Universe,
Who spreads the earth above the waters.
Blessed are You, the Lord our God, King of the Universe,
Who provided me with all my needs.
Blessed are You, the Lord our God, King of the Universe,

Who prepares the steps of man.
Blessed are You, the Lord our God, King of the Universe,
Who girds Israel with might.
Blessed are You, the Lord our God, King of the Universe,
Who crowns Israel with glory.
Blessed are You, the Lord our God, King of the Universe,
Who gives strength to the weary.
Blessed are You, the Lord our God, King of the Universe,
Who removes sleep from my eyes and slumber from my eyelids.

Notes

May it be Your Will

The following prayer, authored by the great sage Rabbi Judah the Prince (135- 217), seeks divine protection against the harmful influences and negative occurrences we face in our daily lives.

Yehi ratzon millefanecha adonai	יְהִי רָצוֹן מִלְּפָנֶיךָ יְהֹוָה
elohai veilohei avotai shettatzileini	אֱלֹהַי וֵאלֹהֵי אֲבוֹתַי שֶׁתַּצִּילֵנִי
hayyom uvechol-yom mei'azzei	הַיּוֹם וּבְכָל־יוֹם מֵעַזֵּי
fanim ume'azzut panim mei'adam	פָנִים וּמֵעַזּוּת פָּנִים מֵאָדָם
ra umeichaver ra umishachein	רָע וּמֵחָבֵר רָע וּמִשָּׁכֵן
ra umippega ra umissatan	רָע וּמִפֶּגַע רָע וּמִשָּׂטָן
hammashchit middin kasheh	הַמַּשְׁחִית מִדִּין קָשֶׁה
umibba'al din kasheh ,bein shehu	וּמִבַּעַל דִּין קָשֶׁה, בֵּין שֶׁהוּא
ven berit uvein she'eino ven berit.	בֶן בְּרִית וּבֵין שֶׁאֵינוֹ בֶן בְּרִית.

May it be Your will, the Lord, my God and God of my fathers, to save me today and every day from arrogant men and from arrogance; from an evil man, from an evil companion, from an evil neighbor; from an evil mishap and from the destructive Satan; from a difficult judgment and a difficult opponent, whether he is a member of the covenant or not a member of the covenant.

Notes

____

____

____

Raise Me Up! - Psalm 30

PSALM 30 WAS originally written to be sung at the inauguration of the Temple. Today, we recite this psalm daily to inaugurate our morning prayers which, the sages tell us, take the place of the offerings that were brought in the Temple. In this psalm, we thank God for lifting us up, even if we have fallen to the lowest of places. We seek His help to raise us from our struggles and transform our sorrow into joy, reaffirming our trust in His ability to elevate us from any hardship.

Mizmor shir chanukkat habbayit
ledavid: aromimcha adonai ki
dillitani velo-simmachta oyevai
li: adonai elohai shivva'ti eleicha
vattirpa'eini: adonai he'elita min-
she'ol nafshi chiyyitani miyyaredi-
vor: zammeru ladonai chasidav
vehodu lezeicher kodsho: ki
rega be'appo chayyim birtzono
ba'erev yalin bechi velabboker
rinnah: va'ani amarti veshalvi
bal-emmot le'olam: adonai
birtzonecha he'emadtah leharri
oz histarta fanecha hayiti nivhal:
eleicha adonai ekra ve'el-adonai
etchannan: mah-betza bedami
beridti el shachat hayodecha
afar hayaggid amittecha: shema
adonai vechanneini adonai

מִזְמוֹר שִׁיר־חֲנֻכַּת הַבַּיִת
לְדָוִד: אֲרוֹמִמְךָ יְהֹוָה כִּי
דִלִּיתָנִי וְלֹא־שִׂמַּחְתָּ אֹיְבַי
לִי: יְהֹוָה אֱלֹהָי שִׁוַּעְתִּי אֵלֶיךָ
וַתִּרְפָּאֵנִי: יְהֹוָה הֶעֱלִיתָ מִן־
שְׁאוֹל נַפְשִׁי חִיִּיתַנִי מִיָּרְדִי־
בוֹר: זַמְּרוּ לַיהֹוָה חֲסִידָיו
וְהוֹדוּ לְזֵכֶר קָדְשׁוֹ: כִּי
רֶגַע בְּאַפּוֹ חַיִּים בִּרְצוֹנוֹ
בָּעֶרֶב יָלִין בֶּכִי וְלַבֹּקֶר
רִנָּה: וַאֲנִי אָמַרְתִּי בְשַׁלְוִי
בַּל־אֶמּוֹט לְעוֹלָם: יְהֹוָה
בִּרְצוֹנְךָ הֶעֱמַדְתָּה לְהַרְרִי
עֹז הִסְתַּרְתָּ פָנֶיךָ הָיִיתִי נִבְהָל:
אֵלֶיךָ יְהֹוָה אֶקְרָא וְאֶל־אֲדֹנָי
אֶתְחַנָּן: מַה־בֶּצַע בְּדָמִי
בְּרִדְתִּי אֶל שָׁחַת הֲיוֹדְךָ
עָפָר הֲיַגִּיד אֲמִתֶּךָ: שְׁמַע
יְהֹוָה וְחָנֵּנִי יְהֹוָה

heyeih-ozeir li: hafachta mispedi
lemachol li pittachta sakki
vatte'azzereni simchah: lema'an
yezammercha chavod velo
yiddom adonai elohai le'olam
odekka:

הֱיֵה־עֹזֵר לִי: הָפַכְתָּ מִסְפְּדִי
לְמָחוֹל לִי פִּתַּחְתָּ שַׂקִּי
וַתְּאַזְּרֵנִי שִׂמְחָה: לְמַעַן
יְזַמֶּרְךָ כָבוֹד וְלֹא
יִדֹּם יְהֹוָה אֱלֹהַי לְעוֹלָם
אוֹדֶךָּ:

A Psalm, a song for the inauguration of the Temple, by David. I will exalt You, O Lord, for You have upheld me, and not let my foes rejoice over me. O Lord, my God, I cried out to You, and You healed me. O Lord, You have raised my soul from the lower world. You have kept me alive, lest I descend to the Pit. Sing to the Lord, [you,] His pious ones, and give thanks to His holy Name. For His anger lasts only a moment, but there is [long] life, in His conciliation. In the evening, one retires weeping, but in the morning there is [a cry of] joy! I said, in my serenity, I would never be moved. [But,] O Lord, it was Your will [alone] that established my mountain as a stronghold. When You concealed Your Presence, I was terrified. To You, O Lord, I called, and my Master I beseeched. What gain is there in [the shedding of] my blood? In my going down to destruction? Will the dust acknowledge You? Will it proclaim Your truth? Hear [me] O Lord, and be gracious to me, O Lord, be a help to me. You have turned my mourning into dancing, You have loosened my sackcloth and supported me with joy. In order that my soul might sing to You and not be stilled, O Lord, my God, forever will I thank You.

Notes

Blessed is He Who Spoke

THIS PRAYER OPENS the section of the morning service in which we praise God, acknowledging Him as the Creator and compassionate Sustainer of all things. By beginning with this praise, we recognize that God is the only One Who can answer our requests. These praises also foster a deeper closeness with Him, increasing the likelihood that our prayers will be heard. Thus, praising God is not just an introduction but an integral part of the essence of prayer.

Baruch she'amar vehayah	בָּרוּךְ שֶׁאָמַר וְהָיָה
ha'olam. Baruch hu. Baruch oseh	הָעוֹלָם. בָּרוּךְ הוּא. בָּרוּךְ עוֹשֶׂה
vereishit. Baruch omer ve'oseh.	בְרֵאשִׁית. בָּרוּךְ אוֹמֵר וְעוֹשֶׂה.
Baruch gozeir umekayyeim.	בָּרוּךְ גּוֹזֵר וּמְקַיֵּם.
Baruch meracheim al-ha'aretz.	בָּרוּךְ מְרַחֵם עַל־הָאָרֶץ.
Baruch meracheim al-habberiyyot.	בָּרוּךְ מְרַחֵם עַל־הַבְּרִיּוֹת.
Baruch meshalleim sachar	בָּרוּךְ מְשַׁלֵּם שָׂכָר
tov lirei'av. Baruch chai la'ad	טוֹב לִירֵאָיו. בָּרוּךְ חַי לָעַד
vekayyam lanetzach. Baruch	וְקַיָּם לָנֶצַח. בָּרוּךְ
podeh umatzil. Baruch shemo.	פּוֹדֶה וּמַצִּיל. בָּרוּךְ שְׁמוֹ.
Baruch attah adonai eloheinu	בָּרוּךְ אַתָּה יְהֹוָה אֱלֹהֵינוּ
melech ha'olam ha'eil ha'av	מֶלֶךְ הָעוֹלָם הָאֵל הָאָב
harachaman hammehullal befi	הָרַחֲמָן הַמְהֻלָּל בְּפִי
ammo meshubbach umefo'ar	עַמּוֹ מְשֻׁבָּח וּמְפֹאָר
bilshon chasidav va'avadav	בִּלְשׁוֹן חֲסִידָיו וַעֲבָדָיו
uveshirei david avdecha.	וּבְשִׁירֵי דָוִד עַבְדֶּךָ.
Nehallelcha adonai eloheinu	נְהַלֶּלְךָ יְהֹוָה אֱלֹהֵינוּ
bishvachot uvizmirot negaddelcha	בִּשְׁבָחוֹת וּבִזְמִירוֹת נְגַדֶּלְךָ
uneshabbeichacha unefa'ercha	וּנְשַׁבֵּחֲךָ וּנְפָאֶרְךָ

venazkir shimcha venamlich'cha   וְנַזְכִּיר שְׁמְךָ וְנַמְלִיכְךָ

malkeinu eloheinu. Yachid chei   מַלְכֵּנוּ אֱלֹהֵינוּ. יָחִיד חֵי

ha'olamim. melech meshubbach   הָעוֹלָמִים. מֶלֶךְ מְשֻׁבָּח

umefo'ar adei-ad shemo   וּמְפֹאָר עֲדֵי־עַד שְׁמוֹ

haggadol. Baruch attah adonai   הַגָּדוֹל. בָּרוּךְ אַתָּה יְהֹוָה

melech mehullal battishbachot.   מֶלֶךְ מְהֻלָּל בַּתִּשְׁבָּחוֹת.

Blessed is He Who spoke, and the world came into being, blessed is He; blessed is He Who maintains the creation; blessed is He Who says and does; blessed is He Who decrees and fulfills; blessed is He Who has compassion on the earth; blessed is He Who has compassion on the creatures; blessed is He Who rewards well those who fear Him, blessed is He Who lives forever and exists eternally; blessed is He Who redeems and saves blessed is His Name. Blessed are You, O Lord, our God, King of the Universe, the Almighty, the merciful Father, Who is verbally extolled by His people, praised and glorified by the tongue of His pious ones, and His servants, and through the songs of David Your servant. We will extoll You, O Lord our God, with praises and psalms; we will exalt, praise, and glorify You; we will mention Your Name, and proclaim You—our King, our God. Unique One, Life of the worlds, King, praised and glorified forever is His great Name. Blessed are You, the Lord, King, Who is extolled with praises.

Notes

____

____

____

____

A Song of Thanksgiving

PSALM 100 WAS recited in the Temple on days when thanksgiving offerings were brought on the altar. The sages included it in our daily prayers to express gratitude for the countless miracles God performs for us every day, many of which we are not even aware.

Mizmor letodah hari'u ladonai
kol-ha'aretz: ivdu et adonai
besimchah bo'u lefanav birnanah:
de'u ki-adonai hu elohim hu
asanu velo anachnu ammo vetzon
mar'ito: bo'u she'arav betodah
chatzeirotav bithillah hodu lo
barechu shemo: ki-tov adonai
le'olam chasdo ve'ad-dor vador
emunato:

מִזְמוֹר לְתוֹדָה הָרִיעוּ לַיהֹוָה
כָּל־הָאָרֶץ: עִבְדוּ אֶת יְהֹוָה
בְּשִׂמְחָה בֹּאוּ לְפָנָיו בִּרְנָנָה:
דְּעוּ כִּי־יְהֹוָה הוּא אֱלֹהִים הוּא
עָשָׂנוּ וְלוֹ אֲנַחְנוּ עַמּוֹ וְצֹאן
מַרְעִיתוֹ: בֹּאוּ שְׁעָרָיו בְּתוֹדָה
חֲצֵרֹתָיו בִּתְהִלָּה הוֹדוּ לוֹ
בָּרְכוּ שְׁמוֹ: כִּי־טוֹב יְהֹוָה
לְעוֹלָם חַסְדּוֹ וְעַד־דֹּר וָדֹר
אֱמוּנָתוֹ:

A song of thanksgiving: Shout for joy to the Lord, everyone on earth. Serve the Lord with joy, come before Him with exultation. Know that the Lord is God, He has made us, and we are His, His people and the sheep of His pasturing. Enter His gates with thanksgiving, His courtyards with praise. Give thanks to Him, bless His Name for the Lord is good, His loving kindness is eternal, and to every generation His faithfulness extends.

God's Glory will Endure Forever

THIS PRAYER INTRODUCES the next group of prayers, Psalms 145-150, which form the main part of the morning service that is dedicated to praising God. It is composed of a collection of verses from Psalms, Chronicles, and Proverbs, in which the Divine Name is mentioned multiple times. The Divine Name should be pronounced with utmost concentration, while remembering that God is the Supreme Master of all existence.

Yehi chevod adonai le'olam	יְהִי כְבוֹד יְהֹוָה לְעוֹלָם
yismach adonai bema'asav: yehi	יִשְׂמַח יְהֹוָה בְּמַעֲשָׂיו: יְהִי
shem adonai mevorach mei'attah	שֵׁם יְהֹוָה מְבֹרָךְ מֵעַתָּה
ve'ad-olam: mimmizrach-shemesh	וְעַד־עוֹלָם: מִמִּזְרַח־שֶׁמֶשׁ
ad-mevo'o mehullal sheim	עַד־מְבוֹאוֹ מְהֻלָּל שֵׁם
adonai: ram al-kol-goyim adonai	יְהֹוָה: רָם עַל־כָּל־גּוֹיִם יְהֹוָה
al hashamayim kevodo: adonai	עַל הַשָּׁמַיִם כְּבוֹדוֹ: יְהֹוָה
shimcha le'olam adonai zichrecha	שִׁמְךָ לְעוֹלָם יְהֹוָה זִכְרְךָ
ledor-vador: adonai bashamayim	לְדֹר־וָדֹר: יְהֹוָה בַּשָּׁמַיִם
heichin kis'o umalchuto bakkol	הֵכִין כִּסְאוֹ וּמַלְכוּתוֹ בַּכֹּל
mashalah: yismechu hashamayim	מָשָׁלָה: יִשְׂמְחוּ הַשָּׁמַיִם
vetageil ha'aretz veyomru	וְתָגֵל הָאָרֶץ וְיֹאמְרוּ
vaggoyim adonai malach: adonai	בַגּוֹיִם יְהֹוָה מָלָךְ: יְהֹוָה
melech adonai malach adonai	מֶלֶךְ יְהֹוָה מָלָךְ יְהֹוָה
yimloch le'olam va'ed: adonai	יִמְלֹךְ לְעֹלָם וָעֶד: יְהֹוָה
melech olam va'ed avedu goyim	מֶלֶךְ עוֹלָם וָעֶד אָבְדוּ גוֹיִם
me'artzo: adonai heifir atzat-goyim	מֵאַרְצוֹ: יְהֹוָה הֵפִיר עֲצַת־גּוֹיִם
heini machshevot ammim: rabbot	הֵנִיא מַחְשְׁבוֹת עַמִּים: רַבּוֹת
machashavot belev-ish va'atzat	מַחֲשָׁבוֹת בְּלֶב־אִישׁ וַעֲצַת
adonai hi takum: atzat adonai	יְהֹוָה הִיא תָקוּם: עֲצַת יְהֹוָה

le'olam ta'amod machshevot libbo   לְעוֹלָם תַּעֲמֹד מַחְשְׁבוֹת לִבּוֹ

ledor vador: ki hu amar vayyehi   לְדֹר וָדֹר: כִּי הוּא אָמַר וַיֶּהִי

hu-tzivvah vayya'amod: ki vachar   הוּא־צִוָּה וַיַּעֲמֹד: כִּי בָחַר

adonai betziyyon ivvah lemoshav   יְהֹוָה בְּצִיּוֹן אִוָּה לְמוֹשָׁב

lo: ki-ya'akov bachar lo yah yisra'el   לוֹ: כִּי־יַעֲקֹב בָּחַר לוֹ יָה יִשְׂרָאֵל

lisgullato: ki lo yittosh adonai   לִסְגֻלָּתוֹ: כִּי לֹא יִטֹּשׁ יְהֹוָה

ammo venachalato lo ya'azov: עַמּוֹ וְנַחֲלָתוֹ לֹא יַעֲזֹב:

vehu rachum yechapper avon   וְהוּא רַחוּם יְכַפֵּר עָוֹן

velo-yashchit vehirbah lehashiv   וְלֹא־יַשְׁחִית וְהִרְבָּה לְהָשִׁיב

appo velo-ya'ir kol-chamato: אַפּוֹ וְלֹא־יָעִיר כָּל־חֲמָתוֹ:

adonai hoshi'ah hammelech   יְהֹוָה הוֹשִׁיעָה הַמֶּלֶךְ

ya'aneinu veyom-kare'einu.   יַעֲנֵנוּ בְיוֹם־קָרְאֵנוּ.

The glory of the Lord will endure forever; the Lord will rejoice in His works. The Name of the Lord will be blessed from now forever. From the rising of the sun to its setting, praised is the Name of the Lord. High above all nations is the Lord, above the heavens is His glory. O Lord, Your Name is forever, O Lord, Your Mention is for generations. The Lord has established His throne in heaven, [but] His dominion rules over all. The heavens will rejoice, the earth will exult, and they will proclaim among the nations: the Lord has begun His reign. The Lord is King, the Lord was King; the Lord will be King forever and ever." The Lord will reign for all eternity [when] nations have perished from His earth. The Lord annuls the counsel of nations, He disrupts the intention of peoples. Many thoughts are in the heart of man, but [only] the Lord's counsel will endure. The counsel of the Lord will stand forever, the thoughts of His heart throughout all generations. For He spoke and it came to be; He commanded and it stood. For the Lord has chosen Zion; He desired it for His dwelling place. For God chose Jacob to be His, Israel for His treasure. For the Lord will not cast off His people, and His inheritance, He will not abandon. And He, the Merciful One, atones iniquity; and does not destroy. He frequently withdraws

His anger and does not arouse all His rage. O Lord, deliver [us!]
The King will answer us on the day we call.

Notes

Fortunate are Those Who Dwell in Your House

P SALM 145 is an important component of our daily prayers. The Sages state that whoever recites it three times every day is worthy of a share in the world to come. To teach us the importance of preparing ourselves through silent contemplation "in the house of God" before approaching God in prayer, the Sages added two verses to the beginning of this psalm. The verses of this psalm are arranged in alphabetical order, representing the highest form of praise for God, as we honor Him with all the sounds we are capable of making.

Ashrei yoshevei veitecha od	אַשְׁרֵי יוֹשְׁבֵי בֵיתֶךָ עוֹד
yehallucha selah: ashrei ha'am	יְהַלְלוּךָ סֶּלָה: אַשְׁרֵי הָעָם
shekkachah lo ashrei ha'am	שֶׁכָּכָה לּוֹ אַשְׁרֵי הָעָם
she'adonai elohav: tehillah	שֶׁיהוָה אֱלֹהָיו: תְּהִלָּה
ledavid aromimcha elohai	לְדָוִד אֲרוֹמִמְךָ אֱלוֹהַי
hammelech va'avarechah shimcha	הַמֶּלֶךְ וַאֲבָרְכָה שִׁמְךָ
le'olam va'ed: bechol-yom	לְעוֹלָם וָעֶד: בְּכָל־יוֹם
avarechekka va'ahallah shimcha	אֲבָרְכֶךָּ וַאֲהַלְלָה שִׁמְךָ
le'olam va'ed: gadol adonai	לְעוֹלָם וָעֶד: גָּדוֹל יְהוָה
umehullal me'od veligdullato ein	וּמְהֻלָּל מְאֹד וְלִגְדֻלָּתוֹ אֵין
cheker: dor ledor yeshabbach	חֵקֶר: דּוֹר לְדוֹר יְשַׁבַּח
ma'asecha ugevurotecha	מַעֲשֶׂיךָ וּגְבוּרֹתֶיךָ
yaggidu: hadar kevod hodecha	יַגִּידוּ: הֲדַר כְּבוֹד הוֹדֶךָ
vedivrei nifle'otecha asichah:	וְדִבְרֵי נִפְלְאֹתֶיךָ אָשִׂיחָה:
ve'ezuz nore'otecha yomeiru	וֶעֱזוּז נוֹרְאֹתֶיךָ יֹאמֵרוּ
ugedullatecha asapperennah:	וּגְדֻלָּתְךָ אֲסַפְּרֶנָּה:

zeicher rav-tuvecha yabbi'u	זֵכֶר רַב־טוּבְךָ יַבִּיעוּ
vetzidkatecha yeranneinu:	וְצִדְקָתְךָ יְרַנֵּנוּ׃
channun verachum adonai	חַנּוּן וְרַחוּם יְהוָֹה
erech appayim ugedal-	אֶרֶךְ אַפַּיִם וּגְדָל־
chased: tov-adonai lakkol	חָסֶד׃ טוֹב־יְהוָֹה לַכֹּל
verachamav al-kol-ma'asav:	וְרַחֲמָיו עַל־כָּל־מַעֲשָׂיו׃
yoducha adonai kol-ma'asecha	יוֹדוּךָ יְהוָֹה כָּל־מַעֲשֶׂיךָ
vachasidecha yevarechuchah:	וַחֲסִידֶיךָ יְבָרְכוּכָה׃
kevod malchutecha yomeiru	כְּבוֹד מַלְכוּתְךָ יֹאמֵרוּ
ugevuratecha yedabbeiru:	וּגְבוּרָתְךָ יְדַבֵּרוּ׃
lehodia' livnei ha'adam gevurotav	לְהוֹדִיעַ לִבְנֵי הָאָדָם גְּבוּרֹתָיו
uchevod hadar malchuto:	וּכְבוֹד הֲדַר מַלְכוּתוֹ׃
malchutecha malchut kol-olamim	מַלְכוּתְךָ מַלְכוּת כָּל־עֹלָמִים
umemshaltecha bechol-dor vador:	וּמֶמְשַׁלְתְּךָ בְּכָל־דּוֹר וָדֹר׃
someich adonai lechol-hannofelim	סוֹמֵךְ יְהוָֹה לְכָל־הַנֹּפְלִים
vezokeif lechol-hakkefufim:	וְזוֹקֵף לְכָל־הַכְּפוּפִים׃
einei-chol eilecha yesabbeiru	עֵינֵי־כֹל אֵלֶיךָ יְשַׂבֵּרוּ
ve'attah notein-lahem et-ochlam	וְאַתָּה נוֹתֵן־לָהֶם אֶת־אָכְלָם
be'itto: Potei'ach et-yadecha	בְּעִתּוֹ׃ פּוֹתֵחַ אֶת־יָדֶךָ
umasbia' lechol-chai ratzon:	וּמַשְׂבִּיעַ לְכָל־חַי רָצוֹן׃
tzaddik adonai bechol-derachav	צַדִּיק יְהוָֹה בְּכָל־דְּרָכָיו
vechasid bechol-ma'asav: karov	וְחָסִיד בְּכָל־מַעֲשָׂיו׃ קָרוֹב
adonai lechol-kore'av lechol asher	יְהוָֹה לְכָל־קֹרְאָיו לְכֹל אֲשֶׁר
yikra'uhu ve'emet: retzon-yerei'av	יִקְרָאֻהוּ בֶאֱמֶת׃ רְצוֹן־יְרֵאָיו
ya'aseh ve'et-shav'atam yishma	יַעֲשֶׂה וְאֶת־שַׁוְעָתָם יִשְׁמַע
veyoshi'em: shomer adonai et-	וְיוֹשִׁיעֵם׃ שׁוֹמֵר יְהוָֹה אֶת־
kol-ohavav ve'eit kol-haresha'im	כָּל־אֹהֲבָיו וְאֵת כָּל־הָרְשָׁעִים
yashmid: tehillat adonai yedabber	יַשְׁמִיד׃ תְּהִלַּת יְהוָֹה יְדַבֶּר
pi vivareich kol-basar sheim	פִּי וִיבָרֵךְ כָּל־בָּשָׂר שֵׁם
kodsho le'olam va'ed: va'anachnu	קָדְשׁוֹ לְעוֹלָם וָעֶד׃ וַאֲנַחְנוּ
nevareich yah mei'attah ve'ad-	נְבָרֵךְ יָהּ מֵעַתָּה וְעַד־
olam halluyah:	עוֹלָם הַלְלוּיָהּ׃

Fortunate are those who dwell in Your house; may they continue to praise You, Selah. Fortunate is the nation whose lot is thus; fortunate is the nation for whom the Lord is their God. A praise by David! I will exalt You, my God, the King, and bless Your Name forever and ever. Every day I will bless You and extol Your Name forever and ever. The Lord is great and highly extolled, and His greatness is unfathomable. One generation to another will praise Your works, and Your mighty acts they will declare. The splendor of Your glorious majesty, and the words of Your wonders I will speak. Of Your awesome might, they will speak, and Your greatness I will recount. Mention of Your bountifulness they will express, and in Your righteousness joyfully exult. The Lord is gracious and merciful, slow to anger and great in kindliness. The Lord is good to all, His mercy encompasses all His works. All Your works will thank You, O Lord, and Your pious ones will bless You. Of the honor of Your kingship, they will speak, and Your might they will declare. To reveal to men His mighty acts, and the glorious splendor of His kingship. Your kingship is the kingship for all times, and Your dominion is in every generation. The Lord supports all the fallen, and straightens all the bent. The eyes of all look expectantly to You, and You give them their food at its proper time. You open Your hand and satisfy the desire of every living being. The Lord is just in all His ways and benevolent in all His deeds. The Lord is near to all who call upon Him, to all who call upon Him in truth. The will of those who fear Him, He fulfills; He hears their cry and delivers them. The Lord watches over all those who love Him, and will destroy all the wicked. Praise of the Lord, my mouth will declare and all flesh will bless His holy Name forever and ever. And we will bless God from now forever. Praise God.

Hallelujah! - Psalms 146-150

Rabbi Samson Raphael Hirsch considers Psalms 146-150, in addition to 145, as the most significant of all the psalms composed by David. These psalms are integral to the section of praise that opens our morning prayers. Each psalm begins and ends with the word "Hallelujah!," "Praise God," and together they represent a sequential progression that invites everyone—Jews and non-Jews alike—to join in King David's praise of God in the restored city of Zion. Ultimately, every nation will unite in universal praise of God, with every soul joining in harmony.

Psalm 146

Halleluyah halli nafshi et-adonai:	הַלְלוּיָהּ הַלְלִי נַפְשִׁי אֶת־יְהֹוָה:
ahallah adonai bechayyai	אֲהַלְלָה יְהֹוָה בְּחַיָּי
azammerah lelohai be'odi: al-	אֲזַמְּרָה לֵאלֹהַי בְּעוֹדִי: אַל־
tivtechu vindivim beven-adam	תִּבְטְחוּ בִנְדִיבִים בְּבֶן־אָדָם
she'ein lo teshu'ah: tetzei rucho	שֶׁאֵין לוֹ תְשׁוּעָה: תֵּצֵא רוּחוֹ
yashuv le'admato bayyom hahu	יָשֻׁב לְאַדְמָתוֹ בַּיּוֹם הַהוּא
avedu eshtonotav: ashrei she'eil	אָבְדוּ עֶשְׁתֹּנֹתָיו: אַשְׁרֵי שֶׁאֵל
ya'akov be'ezro, sivro al-adonai	יַעֲקֹב בְּעֶזְרוֹ, שִׂבְרוֹ עַל־יְהֹוָה
elohav: oseh shamayim va'aretz	אֱלֹהָיו: עֹשֶׂה שָׁמַיִם וָאָרֶץ
et-hayyam ve'et-kol-asher-bam,	אֶת־הַיָּם וְאֶת־כָּל־אֲשֶׁר־בָּם,
hashomer emet le'olam: oseh	הַשֹּׁמֵר אֱמֶת לְעוֹלָם: עֹשֶׂה
mishpat la'ashukim notein lechem	מִשְׁפָּט לַעֲשׁוּקִים נֹתֵן לֶחֶם
lare'eivim adonai mattir asurim:	לָרְעֵבִים יְהֹוָה מַתִּיר אֲסוּרִים:
adonai pokei'ach ivrim adonai	יְהֹוָה פֹּקֵחַ עִוְרִים יְהֹוָה
zokeif kefufim adonai oheiv	זֹקֵף כְּפוּפִים יְהֹוָה אֹהֵב
tzaddikim: adonai shomeir et-	צַדִּיקִים: יְהֹוָה שֹׁמֵר אֶת־

geirim yatom ve'almanah ye'oded   גֵּרִים יָתוֹם וְאַלְמָנָה יְעוֹדֵד

vederech resha'im ye'avveit: וְדֶרֶךְ רְשָׁעִים יְעַוֵּת:

yimloch adonai le'olam elohayich   יִמְלֹךְ יְהוָֹה לְעוֹלָם אֱלֹהַיִךְ

tziyyon ledor vador halleluyah: צִיּוֹן לְדֹר וָדֹר הַלְלוּיָהּ:

Praise God! My soul, praise the Lord. I will praise the Lord with my life; I will sing to my God as long as I live. Do not place your trust [even] in noble men, in man who has no [power of] deliverance. [When] his spirit departs, he returns to his earth; on that day his plans come to naught. Fortunate [is he] when the Almighty of Jacob is his help, whose expectation is on the Lord, his God. He makes heaven and earth, the sea and all that is in them; He keeps His promises faithfully forever. He performs justice for the oppressed; He gives bread to the hungry; the Lord releases the imprisoned. The Lord gives sight to the blind; the Lord straightens the bent. The Lord loves the righteous. The Lord protects strangers; the orphan and widow He enables to stand firm; and the way of the wicked He thwarts. the Lord will reign forever; your God, Zion, throughout all generations. Praise God.

Psalm 147

Halleluyah ki-tov zammerah   הַלְלוּיָהּ כִּי־טוֹב זַמְּרָה

eloheinu, ki-na'im navah tehillah: אֱלֹהֵינוּ, כִּי־נָעִים נָאוָה תְהִלָּה:

boneh yerushalayim adonai   בּוֹנֵה יְרוּשָׁלַם יְהוָֹה

nidchei yisra'el yechanneis: נִדְחֵי יִשְׂרָאֵל יְכַנֵּס:

harofei lishvurei lev umechabbesh   הָרוֹפֵא לִשְׁבוּרֵי לֵב וּמְחַבֵּשׁ

le'atzevotam: moneh mispar   לְעַצְּבוֹתָם: מוֹנֶה מִסְפָּר

lakkochavim lechullam sheimot   לַכּוֹכָבִים לְכֻלָּם שֵׁמוֹת

yikra: gadol adoneinu verav-koach   יִקְרָא: גָּדוֹל אֲדוֹנֵינוּ וְרַב־כֹּחַ

litvunato ein mispar: me'odeid   לִתְבוּנָתוֹ אֵין מִסְפָּר: מְעוֹדֵד

anavim adonai mashpil resha'im   עֲנָוִים יְהוָה מַשְׁפִּיל רְשָׁעִים

adei-aretz: enu ladonai betodah   עֲדֵי־אָרֶץ: עֱנוּ לַיהוָה בְּתוֹדָה

zammeru leiloheinu vechinnor: זַמְּרוּ לֵאלֹהֵינוּ בְכִנּוֹר:

hammechasseh shamayim   הַמְכַסֶּה שָׁמַיִם

be'avim hammeichin la'aretz matar   בְּעָבִים הַמֵּכִין לָאָרֶץ מָטָר

hammatzmiach harim chatzir: הַמַּצְמִיחַ הָרִים חָצִיר:

notein livheimah lachmah livnei   נוֹתֵן לִבְהֵמָה לַחְמָהּ לִבְנֵי

oreiv asher yikra'u: lo vigvurat   עֹרֵב אֲשֶׁר יִקְרָאוּ: לֹא בִגְבוּרַת

hassus yechpatz lo veshokei   הַסּוּס יֶחְפָּץ לֹא בְשׁוֹקֵי

ha'ish yirtzeh: rotzeh adonai   הָאִישׁ יִרְצֶה: רוֹצֶה יְהוָה

et-yere'av et-hammeyachalim   אֶת־יְרֵאָיו אֶת־הַמְיַחֲלִים

lechasdo: shabbechi yerushalayim   לְחַסְדּוֹ: שַׁבְּחִי יְרוּשָׁלַם

et adonai halli elohayich tziyyon: אֶת יְהוָה הַלְלִי אֱלֹהַיִךְ צִיּוֹן:

ki-chizzak berichei she'arayich   כִּי־חִזַּק בְּרִיחֵי שְׁעָרָיִךְ

beirach banayich bekirbeich: בֵּרַךְ בָּנַיִךְ בְּקִרְבֵּךְ:

hassam-gevuleich shalom cheilev   הַשָּׂם־גְּבוּלֵךְ שָׁלוֹם חֵלֶב

chittim yasbi'ech: hasholei'ach   חִטִּים יַשְׂבִּיעֵךְ: הַשֹּׁלֵחַ

imrato aretz ad-meheirah yarutz   אִמְרָתוֹ אָרֶץ עַד־מְהֵרָה יָרוּץ

devaro: hannotein sheleg   דְּבָרוֹ: הַנֹּתֵן שֶׁלֶג

katzamer kefor ka'eifer yefazzer: כַּצָּמֶר כְּפוֹר כָּאֵפֶר יְפַזֵּר:

mashliach karcho chefittim lifnei   מַשְׁלִיךְ קַרְחוֹ כְפִתִּים לִפְנֵי

karato mi ya'amod: yishlach   קָרָתוֹ מִי יַעֲמֹד: יִשְׁלַח

devaro veyamseim yasheiv rucho   דְּבָרוֹ וְיַמְסֵם יַשֵּׁב רוּחוֹ

yizzelu-mayim: maggid devarav   יִזְּלוּ־מָיִם: מַגִּיד דְּבָרָיו

leya'akov chukkav umishpatav   לְיַעֲקֹב חֻקָּיו וּמִשְׁפָּטָיו

leyisra'el: lo asah chein lechol-   לְיִשְׂרָאֵל: לֹא עָשָׂה כֵן לְכָל־

goy umishpatim bal-yeda'um   גּוֹי וּמִשְׁפָּטִים בַּל־יְדָעוּם

halleluyah: הַלְלוּיָהּ:

Praise God! for it is good to sing to our God; for [His] praise is pleasant, befitting. The builder of Jerusalem is the Lord; the banished ones of Israel He will gather. [He is] the Healer of the broken-hearted and [also] binds up their wounds. He fixes the number of stars; He calls all of them by names. Great is our Master and abundant in power; His understanding is beyond reckoning. The Lord causes the humble to stand firm; He casts down the wicked to the ground. Cry out to the Lord in thanksgiving; sing to our God with the harp. [He] Who covers the heaven with clouds, Who prepares rain for the earth; Who causes grass to grow upon the hills. Who gives the animal its fodder; [also] to the young ravens which call. Not the power of the horse does He desire, nor the thighs of man does He want. The Lord wants those who fear Him, those who hope for His kindliness. Jerusalem, praise the Lord; Zion, extol your God. For He has fortified the bars of your gates; He has blessed your children in your midst. He established peace at your border; with prime wheat He satisfies you. He dispatches His command earthward; His word races swiftly. He provides snow like fleece, He scatters frost like ashes. He hurls His ice like crumbs; who can withstand His cold? He dispatches His word and melts them; He blows His wind, they flow as water. He declares His word to Jacob, His statutes and His laws to Israel. He did not do so to any [other] nation; and of His laws they were not informed. Praise God.

Psalm 148

Halleluyah halelu et-adonai	הַלְלוּיָהּ הַלְלוּ אֶת־יְהֹוָה
min hashamayim haleluhu	מִן הַשָּׁמַיִם הַלְלוּהוּ
bammeromim: haleluhu kol-	בַּמְּרוֹמִים: הַלְלוּהוּ כָל־
mal'achav haleluhu kol-tzeva'av:	מַלְאָכָיו הַלְלוּהוּ כָּל־צְבָאָיו:
haleluhu shemesh veyarei'ach	הַלְלוּהוּ שֶׁמֶשׁ וְיָרֵחַ
haleluhu kol-kochevei or: haleluhu	הַלְלוּהוּ כָּל־כּוֹכְבֵי אוֹר: הַלְלוּהוּ
shemei hashamayim vehammayim	שְׁמֵי הַשָּׁמַיִם וְהַמַּיִם
asher mei'al hashamayim:	אֲשֶׁר מֵעַל הַשָּׁמָיִם:
yehalelu et-sheim adonai ki hu	יְהַלְלוּ אֶת־שֵׁם יְהֹוָה כִּי הוּא

tzivvah venivra'u: vayya'amideim	צִוָּה וְנִבְרָאוּ: וַיַּעֲמִידֵם
la'ad le'olam chak-natan velo	לָעַד לְעוֹלָם חָק־נָתַן וְלֹא
ya'avor: halelu et-adonai min-	יַעֲבוֹר: הַלְלוּ אֶת־יְהֹוָה מִן־
ha'aretz tanninim vechol-tehomot:	הָאָרֶץ תַּנִּינִים וְכָל־תְּהֹמוֹת:
eish uvarad sheleg vekitor ruach	אֵשׁ וּבָרָד שֶׁלֶג וְקִיטוֹר רוּחַ
se'arah osah devaro: heharim	סְעָרָה עֹשָׂה דְבָרוֹ: הֶהָרִים
vechol-geva'ot eitz peri vechol-	וְכָל־גְּבָעוֹת עֵץ פְּרִי וְכָל־
arazim: hachayyah vechol-	אֲרָזִים: הַחַיָּה וְכָל־
beheimah remes vetzippor kanaf:	בְּהֵמָה רֶמֶשׂ וְצִפּוֹר כָּנָף:
malchei-eretz vechol-le'ummim	מַלְכֵי־אֶרֶץ וְכָל־לְאֻמִּים
sarim vechol-shofetei aretz:	שָׂרִים וְכָל־שֹׁפְטֵי אָרֶץ:
bachurim vegam-betulot zekeinim	בַּחוּרִים וְגַם־בְּתוּלוֹת זְקֵנִים
im-ne'arim: yehalelu et-sheim	עִם־נְעָרִים: יְהַלְלוּ אֶת־שֵׁם
adonai ki-nisgav shemo levaddo	יְהֹוָה כִּי־נִשְׂגָּב שְׁמוֹ לְבַדּוֹ
hodo al-eretz veshamayim:	הוֹדוֹ עַל־אֶרֶץ וְשָׁמָיִם:
vayyarem keren le'ammo tehillah	וַיָּרֶם קֶרֶן לְעַמּוֹ תְּהִלָּה
lechol-chasidav livnei yisra'el am	לְכָל־חֲסִידָיו לִבְנֵי יִשְׂרָאֵל עַם
kerovo halleluyah:	קְרֹבוֹ הַלְלוּיָהּ:

Praise God. Praise the Lord from the sky; Praise Him in the heights! Praise Him, all His angels; Praise Him, all His hosts! Praise Him, sun and moon; Praise Him, all the stars of light. Praise Him, skies of skies, and the waters that are above the skies. They will praise the Name of the Lord, for He commanded it and they were created. He established them for all time, for as long as the world exists; He decreed it and it is unalterable. Praise the Lord from the earth, sea-monsters and all [that dwell in] the depths. Fire and hail, snow and vapor, stormwind, [all] fulfilling His word. The mountains and all the hills, fruit trees and all cedars. Wild beasts and all animals, creeping things and winged fowl. Earthly kings and all peoples, ministers and all earthly judges. Young men and also maidens, elders together with lads. They will praise the Name of the Lord, for His Name alone is exalted; His majesty is over the earth and the skies. He will raise the might of His people, [which is] praise for all His pious ones, for the Children of Israel, the people near to Him. Praise God.

Psalm 149

Halleluyah shiru ladonai shir
chadash tehillato bik'hal chasidim:
yismach yisra'el be'osav benei-
tziyyon yagilu vemalkam: yehalelu
shemo vemachol betof vechinnor
yezammeru-lo: ki-rotzeh adonai
be'ammo yefa'eir anavim bishu'ah:
ya'lezu chasidim bechavod
yerannenu al-mishkevotam:
romemot el bigronam vecherev
pifiyyot beyadam: la'asot nekamah
vaggoyim tocheichot bal'ummim:
le'sor malcheihem bezikkim
venichbedeihem bechavlei
varzel: la'asot bahem mishpat
katuv hadar hu lechol-chasidav
halleluyah:

הַלְלוּיָהּ שִׁירוּ לַיהוָה שִׁיר
חָדָשׁ תְּהִלָּתוֹ בִּקְהַל חֲסִידִים:
יִשְׂמַח יִשְׂרָאֵל בְּעֹשָׂיו בְּנֵי־
צִיּוֹן יָגִילוּ בְמַלְכָּם: יְהַלְלוּ
שְׁמוֹ בְמָחוֹל בְּתֹף וְכִנּוֹר
יְזַמְּרוּ־לוֹ: כִּי־רוֹצֶה יְהוָה
בְּעַמּוֹ יְפָאֵר עֲנָוִים בִּישׁוּעָה:
יַעְלְזוּ חֲסִידִים בְּכָבוֹד
יְרַנְּנוּ עַל־מִשְׁכְּבוֹתָם:
רוֹמְמוֹת אֵל בִּגְרוֹנָם וְחֶרֶב
פִּיפִיּוֹת בְּיָדָם: לַעֲשׂוֹת נְקָמָה
בַּגּוֹיִם תּוֹכֵחֹת בַּלְאֻמִּים:
לֶאְסֹר מַלְכֵיהֶם בְּזִקִּים
וְנִכְבְּדֵיהֶם בְּכַבְלֵי
בַרְזֶל: לַעֲשׂוֹת בָּהֶם מִשְׁפָּט
כָּתוּב הָדָר הוּא לְכָל־חֲסִידָיו
הַלְלוּיָהּ:

Praise God. Sing a new song to the Lord, His praise in the assembly of the pious. Israel will rejoice in its Maker; the children of Zion will exult in their King. They will praise His Name with dance; with drum and harp they will make music to Him. Because the Lord desires His people; He will adorn the humble with deliverance. The pious will rejoice in honor; they will sing joyously upon their beds. High praises of the Almighty in their throats, and a double-edged sword in their hand. To perform vengeance upon the nations, chastisement upon

*the peoples. To bind their kings with chains, and their nobles with
iron fetters. To execute upon them [the] written judgment; it is the
splendor of all His pious ones. Praise God.*

Psalm 150

Halleluyah hallu-el bekodsho
halleluhu birkia' uzzo: halleluhu
bigvurotav halleluhu kerov gudlo:
halleluhu beteika shofar halleluhu
beneivel vechinnor: halleluhu
betof umachol halleluhu beminnim
ve'ugav: halleluhu vetziltzelei-
shama halleluhu betziltzelei
teru'ah: kol hanneshamah tehallel
yah halleluyah: kol hanneshamah
tehallel yah halleluyah:

הַלְלוּיָהּ הַלְלוּ־אֵל בְּקָדְשׁוֹ
הַלְלוּהוּ בִּרְקִיעַ עֻזּוֹ: הַלְלוּהוּ
בִּגְבוּרֹתָיו הַלְלוּהוּ כְּרֹב גֻּדְלוֹ:
הַלְלוּהוּ בְּתֵקַע שׁוֹפָר הַלְלוּהוּ
בְּנֵבֶל וְכִנּוֹר: הַלְלוּהוּ
בְּתֹף וּמָחוֹל הַלְלוּהוּ בְּמִנִּים
וְעֻגָב: הַלְלוּהוּ בְּצִלְצְלֵי־
שָׁמַע הַלְלוּהוּ בְּצִלְצְלֵי
תְרוּעָה: כֹּל הַנְּשָׁמָה תְּהַלֵּל
יָהּ הַלְלוּיָהּ: כֹּל הַנְּשָׁמָה
תְּהַלֵּל יָהּ הַלְלוּיָהּ:

*Praise God. Praise the Almighty in His Sanctuary Praise God in the
firmament of His might Praise Him for His mighty deeds; Praise
Him according to the abundance of His greatness. Praise Him with
the blowing of the shofar (ram's horn); praise Him with lyre and
harp. Praise Him with drum and dance. Praise Him with stringed
instruments and flute. Praise Him with resounding cymbals. Praise
Him with clanging cymbals. Let every soul praise God. Praise God.
Let every soul praise God. Praise God.*

Notes

Praised be Your Name

THE FOLLOWING BLESSING concludes the section of praise in the morning prayers. It acknowledges that God is worthy of endless praise and that we should indeed continue praising Him forever. By reciting these words, we recognize that, although we can never fully express adequate recognition and praise for our Creator, our hearts remain filled with gratitude as we transition to the next part of our prayers.

Yishtabbach shimcha la'ad malkeinu. Ha'eil hammelech haggadol vehakkadosh bashamayim uva'aretz. Ki lecha na'eh adonai eloheinu veilohei avoteinu. Shir ushevachah halleil vezimrah. Oz umemshalah. netzach gedullah ugevurah. Tehillah vetif'eret. Kedushah umalchut. Berachot vehoda'ot mei'attah ve'ad-olam. Baruch attah adonai el melech gadol battishbachot. El hahoda'ot adon hannifla'ot habbocheir beshirei zimrah. melech el chei ha'olamim.

יִשְׁתַּבַּח שִׁמְךָ לָעַד מַלְכֵּנוּ. הָאֵל הַמֶּלֶךְ הַגָּדוֹל וְהַקָּדוֹשׁ בַּשָּׁמַיִם וּבָאָרֶץ. כִּי לְךָ נָאֶה יְהֹוָה אֱלֹהֵינוּ וֵאלֹהֵי אֲבוֹתֵינוּ. שִׁיר וּשְׁבָחָה הַלֵּל וְזִמְרָה. עֹז וּמֶמְשָׁלָה. נֶצַח גְּדֻלָּה וּגְבוּרָה. תְּהִלָּה וְתִפְאֶרֶת. קְדֻשָּׁה וּמַלְכוּת. בְּרָכוֹת וְהוֹדָאוֹת מֵעַתָּה וְעַד־עוֹלָם. בָּרוּךְ אַתָּה יְהֹוָה אֵל מֶלֶךְ גָּדוֹל בַּתִּשְׁבָּחוֹת. אֵל הַהוֹדָאוֹת אֲדוֹן הַנִּפְלָאוֹת הַבּוֹחֵר בְּשִׁירֵי זִמְרָה. מֶלֶךְ אֵל חֵי הָעוֹלָמִים.

Praised be Your Name forever, our King, Almighty the great and holy King in heaven and on earth. For to You it is fitting [to offer] the Lord, our God, and God of our fathers, song and praise, glorification and hymns, [to proclaim Your] strength and dominion, victory, grandeur, and might, praise and glory, holiness and sovereignty, blessings and thanksgivings, from now and forever. Blessed are You, the Lord, Almighty, King [Who is] great in [our] praise Almighty, of [to Whom we offer our] thanksgiving, Master of [Whom we praise for His] wonders, the Selector of song-hymns, You are the King, Almighty, Life of [all] the worlds.

Notes

Shema Yisrael - Hear O' Israel!

THE *SHEMA YISRAEL* prayer begins with one of the most sacred and powerful verses in the Bible, central to Jewish faith and practice. By reciting this verse, we acknowledge the singularity and oneness of God and accept His sovereignty over us. The Shema prayer is recited both at night and in the morning, to fulfill the verse in Deuteronomy 6:7, "And you shall say them... when you lie down and when you get up."

Shema yisra'el adonai eloheinu
adonai echad.

שְׁמַע יִשְׂרָאֵל יְהֹוָה אֱלֹהֵינוּ
יְהֹוָה אֶחָד.

Hear, Israel: the Lord is our God, the Lord is One.

The next two paragraphs of the *Shema Yisrael* prayer describe the rewards and punishments for keeping or violating God's commands. Once we accept Him as our ruler, we can accept and commit ourselves to following His laws.

Deuteronomy 6:5-9

Ve'ahavta eit adonai elhecha
bechol levavecha uvechol
nafshecha uvechol meodecha:
vehayu haddevarim ha'eilleh
asher anochi metzavvecha hayom
al levavecha: veshinnantam
levanecha vedibbarta bam

וְאָהַבְתָּ אֵת ה׳ אֱלֹהֶיךָ
בְּכָל לְבָבְךָ וּבְכָל
נַפְשְׁךָ וּבְכָל מְאֹדֶךָ:
וְהָיוּ הַדְּבָרִים הָאֵלֶּה
אֲשֶׁר אָנֹכִי מְצַוְּךָ הַיּוֹם
עַל לְבָבֶךָ: וְשִׁנַּנְתָּם
לְבָנֶיךָ וְדִבַּרְתָּ בָּם

beshivtecha beveitecha	בְּשִׁבְתְּךָ בְּבֵיתֶךָ
uvelechtecha vadderech	וּבְלֶכְתְּךָ בַדֶּרֶךְ
uveshochbecha uvekumecha:	וּבְשָׁכְבְּךָ וּבְקוּמֶךָ:
ukeshartam le'ot al yadecha	וּקְשַׁרְתָּם לְאוֹת עַל יָדֶךָ
vehayu letotafot bein einecha:	וְהָיוּ לְטֹטָפֹת בֵּין עֵינֶיךָ:
uchetavtam al mezuzot beitecha	וּכְתַבְתָּם עַל מְזֻזוֹת בֵּיתֶךָ
uvish'arecha:	וּבִשְׁעָרֶיךָ:

*And you shall love the Lord your God with all your heart and with
all your soul and with all your possessions. And these words which I
command you today, shall be upon your heart. And you shall teach
them sharply to your children. And you shall discuss them when
you sit in your house, and when you travel on the road, and when
you lie down and when you rise. And you shall bind them for a sign
upon your hand, and they shall be for ornaments between your
eyes. And you shall write them upon the doorposts of your house
and upon your gateways.*

Deuteronomy 11:13-21

Vehayah im shamo'a tishme'u	וְהָיָה אִם שָׁמֹעַ תִּשְׁמְעוּ
el mitzvotai asher anochi	אֶל מִצְוֹתַי אֲשֶׁר אָנֹכִי
metzavecha etchem hayom	מְצַוֶּה אֶתְכֶם הַיּוֹם
le'ahavah et adonai eloheichem	לְאַהֲבָה אֶת ה׳ אֱלֹהֵיכֶם
ule'avedo bechol levavechem	וּלְעָבְדוֹ בְּכָל לְבַבְכֶם
uvechol nafshechem: venatatti	וּבְכָל נַפְשְׁכֶם: וְנָתַתִּי
metar artzechem be'itto yoreh	מְטַר אַרְצְכֶם בְּעִתּוֹ יוֹרֶה
umalkosh ve'asafta deganecha	וּמַלְקוֹשׁ וְאָסַפְתָּ דְגָנֶךָ
vetiroshecha veyitzharecha:	וְתִירֹשְׁךָ וְיִצְהָרֶךָ:
venatatti eisev besadcha	וְנָתַתִּי עֵשֶׂב בְּשָׂדְךָ
livhemtecha ve'achalta vesava'ta:	לִבְהֶמְתֶּךָ וְאָכַלְתָּ וְשָׂבָעְתָּ:
hishameru lachem pen yifteh	הִשָּׁמְרוּ לָכֶם פֶּן יִפְתֶּה
levav'chem vesartem va'avad'tem	לְבַבְכֶם וְסַרְתֶּם וַעֲבַדְתֶּם

elohim acheirim vehishtachavitem	אֱלֹהִים אֲחֵרִים וְהִשְׁתַּחֲוִיתֶם
lahem: vecharah af adonai	לָהֶם: וְחָרָה אַף ה'
bachem ve'atzar et hashamayim	בָּכֶם וְעָצַר אֶת הַשָּׁמַיִם
velo yihyeh matar veha'adamah	וְלֹא יִהְיֶה מָטָר וְהָאֲדָמָה
lo titten et yevulah va'avadtem	לֹא תִתֵּן אֶת יְבוּלָהּ וַאֲבַדְתֶּם
meheirah mei'al ha'aretz hattovah	מְהֵרָה מֵעַל הָאָרֶץ הַטֹּבָה
asher adonai notein lachem:	אֲשֶׁר ה' נֹתֵן לָכֶם:
vesamtem et devarai eilleh al	וְשַׂמְתֶּם אֶת דְּבָרַי אֵלֶּה עַל
levavchem ve'al nafshechem	לְבַבְכֶם וְעַל נַפְשְׁכֶם
ukeshartem otam le'ot al yedchem	וּקְשַׁרְתֶּם אֹתָם לְאוֹת עַל יֶדְכֶם
vehayu letotafot bein eineichem:	וְהָיוּ לְטוֹטָפֹת בֵּין עֵינֵיכֶם:
velimmad'tem otam et beneichem	וְלִמַּדְתֶּם אֹתָם אֶת בְּנֵיכֶם
ledabbeir bam beshivtecha	לְדַבֵּר בָּם בְּשִׁבְתְּךָ
beveitecha uvelechtecha	בְּבֵיתֶךָ בְלֶכְתְּךָ
vadderech uv'shochbecha	בַדֶּרֶךְ וּבְשָׁכְבְּךָ
uv'kumecha: uch'tavtam al	וּבְקוּמֶךָ: וּכְתַבְתָּם עַל
mezuzot beitecha uvish'arecha:	מְזוּזוֹת בֵּיתֶךָ וּבִשְׁעָרֶיךָ:
lema'an yirbu yemeichem vimei	לְמַעַן יִרְבּוּ יְמֵיכֶם וִימֵי
veneichem al ha'adamah asher	בְנֵיכֶם עַל הָאֲדָמָה אֲשֶׁר
nishba adonai la'avoteichem	נִשְׁבַּע ה' לַאֲבֹתֵיכֶם
lateit lahem kimei hashamayim al	לָתֵת לָהֶם כִּימֵי הַשָּׁמַיִם עַל
ha'aretz:	הָאָרֶץ:

And it will be— if you vigilantly obey My commandments which I command you this day, to love the Lord your God, and serve Him with your entire hearts and with your entire souls— that I will give rain for your land in its proper time, the early (autumn) rain and the late (spring) rain; and you will harvest your grain and your wine and your oil. And I will put grass in your fields for your cattle, and you will eat and be satisfied. Beware lest your hearts be swayed and you turn astray, and you worship alien gods and bow to them. And the Lord's fury will blaze among you, and He will close off the heavens and there will be no rain and the earth will not yield its produce; and you will perish swiftly from the good land which the Lord gives you. Place these words of Mine upon your hearts and upon your souls, and bind them for a sign upon your hands, and they shall be ornaments between your eyes. And you shall teach them to your sons, to speak of them when you sit in your house, and when you travel on the road, and when you lie down and when you rise. And you shall write them upon the doorposts of your house and upon your gateways. In order that your days be prolonged, and the days of your children, upon the land which the Lord swore to your fathers to give them [for as long] as the heavens are above the earth.

Notes

Standing before God: The Silent Amidah Prayer

THE SILENT *AMIDAH* (standing) prayer, recited in the morning, afternoon, and evening, is the central prayer of our daily worship, when we truly feel that we are standing in God's presence. It consists of 19 blessings, beginning with three blessings of praise, followed by blessings in which we make requests of God, and concluding with three blessings of gratitude and thanks. We include here some selected blessings from this prayer.

Who is Like You? An Introduction to the Silent Amidah Prayer

The following prayer introduces the silent *Amidah* prayer. These verses were selected for their deep reverence of God's unfathomable and awe-inspiring works. Our ancestors, despite witnessing incredible miracles, recognized that God's actions transcend human comprehension. By opening the silent *Amidah* with these words, we approach God humbly, offering praise and gratitude for His everlasting kindness, while acknowledging the mystery of His ways.

Mi chamochah ba'eilim adonai.	מִי כָמֹכָה בָּאֵלִים ה׳.
Mi kamochah ne'dar bakkodesh.	מִי כָּמֹכָה נֶאְדָּר בַּקֹּדֶשׁ.
Nora tehillot. oseh fele.	נוֹרָא תְהִלֹּת. עשה כֶּלֶא.
Shirah chadashah shibbechu	שִׁירָה חֲדָשָׁה שִׁבְּחוּ
ge'ulim leshimcha al s'fat hayyam.	גְאוּלִים לְשִׁמְךָ עַל שְׂפַת הַיָּם.

yachad kullam hodu vehimlichu
ve'ameru: adonai yimloch le'olam
va'ed.

יַֽחַד כֻּלָּם הוֹדוּ וְהִמְלִֽיכוּ
וְאָמְרוּ: ה׳ יִמְלֹךְ לְעוֹלָם
וָעֶד.

Tzur yisra'el kumah be'ezrat
yisra'el ufedeih chin'umecha
yehudah veyisra'el, go'aleinu
adonai tzeva'ot shemo kedosh
yisra'el. Baruch attah adonai ga'al
yisra'el.

צוּר יִשְׂרָאֵל קֽוּמָה בְּעֶזְרַת
יִשְׂרָאֵל וּפְדֵה כִנְאֻמֶֽךָ
יְהוּדָה וְיִשְׂרָאֵל, גֹּאֲלֵֽנוּ
יְהֹוָה צְבָאוֹת שְׁמוֹ קְדוֹשׁ
יִשְׂרָאֵל. בָּרוּךְ אַתָּה יְהֹוָה גָּאַל
יִשְׂרָאֵל.

Who is like You among the mighty, O Lord! Who is like You— [You are] adorned in holiness, awesome in praise, performing wonders!

With a new song the redeemed people praised Your Name at the seashore! All of them gave thanks in unison and proclaimed Your sovereignty and said: "The Lord will reign forever and ever."

Rock of Israel, arise to the aid of Israel, and liberate Judah and Israel as You promised. Our Redeemer—'Lord of hosts' is His Name, the Holy One of Israel. Blessed are You, O Lord, Who redeemed Israel.

Open My Lips

Before beginning the silent *Amidah* prayer, we recite a verse from Psalm 51. We ask God to open up our lips so that we can declare His praise. With this verse, we acknowledge that standing before God can fill us with such awe and fear that we might be rendered speechless. We therefore ask God for the ability to speak in His presence. This verse also reminds us that the ability to speak, often taken for granted, is itself a daily miracle, granted to us by the Creator.

Adonai sefatai tiftach ufi yaggid
tehillatecha.

אֲדֹנָי שְׂפָתַי תִּפְתָּח וּפִי יַגִּיד
תְּהִלָּתֶךָ.

My Master, open my lips, and my mouth will declare Your praise.

The Shield of Abraham

The silent *Amidah* prayer begins with three blessings of praise, exalting God as the ultimate Source of existence and the Master of nature. These blessings are a necessary prelude to making requests of the Almighty, as it would be improper to begin our dialogue with God by immediately presenting our needs. The first blessing invokes Abraham, Isaac, and Jacob, acknowledging their role as the pioneers of prayer to God.

Baruch attah adonai eloheinu
veilohei avoteinu elohei avraham
elohei yitzchak veilohei ya'akov
ha'eil haggadol haggibbor
vehannora el elyon gomeil
chasadim tovim vekoneih hakkol
vezocheir chasdei avot umeivi
go'el livnei veneihem lema'an
shemo be'ahavah: melech ozeir
umoshia' umagein. Baruch attah
adonai magein avraham.

בָּרוּךְ אַתָּה יְהֹוָה אֱלֹהֵינוּ
וֵאלֹהֵי אֲבוֹתֵינוּ אֱלֹהֵי אַבְרָהָם
אֱלֹהֵי יִצְחָק וֵאלֹהֵי יַעֲקֹב
הָאֵל הַגָּדוֹל הַגִּבּוֹר
וְהַנּוֹרָא אֵל עֶלְיוֹן גּוֹמֵל
חֲסָדִים טוֹבִים וְקוֹנֵה הַכֹּל
וְזוֹכֵר חַסְדֵי אָבוֹת וּמֵבִיא
גוֹאֵל לִבְנֵי בְנֵיהֶם לְמַעַן
שְׁמוֹ בְּאַהֲבָה: מֶלֶךְ עוֹזֵר
וּמוֹשִׁיעַ וּמָגֵן: בָּרוּךְ אַתָּה
יְהֹוָה מָגֵן אַבְרָהָם

Blessed are You, the Lord, our God, and God of our fathers, God of Abraham, God of Isaac, and God of Jacob, the Almighty, the Great, the Powerful, the Awesome, most high Almighty, Who bestows beneficent kindness, Who possesses everything, Who remembers the piety of the Patriarchs, and Who brings a redeemer to their children's children, for the sake of His Name, with love. King, Helper, and Deliverer and Shield. Blessed are You, the Lord, Shield of Abraham.

The Revival of the Dead

The second blessing mentions God's power to revive the dead five times. Rabbi Isaiah Wohlgemuth explains that this repetition alludes to the various ways God "revives the dead." While one reference is to the great resurrection prophesied for the end of times, it also encompasses other forms of revival. These include restoring our souls each morning, providing life-giving rain, and supporting those whose misfortunes have left them experiencing a meta-phorical "living death."

Attah gibbor le'olam adonai	אַתָּה גִבּוֹר לְעוֹלָם אֲדֹנָי
mechayyeih meitim attah rav	מְחַיֶּה מֵתִים אַתָּה רַב
lehoshia'	לְהוֹשִׁיעַ
(in the summer, say) morid hattal	בקיץ: מוֹרִיד הַטָּל
(in the winter, say) mashiv haruach	בחורף: מַשִּׁיב הָרוּחַ
umorid haggeshem	וּמוֹרִיד הַגֶּשֶׁם
mechalkeil chayyim bechesed	מְכַלְכֵּל חַיִּים בְּחֶסֶד
mechayyeih meitim berachamim	מְחַיֶּה מֵתִים בְּרַחֲמִים
rabbim someich nofelim verofei	רַבִּים סוֹמֵךְ נוֹפְלִים
cholim umattir asurim umekayyeim	וְרוֹפֵא חוֹלִים וּמַתִּיר אֲסוּרִים
emunato lisheinei afar, mi	וּמְקַיֵּם אֱמוּנָתוֹ לִישֵׁנֵי
chamocha ba'al gevurot umi	עָפָר, מִי כָמוֹךָ בַּעַל גְּבוּרוֹת
domeh lach melech meimit	וּמִי דוֹמֶה לָּךְ מֶלֶךְ מֵמִית

umechayyeh umatzmiach

yeshu'ah. Vene'eman attah

lehachayot meitim: baruch attah

adonai mechayyeih hammeitim:

וּמְחַיֶּה וּמַצְמִיחַ

יְשׁוּעָה. וְנֶאֱמָן אַתָּה

לְהַחֲיוֹת מֵתִים: בָּרוּךְ אַתָּה

יְהֹוָה מְחַיֵּה הַמֵּתִים.

You are mighty forever, my Master; You are the Resurrector of the dead the Powerful One to deliver us.

In the summer season, say: He causes the dew to descend. In the winter season, say: Causer of the wind to blow and of the rain to fall.

Sustainer of the living with kindliness, Resurrector of the dead with great mercy, Supporter of the fallen, and Healer of the sick, and Releaser of the imprisoned, and Fulfiller of His faithfulness to those who sleep in the dust. Who is like You, Master of mighty deeds, and who can be compared to You? King Who causes death and restores life, and causes deliverance to sprout forth. And You are faithful to restore the dead to life. Blessed are You, the Lord, Resurrector of the dead.

The Holiness of God

The third blessing in the silent *Amidah* prayer highlights the holiness of God. Leviticus 19:2 teaches us that because God is holy, we have an obligation to conduct ourselves in a way that is holy and dignified. As we recite this blessing, we reflect on God's holiness and reaffirm our commitment to live according to His divine standards.

Attah kadosh veshimcha kadosh

ukedoshim bechol-yom

אַתָּה קָדוֹשׁ וְשִׁמְךָ

קָדוֹשׁ וּקְדוֹשִׁים בְּכָל־יוֹם

yehallelucha selah. Baruch attah   יְהַלְלוּךָ סֶּלָה. בָּרוּךְ אַתָּה

adonai ha'eil hakkadosh.   יְהֹוָה הָאֵל הַקָּדוֹש.

You are holy and Your Name is holy and holy beings praise You every day, forever. For You are an Almighty King – great and holy.

A Plea for Wisdom

This is the first blessing in which we make a request of God. Just as King Solomon requested wisdom and knowledge when given the chance by God to ask for a gift of value (I Kings 3), the first thing we ask for is knowledge and understanding.

Attah chonein le'adam da'at   אַתָּה חוֹנֵן לְאָדָם דַּעַת

umelammeid le'enosh binah: וּמְלַמֵּד לֶאֱנוֹש בִּינָה:

channeinu mei'ittecha dei'ah   חָנֵּנוּ מֵאִתְּךָ דֵּעָה

binah vehaskeil: baruch attah   בִּינָה וְהַשְׂכֵּל: בָּרוּךְ אַתָּה

adonai chonein hadda'at.   יְהֹוָה חוֹנֵן הַדָּעַת.

You favor man with perception and teach mankind understanding. Grant us knowledge, understanding and intellect from You. Blessed are You, the Lord, Grantor of perception.

Return Us to You!

In the next two blessings, we ask God to help us return to Him and repent, and to forgive us for all of our sins. While many of our characteristics are predetermined, it is up to each of us to choose between good and evil. In Ecclesiastes 7:20, King Solomon says that there isn't a single person in this world who does not sin. We are all

Hashiveinu avinu letoratecha	הֲשִׁיבֵנוּ אָבִינוּ לְתוֹרָתֶךָ
vekareveinu malkeinu	וְקָרְבֵנוּ מַלְכֵּנוּ
la'avodatecha vehachazireinu	לַעֲבוֹדָתֶךָ וְהַחֲזִירֵנוּ
bitshuvah sheleimah lefanecha:	בִּתְשׁוּבָה שְׁלֵמָה לְפָנֶיךָ:
baruch attah adonai harotzeh	בָּרוּךְ אַתָּה יְהֹוָה הָרוֹצֶה
bitshuvah.	בִּתְשׁוּבָה.

Cause us to return, our Father, to Your Law, and bring us near, our King, to Your service; and bring us back in whole-hearted repentance before You. Blessed are You, O Lord, Who desires penitence.

Selach lanu avinu ki chatanu	סְלַח לָנוּ אָבִינוּ כִּי חָטָאנוּ
mechal lanu malkeinu ki fasha'nu	מְחַל לָנוּ מַלְכֵּנוּ כִּי פָשָׁעְנוּ
ki mocheil vesolei'ach attah:	כִּי מוֹחֵל וְסוֹלֵחַ אָתָּה:
baruch attah adonai channun	בָּרוּךְ אַתָּה יְהֹוָה חַנּוּן
hammarbeh lisloach.	הַמַּרְבֶּה לִסְלוֹחַ.

Pardon us, our Father, for we have sinned, forgive us, our King, for we have transgressed; for You forgive and pardon. Blessed are You, O Lord, Gracious One, Who pardons abundantly.

Refa'einu adonai veneirafei	רְפָאֵנוּ יְהֹוָה וְנֵרָפֵא
hoshi'einu venivvashei'ah ki	הוֹשִׁיעֵנוּ וְנִוָּשֵׁעָה כִּי
tehillateinu attah veha'aleih	תְהִלָּתֵנוּ אָתָּה וְהַעֲלֵה רְפוּאָה
refu'ah sheleimah lechol	שְׁלֵמָה לְכָל
makkoteinu	מַכּוֹתֵינוּ

If you wish to pray for	מי שרוצה להתפלל על
the recovery of a sick person, you	החולה יאמר כאן
may do so here.	תחנה זו:
Yehi ratzon millefanecha adonai	יְהִי רָצוֹן מִלְּפָנֶיךָ יְהֹוָה
eloheinu veilohei avoteinu	אֱלֹהֵינוּ וֵאלֹהֵי אֲבוֹתֵינוּ
shettishlach meheirah refu'ah	שֶׁתִּשְׁלַח מְהֵרָה רְפוּאָה
sheleimah min hashamayim,	שְׁלֵמָה מִן הַשָּׁמַיִם,
refu'at hannefesh urefu'at hagguf,	רְפוּאַת הַנֶּפֶשׁ וּרְפוּאַת הַגּוּף,
lacholeh (*name*) son/daughter of	לַחוֹלֶה (פלוני/פלונית) בֶּן/בַּת
(*mother's name*) betoch she'ar	(פלונית) בְּתוֹךְ שְׁאָר
cholei yisra'el.	חוֹלֵי יִשְׂרָאֵל.

ki el melech rofei ne'eman	כִּי אֵל מֶלֶךְ רוֹפֵא נֶאֱמָן
verachaman attah :baruch attah	וְרַחֲמָן אָתָּה: בָּרוּךְ אַתָּה
adonai rofei cholei ammo yisra'el.	יְהֹוָה רוֹפֵא חוֹלֵי עַמּוֹ יִשְׂרָאֵל.

Heal us, O Lord, and we will be healed, deliver us and we will be delivered;
for You are our praise. Grant a complete healing to all our affliction
If you wish to pray for the recovery of a sick person, you may do so here.
May it be Your will, O Lord, our God, and the God of our fathers,

*that You send, quickly ,a complete recovery from the heavens,
healing for the soul ,and healing for the body ,for the ailing) name(
son/daughter of) mother's name (among the ailing of Israel.*

*Because You are the Almighty, King, Who is a faithful and merciful
Healer. Blessed are You, O Lord, Healer of the sick of His people Israel.*

Bless Us with Sustenance

Just as we are dependent on God for healing and salvation,
our sustenance comes from the Almighty as well. The following blessing is a request for sustenance. Since it only
rains during the winter in the land of Israel, in the winter
months we ask for rain but during the summer months we
ask more generically for God's blessing.

Bareich aleinu adonai eloheinu et-
hashanah hazzot ve'et-kol-minei
tevu'atah letovah, vetein

בָּרֵךְ עָלֵינוּ יְהֹוָה אֱלֹהֵינוּ אֶת־
הַשָּׁנָה הַזֹּאת וְאֶת־כָּל־מִינֵי
תְבוּאָתָהּ לְטוֹבָה, וְתֵן

*From the first day of Passover until
the evening of December 4, or, on
a civil leap year, December 5, say:*
berachah

בימות החמה:
בְּרָכָה

*From the evening service on
December 4, or, on a civil leap
year, December 5, until the First
day of Passover say:*
tal umatar livrachah

בימות הגשמים:
טַל וּמָטָר לִבְרָכָה

al penei ha'adamah vesabbe'einu

עַל פְּנֵי הָאֲדָמָה וְשַׂבְּעֵנוּ

mittuvecha uvareich shenateinu   מְטוּבֶךְ וּבָרֵךְ שְׁנָתֵנוּ

kashanim hattovot: baruch attah   כַּשָּׁנִים הַטּוֹבוֹת: בָּרוּךְ אַתָּה

adonai mevareich hashanim.   יְהֹוָה מְבָרֵךְ הַשָּׁנִים.

Bless for us, O Lord our God, this year and all the varieties of its produce for good; and bestow

From the first say of Passover until the evening of December 4, or, on a civil leap year, December 5, say: blessing

From the evening service on December 4, or, on a civil leap year, December 5, until the First day of Passover say: dew and rain for a blessing

upon the face of the earth; satisfy us from Your bounty and bless our year, like the good years. Blessed are You, the Lord, Blesser of the years.

A Call for Justice

This next blessing recalls the prophecy in Isaiah 1:26: "I will restore your magistrates as of old, and your counselors as of yore. After that, you shall be called the City of Righteousness, Faithful City." The restoration of justice is a key element in the process of redemption. Corruption and injustice are, unfortunately, very common among our leaders and judges. We await the day when God, our true Ruler, will govern us and the entire world with kindness and compassion, and our human judges will judge according to His will.

Hashivah shofeteinu kevarishonah   הָשִׁיבָה שׁוֹפְטֵינוּ כְּבָרִאשׁוֹנָה

veyo'atzeinu kevattechillah   וְיוֹעֲצֵינוּ כְּבַתְּחִלָּה

vehaser mimmennu yagon   וְהָסֵר מִמֶּנּוּ יָגוֹן

va'anachah umeloch aleinu attah   וַאֲנָחָה וּמְלוֹךְ עָלֵינוּ אַתָּה

adonai levadd'cha bechesed   יְהֹוָה לְבַדְּךָ בְּחֶסֶד

uverachamim vetzaddekeinu   וּבְרַחֲמִים וְצַדְּקֵנוּ

bamishpat: baruch attah adonai   בַּמִּשְׁפָּט: בָּרוּךְ אַתָּה יְהֹוָה

melech oheiv tzedakah umishpat.   מֶלֶךְ אֹהֵב צְדָקָה וּמִשְׁפָּט.

Restore our judges as before and our counselors as at first. Remove sorrow and sighing from us, and reign over us You, O Lord, alone with kindness and compassion; and make us righteous with justice, Blessed are You, O Lord, King, Lover of righteousness and justice.

Uproot our Enemies

In this next blessing we ask God to uproot and subdue all of our enemies. This blessing was a later addition to the silent *Amidah* prayer, authored by a sage known as "Samuel the Small", who was known for quoting the verse in Proverbs 24:17: "If your enemy falls, do not exult; If he trips, let your heart not rejoice." Though we must destroy the evil enemies of Israel who seek to harm God's people, our goal is not vengeance but a world of peace and righteousness.

Velammalshinim al tehi tikvah   וְלַמַּלְשִׁינִים אַל תְּהִי תִקְוָה

vechol harish'ah kerega toveid   וְכָל הָרִשְׁעָה כְּרֶגַע תֹּאבֵד

vechol oyevecha meheirah   וְכָל אֹיְבֶיךָ מְהֵרָה

yikkareitu vehazzeidim meheirah   יִכָּרֵתוּ וְהַזֵּדִים מְהֵרָה

te'akkeir uteshabbeir utemaggeir   תְעַקֵּר וּתְשַׁבֵּר וּתְמַגֵּר

vetachnia' bimheirah veyameinu: וְתַכְנִיעַ בִּמְהֵרָה בְיָמֵינוּ:

baruch attah adonai shoveir   בָּרוּךְ אַתָּה יְהֹוָה שׁוֹבֵר

oyevim umachnia' zeidim.   אֹיְבִים וּמַכְנִיעַ זֵדִים.

Let there be no hope for informers and may all wickedness instantly perish; may all the enemies of Your people be swiftly cut off, and may You quickly uproot, crush, rout and subdue the insolent, speedily in our days. Blessed are You, O Lord, Crusher of enemies. and Subduer of the insolent.

Have Mercy Upon the Righteous

This blessing asks God to have mercy on the righteous. Why do we pray for the righteous? If they are indeed righteous, do they really need our prayers? The righteous are those people who choose to give of themselves for the greater good, sacrificing their personal time and needs for the sake of others. According to Rabbi Yaakov Emden, this is our way of repaying them for everything that they do for us. We ask God to give them what they need to continue impacting us and the world at large.

Al-hatzaddikim ve'al-hachasidim	עַל־הַצַּדִּיקִים וְעַל־הַחֲסִידִים
ve'al-ziknei ammecha beit	וְעַל־זִקְנֵי עַמְּךָ בֵּית
yisra'el ve'al peleitat sofereihem	יִשְׂרָאֵל וְעַל פְּלֵיטַת סוֹפְרֵיהֶם
ve'al gerei hatzedek ve'aleinu	וְעַל גֵּרֵי הַצֶּדֶק וְעָלֵינוּ
yehemu rachamecha adonai	יֶהֱמוּ רַחֲמֶיךָ יְהֹוָה
eloheinu vetein sachar tov lechol	אֱלֹהֵינוּ וְתֵן שָׂכָר טוֹב לְכָל
habbotechim beshimcha be'emet	הַבּוֹטְחִים בְּשִׁמְךָ בֶּאֱמֶת
vesim chelkeinu immahem le'olam	וְשִׂים חֶלְקֵנוּ עִמָּהֶם לְעוֹלָם
velo nevosh ki vecha batachenu:	וְלֹא נֵבוֹשׁ כִּי בְךָ בָּטָחְנוּ:
baruch attah adonai mish'an	בָּרוּךְ אַתָּה יְהֹוָה מִשְׁעָן
umivtach latzaddikim.	וּמִבְטָח לַצַּדִּיקִים.

May Your mercy be aroused, O Lord, our God, upon the righteous, upon the pious, upon the elders of Your people, Israel, upon the

*remnant of their scholars, upon the true proselytes and upon us.
Grant a bountiful reward to all who trust in Your Name in truth;
and place our lot among them, and may we never be put to shame,
for we have put our trust in You. Blessed are You, O Lord, Support
and Trust of the righteous.*

Rebuild Jerusalem

In this blessing, we ask God to return to Jerusalem and
restore His sacred city and the kingdom of David. It cap-
tures the hope and anticipation for the return of the Divine
Presence and the re-establishment of Jerusalem as a bea-
con of spirituality, a hope that began to be fulfilled with
the liberation of the holy city in the Six-Day War of 1967.
This blessing reminds us of our enduring connection to
Jerusalem and our faith in its ultimate redemption.

Velirushalayim ircha berachamim	וְלִירוּשָׁלַיִם עִירְךָ בְּרַחֲמִים
tashuv vetishkon betochah	תָּשׁוּב וְתִשְׁכּוֹן בְּתוֹכָהּ
ka'asher dibbarta uveneih otah	כַּאֲשֶׁר דִּבַּרְתָּ וּבְנֵה אוֹתָהּ
bekarov beyameinu binyan	בְּקָרוֹב בְּיָמֵינוּ בִּנְיַן
olam vechissei david meheirah	עוֹלָם וְכִסֵּא דָוִד מְהֵרָה
letochah tachin: baruch attah	לְתוֹכָהּ תָּכִין: בָּרוּךְ אַתָּה
adonai boneih yerushalayim.	יְהֹוָה בּוֹנֵה יְרוּשָׁלָיִם.

*And return in mercy to Jerusalem, Your city, and dwell therein as
You have spoken; and rebuild it soon, in our days, as an everlasting
structure, and may You speedily establish the throne of David
therein. Blessed are You, the Lord, Builder of Jerusalem.*

Et-tzemach david avdecha
meheirah tatzmiach vekarno
tarum bishu'atecha ki lishu'atecha
kivvinu kol hayyom: baruch
attah adonai matzmiach keren
yeshu'ah.

אֶת־צֶמַח דָּוִד עַבְדְּךָ
מְהֵרָה תַצְמִיחַ וְקַרְנוֹ
תָּרוּם בִּישׁוּעָתֶךָ כִּי לִישׁוּעָתְךָ
קִוִּינוּ כָּל הַיּוֹם: בָּרוּךְ אַתָּה
יְהֹוָה מַצְמִיחַ קֶרֶן יְשׁוּעָה.

Speedily cause the sprout of David, Your servant, to flourish and exalt his power with Your deliverance. We hope all day for Your deliverance. Blessed are You, the Lord, Who causes the power of salvation to sprout.

Shema koleinu adonai eloheinu
chus veracheim aleinu vekabbeil

שְׁמַע קוֹלֵנוּ יְהֹוָה אֱלֹהֵינוּ
חוּס וְרַחֵם עָלֵינוּ וְקַבֵּל

berachamim uveratzon et-
tefillateinu ki el shomei'a tefillot
vetachanunim attah umillefanecha
malkeinu reikam al-teshiveinu
(insert personal requests here)
ki attah shomei'a tefillat ammecha
yisra'el berachamim. Baruch attah
adonai shomei'a tefillah.

בְּרַחֲמִים וּבְרָצוֹן אֶת־
תְּפִלָּתֵנוּ כִּי אֵל שׁוֹמֵעַ תְּפִלּוֹת
וְתַחֲנוּנִים אַתָּה וּמִלְּפָנֶיךָ
מַלְכֵּנוּ רֵיקָם אַל־תְּשִׁיבֵנוּ
(insert personal requests here)
כִּי אַתָּה שׁוֹמֵעַ תְּפִלַּת עַמְּךָ
יִשְׂרָאֵל בְּרַחֲמִים. בָּרוּךְ אַתָּה
יְהֹוָה שׁוֹמֵעַ תְּפִלָּה.

*Hear our voice, the Lord, our God; spare us and have compassion
on us, and accept our prayers compassionately and willingly, for
You are Almighty Who hears prayers and supplications; and do
not turn us away empty-handed from Your Presence, our King
(insert personal requests here), for You hear the prayers of Your
people, Israel, with compassion. Blessed are You, the Lord, Who
hears prayers.*

Thank You Lord!

We conclude the silent *Amidah* prayer with blessings of
gratitude and thanks. This prayer acknowledges the divine
providence that guides and sustains our lives. Earlier, we
recited Psalm 100 to thank God for the miracles we are
unaware of. In this prayer, we thank Him for the miracles
we are aware of, celebrating His everlasting kindness and
recognizing Him as our constant protector and benefac-
tor. Through this prayer, we affirm our unwavering faith and
gratitude towards the Almighty, whose mercy and compassion never cease.

Modim anachnu lach sha'attah hu
adonai eloheinu veilohei avoteinu

מוֹדִים אֲנַחְנוּ לָךְ שָׁאַתָּה הוּא
יְהֹוָה אֱלֹהֵינוּ וֵאלֹהֵי אֲבוֹתֵינוּ

le'olam va'ed, tzur chayyeinu   לְעוֹלָם וָעֶד צוּר חַיֵּינוּ
magein yish'einu attah hu ledor   מָגֵן יִשְׁעֵנוּ אַתָּה הוּא לְדוֹר
vador, nodeh lecha unesappeir   וָדוֹר נוֹדֶה לְךָ וּנְסַפֵּר
tehillatecha al-chayyeinu   תְּהִלָּתֶךָ עַל־חַיֵּינוּ
hammesurim beyadecha ve'al   הַמְּסוּרִים בְּיָדֶךָ וְעַל
nishmoteinu happekudot lach   נִשְׁמוֹתֵינוּ הַפְּקוּדוֹת לָךְ
ve'al nissecha shebbechol   וְעַל נִסֶּיךָ שֶׁבְּכָל
yom immanu ve'al nifle'otecha   יוֹם עִמָּנוּ וְעַל נִפְלְאוֹתֶיךָ
vetovotecha shebbechol eit,   וְטוֹבוֹתֶיךָ שֶׁבְּכָל עֵת
erev vavoker vetzohorayim,   עֶרֶב וָבֹקֶר וְצָהֳרָיִם
hattov ki lo chalu rachamecha   הַטּוֹב כִּי לֹא כָלוּ רַחֲמֶיךָ
vehammeracheim ki lo tammu   וְהַמְרַחֵם כִּי לֹא תַמּוּ
chasadecha mei'olam kivvinu lach.   חֲסָדֶיךָ מֵעוֹלָם קִוִּינוּ לָךְ.

Ve'al-kullam yitbarach veyitromam   וְעַל־כֻּלָּם יִתְבָּרַךְ וְיִתְרוֹמַם
shimcha malkeinu tamid le'olam   שִׁמְךָ מַלְכֵּנוּ תָּמִיד לְעוֹלָם
va'ed: vechol hachayyim yoducha   וָעֶד. וְכֹל הַחַיִּים יוֹדוּךָ
selah vihallu et-shimcha be'emet   סֶלָה וִיהַלְלוּ אֶת־שִׁמְךָ בֶּאֱמֶת
ha'el yeshu'ateinu ve'ezrateinu   הָאֵל יְשׁוּעָתֵנוּ וְעֶזְרָתֵנוּ
selah. Baruch attah adonai hattov   סֶלָה: בָּרוּךְ אַתָּה יְהֹוָה הַטּוֹב
shimcha ulecha na'eh lehodot.   שִׁמְךָ וּלְךָ נָאֶה לְהוֹדוֹת.

*We are thankful to You that You, O Lord, are our God and the
God of our fathers forever; Rock of our lives, You are the Shield
of our deliverance in every generation. We will give thanks to You
and recount Your praise, for our lives which are committed into
Your hand, and for our souls which are entrusted to You, and for
Your miracles of every day with us, and for Your wonders and
benefactions at all times— evening, morning and noon. (You are)
The Beneficent One— for Your compassion is never withheld; And
(You are) the Merciful One— for Your kindness never ceases; we
have always placed our hope in You. And for all the foregoing may
Your Name, our King, constantly be blessed and extolled, forever*

and ever. And all the living shall thank You forever and praise Your Name with sincerity — the Almighty, Who is our deliverance and our help forever. Blessed are You, the Lord; Your Name is The Beneficent and You it is fitting to praise.

Grant Us Peace

The sages teach that peace is the vessel that holds all of God's blessings. One might possess great material wealth, fulfilling relationships, and numerous other blessings. However, if one's life is marred by tension, conflict, and a toxic environment devoid of peace, those blessings seem to lose their value and may even be lost. This is why the final blessing of the silent *Amidah* prayer is a plea for peace.

Sim shalom tovah uverachah	שִׂים שָׁלוֹם טוֹבָה וּבְרָכָה
chein vachesed verachamim	חֵן וָחֶסֶד וְרַחֲמִים
aleinu ve'al kol-yisra'el ammecha.	עָלֵינוּ וְעַל כָּל־יִשְׂרָאֵל עַמֶּךָ.
Barecheinu avinu kullanu	בָּרְכֵנוּ אָבִינוּ כֻּלָּנוּ
ke'echad be'or panecha. Ki ve'or	כְּאֶחָד בְּאוֹר פָּנֶיךָ. כִּי בְאוֹר
panecha natatta lanu adonai	פָּנֶיךָ נָתַתָּ לָּנוּ יְהֹוָה
eloheinu torat chayyim ve'ahavat	אֱלֹהֵינוּ תּוֹרַת חַיִּים וְאַהֲבַת
chesed utzedakah uverachah	חֶסֶד וּצְדָקָה וּבְרָכָה
verachamim vechayyim veshalom.	וְרַחֲמִים וְחַיִּים וְשָׁלוֹם.
Vetov be'einecha levareich et	וְטוֹב בְּעֵינֶיךָ לְבָרֵךְ אֶת
ammecha yisra'el bechol-eit	עַמְּךָ יִשְׂרָאֵל בְּכָל־עֵת
uvechol-sha'ah bishlomecha.	וּבְכָל־שָׁעָה בִּשְׁלוֹמֶךָ.
Baruch attah adonai hamvareich	בָּרוּךְ אַתָּה יְהֹוָה הַמְבָרֵךְ
et-ammo yisra'el bashalom.	אֶת־עַמּוֹ יִשְׂרָאֵל בַּשָּׁלוֹם.

Grant peace, goodness, and blessing, favor, kindness and compassion upon us and upon all Israel, Your people. Bless us, our Father, all of us as one with the light of Your countenance. For by the light of Your countenance You gave us, Lord, our God, a living Torah and the love of kindliness, righteousness, blessing, compassion, life and peace. And may it be good in Your sight to bless Your people, Israel, at all times and at every moment with Your peace. Blessed are You, O Lord, Who blesses His people Israel with peace.

Conclusion of the Silent Amidah Prayer

At the end of the silent *Amidah* prayer, we recite one final personal supplication. We ask for God's help to avoid speaking evil, remain humble, follow His commandments, and thwart our adversaries. Finally, we ask Him to answer our prayers for His sake, not ours.

Elohai netzor leshoni meira	אֱלֹהַי נְצוֹר לְשׁוֹנִי מֵרָע
usefatai middabber mirmah.	וּשְׂפָתַי מִדַּבֵּר מִרְמָה.
Velimkal'lai nafshi tiddom venafshi	וְלִמְקַלְלַי נַפְשִׁי תִדּוֹם וְנַפְשִׁי
ke'afar lakkol tihyeh. Petach libbi	כֶּעָפָר לַכֹּל תִּהְיֶה. פְּתַח לִבִּי
betoratecha uvemitzvotecha tirdof	בְּתוֹרָתֶךָ וּבְמִצְוֹתֶיךָ תִּרְדֹּף
nafshi. Vechol hachoshevim alai	נַפְשִׁי. וְכֹל הַחוֹשְׁבִים עָלַי
ra'ah meheirah hafeir atzatam	רָעָה מְהֵרָה הָפֵר עֲצָתָם
vekalkeil machashavtam: aseih	וְקַלְקֵל מַחֲשַׁבְתָּם: עֲשֵׂה
lema'an shemecha aseih lema'an	לְמַעַן שְׁמֶךָ עֲשֵׂה לְמַעַן
yeminecha aseih lema'an	יְמִינֶךָ עֲשֵׂה לְמַעַן
kedushatecha aseih lema'an	קְדֻשָּׁתֶךָ עֲשֵׂה לְמַעַן
toratecha. Lema'an yeichaletzun	תוֹרָתֶךָ. לְמַעַן יֵחָלְצוּן
yedidecha hoshi'ah yemincha	יְדִידֶיךָ הוֹשִׁיעָה יְמִינְךָ
va'aneini: yihyu leratzon imrei fi	וַעֲנֵנִי: יִהְיוּ לְרָצוֹן אִמְרֵי פִי
vehegyon libbi lefanecha adonai	וְהֶגְיוֹן לִבִּי לְפָנֶיךָ יְהֹוָה
tzuri vego'ali: Oseh shalom	צוּרִי וְגוֹאֲלִי: עֹשֶׂה שָׁלוֹם

בִּמְרוֹמָיו הוּא יַעֲשֶׂה שָׁלוֹם
עָלֵינוּ וְעַל כָּל־יִשְׂרָאֵל וְאִמְרוּ
אָמֵן׃

My God, guard my tongue from evil and my lips from speaking deceitfully. May my soul be unresponsive to those who curse me; and let my soul be like dust to all. Open my heart to Your Torah and let my soul pursue Your commandments. And all who plan evil against me, quickly annul their counsel and frustrate their intention. Act for the sake of Your Name. Act for the sake of Your right hand. Act for the sake of Your holiness. Act for the sake of Your Torah. In order that Your loved ones be released, deliver [with] Your right hand and answer me. May the words of my mouth and the thoughts of my heart be acceptable before You the Lord, my Rock and my Redeemer. He Who makes peace in His high heavens may He make peace upon us and upon all Israel and say Amen.

Notes

____

____

____

____

____

____

____

Grant Us Atonement

*T*ACHANUN, WHICH MEANS "supplication," is a set of peniten-
tial prayers recited after the morning and afternoon
Amidah prayers on non-festive days. When recited with
proper intent, *Tachanun* invokes God's mercy and brings
atonement. The main section of this prayer opens with a
verse from II Samuel 24:14 and includes Psalm 6 (with the
exception of the first verse), composed by David during a
time of great physical and emotional distress.

Vayyomer david el-gad tzar-li	וַיֹּאמֶר דָּוִד אֶל־גָּד צַר־לִי
me'od nippelah-na veyad-adonai	מְאֹד נִפְּלָה־נָּא בְיַד־יְהֹוָה
ki-rabbim rachamav uveyad-adam	כִּי־רַבִּים רַחֲמָיו וּבְיַד־אָדָם
al-eppolah	אַל־אֶפֹּלָה
Rachum vechannun chatati	רַחוּם וְחַנּוּן חָטָאתִי
lefanecha adonai malei	לְפָנֶיךָ יְהֹוָה מָלֵא
rachamim racheim alai vekabbeil	רַחֲמִים רַחֵם עָלַי וְקַבֵּל
tachanunai: adonai al-be'appecha	תַחֲנוּנָי: יְהֹוָה אַל־בְּאַפְּךָ
tochicheini ve'al-bachamatecha	תוֹכִיחֵנִי וְאַל־בַּחֲמָתְךָ
teyassereini: channeini adonai	תְיַסְּרֵנִי: חָנֵּנִי יְהֹוָה
ki umlal ani refa'eini adonai ki	כִּי אֻמְלַל אָנִי רְפָאֵנִי יְהֹוָה כִּי
nivhalu atzamai: venafshi nivhalah	נִבְהֲלוּ עֲצָמָי: וְנַפְשִׁי נִבְהֲלָה
me'od ve'attah adonai ad-matai:	מְאֹד וְאַתָּה יְהֹוָה עַד־מָתָי:
shuvah adonai challetzah nafshi	שׁוּבָה יְהֹוָה חַלְּצָה נַפְשִׁי
hoshi'eini lema'an chasdecha: ki	הוֹשִׁיעֵנִי לְמַעַן חַסְדֶּךָ: כִּי
ein bammavet zichrecha bish'ol	אֵין בַּמָּוֶת זִכְרֶךָ בִּשְׁאוֹל
mi-yodeh lach: yaga'ti-be'anchati	מִי־יוֹדֶה לָּךְ: יָגַעְתִּי־בְּאַנְחָתִי
ascheh vechol-layyelah mittati	אַשְׂחֶה בְכָל־לַיְלָה מִטָּתִי
bedim'ati arsi amseh: asheshah	בְּדִמְעָתִי עַרְשִׂי אַמְסֶה: עָשְׁשָׁה

mikka'as eini atekah bechol-
tzorerai: suru mimmenni kol-
po'alei aven ki-shama adonai kol
bichyi: shama adonai techinnati
adonai tefillati yikkach: yevoshu
veyibbahalu me'od kol-oyevai
yashuvu yeivoshu raga:

מִכַּעַס עֵינִי עָתְקָה בְּכָל־
צוֹרְרָי: סוּרוּ מִמֶּנִּי כָּל־
פֹּעֲלֵי אָוֶן כִּי־שָׁמַע יְהוָֹה קוֹל
בִּכְיִי: שָׁמַע יְהוָֹה תְּחִנָּתִי
יְהוָֹה תְּפִלָּתִי יִקָּח: יֵבֹשׁוּ
וְיִבָּהֲלוּ מְאֹד כָּל־אֹיְבָי
יָשֻׁבוּ יֵבֹשׁוּ רָגַע:

David said to Gad, "I am in great distress. Let us fall into the hands of the Lord, for His compassion is great; and let me not fall into the hands of men."

Merciful and Gracious One, I have sinned before You; O Lord, full of mercy, have compassion upon me and accept my supplications: O Lord, do not punish me in anger, do not chastise me in fury. Have mercy on me, O Lord, for I languish; heal me, O Lord, for my bones shake with terror. My whole being is stricken with terror, while You, O Lord —O, how long! O Lord, turn! Rescue me! Deliver me as befits Your faithfulness. For there is no praise of You among the dead; in Sheol, who can acclaim You? I am weary with groaning; every night I drench my bed, I melt my couch in tears. My eyes are wasted by vexation, worn out because of all my foes. Away from me, all you evildoers, for the Lord heeds the sound of my weeping. The Lord heeds my plea, the Lord accepts my prayer. All my enemies will be frustrated and stricken with terror; they will turn back in an instant, frustrated.

Notes

Concluding Prayer - *Aleinu*

THE *ALEINU* PRAYER is the concluding prayer of the daily services. The first part highlights how belief in the one and only God sets us apart from other nations that do not recognize Him. We have an obligation to praise God for giving our lives meaning, unlike those who worship false gods. The prayer concludes with a hopeful vision for the future, anticipating a time when idolatry and false beliefs will be eradicated and all humanity will acknowledge and honor God's sovereignty.

Aleinu leshabbei'ach la'adon	עָלֵינוּ לְשַׁבֵּחַ לַאֲדוֹן
hakkol lateit gedullah leyotzeir	הַכֹּל לָתֵת גְּדֻלָּה לְיוֹצֵר
bereishit shello asanu kegoyei	בְּרֵאשִׁית שֶׁלֹּא עָשָׂנוּ כְּגוֹיֵי
ha'aratzot velo samanu	הָאֲרָצוֹת וְלֹא שָׂמָנוּ
kemishpechot ha'adamah	כְּמִשְׁפְּחוֹת הָאֲדָמָה
shello sam chelkeinu kahem	שֶׁלֹּא שָׂם חֶלְקֵנוּ כָּהֶם
vegoraleinu kechol hamonam:	וְגוֹרָלֵנוּ כְּכָל הֲמוֹנָם:
sheheim mishtachavim lahevel	שֶׁהֵם מִשְׁתַּחֲוִים לְהֶבֶל
varik umitpallelim el eil lo	וָרִיק וּמִתְפַּלְּלִים אֶל אֵל לֹא
yoshi'a, va'anachnu kore'im	יוֹשִׁיעַ, וַאֲנַחְנוּ כּוֹרְעִים
umishtachavim umodim lifnei	וּמִשְׁתַּחֲוִים וּמוֹדִים לִפְנֵי
melech malchei hammelachim	מֶלֶךְ מַלְכֵי הַמְּלָכִים
hakkadosh baruch hu, shehu	הַקָּדוֹשׁ בָּרוּךְ הוּא, שֶׁהוּא
noteh shamayim veyosed aretz,	נוֹטֶה שָׁמַיִם וְיוֹסֵד אָרֶץ,
umoshav yekaro bashamayim	וּמוֹשַׁב יְקָרוֹ בַּשָּׁמַיִם
mimma'al, ushechinat uzzo	מִמַּעַל, וּשְׁכִינַת עֻזּוֹ
begavehei meromim, hu eloheinu	בְּגָבְהֵי מְרוֹמִים, הוּא אֱלֹהֵינוּ
ein od, emet malkeinu efes zulato	אֵין עוֹד, אֱמֶת מַלְכֵּנוּ אֶפֶס זוּלָתוֹ
kakkatuv betorato veyada'ta	כַּכָּתוּב בְּתוֹרָתוֹ וְיָדַעְתָּ

hayyom vahasheivota
el levavecha ki adonai hu
ha'elohim bashamayim mimma'al
ve'al ha'aretz mittachat ein od
(Deuteronomy 4:39).

הַיּוֹם וַהֲשֵׁבֹתָ
אֶל לְבָבֶךָ כִּי יְהֹוָה הוּא
הָאֱלֹהִים בַּשָּׁמַיִם מִמַּעַל
וְעַל הָאָרֶץ מִתָּחַת אֵין עוֹד
(דברים ד:לט).

Al kein nekavveh lecha adonai
eloheinu lir'ot meheirah betif'eret
uzzecha leha'avir gillulim
min ha'aretz veha'elilim karot
yikkareitun letakkein olam
bemalchut shaddai vechol benei
vasar yikre'u vishmecha, lehafnot
eleicha kol rish'ei aretz, yakkiru
veyeide'u kol yoshevei teivel ki
lecha tichra kol berech tishava kol
lashon: lefanecha adonai eloheinu
yichre'u veyippolu, velichvod
shimcha yekar yitteinu, vikabbelu
chullam et ol malchutecha,
vetimloch aleihem meheirah
le'olam va'ed, ki hammalchut
shellecha hi ule'olemei ad timloch
bechavod, kakkatuv betoratecha
adonai yimloch le'olam va'ed:
vene'emar vehayah adonai
lemelech al kol ha'aretz bayyom
hahu yihyeh adonai echad
ushemo echad.

עַל כֵּן נְקַוֶּה לְךָ יְהֹוָה
אֱלֹהֵינוּ לִרְאוֹת מְהֵרָה בְּתִפְאֶרֶת
עֻזֶּךָ לְהַעֲבִיר גִּלּוּלִים
מִן הָאָרֶץ וְהָאֱלִילִים כָּרוֹת
יִכָּרֵתוּן לְתַקֵּן עוֹלָם
בְּמַלְכוּת שַׁדַּי וְכָל בְּנֵי
בָשָׂר יִקְרְאוּ בִשְׁמֶךָ, לְהַפְנוֹת
אֵלֶיךָ כָּל רִשְׁעֵי אָרֶץ, יַכִּירוּ
וְיֵדְעוּ כָּל יוֹשְׁבֵי תֵבֵל כִּי
לְךָ תִכְרַע כָּל בֶּרֶךְ תִּשָּׁבַע כָּל
לָשׁוֹן: לְפָנֶיךָ יְהֹוָה אֱלֹהֵינוּ
יִכְרְעוּ וְיִפֹּלוּ, וְלִכְבוֹד
שִׁמְךָ יְקָר יִתֵּנוּ, וִיקַבְּלוּ
כֻלָּם אֶת עֹל מַלְכוּתֶךָ,
וְתִמְלֹךְ עֲלֵיהֶם מְהֵרָה
לְעוֹלָם וָעֶד, כִּי הַמַּלְכוּת
שֶׁלְּךָ הִיא וּלְעוֹלְמֵי עַד תִּמְלוֹךְ
בְּכָבוֹד, כַּכָּתוּב בְּתוֹרָתֶךְ
יְהֹוָה יִמְלֹךְ לְעֹלָם וָעֶד:
וְנֶאֱמַר וְהָיָה יְהֹוָה
לְמֶלֶךְ עַל כָּל הָאָרֶץ בַּיּוֹם
הַהוּא יִהְיֶה יְהֹוָה אֶחָד
וּשְׁמוֹ אֶחָד.

*It is our obligation to praise the Master of all, to ascribe greatness
to the Creator of the world in the beginning: that He has not made
us like the nations of the lands, and has not positioned us like*

the families of the earth; that He has not assigned our portion like theirs, nor our lot like that of all their multitudes. For they prostrate themselves to vanity and nothingness, and pray to gods that cannot deliver. But we bow, prostrate ourselves, and offer thanks before the Supreme King of Kings, the Holy One blessed is He, Who spreads the heavens, and establishes the earth, and the seat of His glory is in heaven above, and the abode of His invincible might is in the loftiest heights. He is our God, there is nothing else. Our King is true, all else is insignificant, as it is written in His Bible: And You shall know this day and take into Your heart that the Lord is God in the heavens above and upon the earth below; there is nothing else. (Deuteronomy 4:39).

We, therefore, put our hope in You, the Lord our God, to soon behold the glory of Your might in banishing idolatry from the earth, and the false gods will be utterly exterminated to perfect the world as the kingdom of Shadai. And all mankind will invoke Your Name, to turn back to You, all the wicked of the earth. They will realize and know, all the inhabitants of the world, that to You, every knee must bend, every tongue must swear [allegiance to You]. Before You, O Lord, our God, they will bow and prostrate themselves, and to the glory of Your Name give honor. And they will all accept [upon themselves] the yoke of Your kingdom, and You will reign over them, soon, forever and ever. For the kingdom is Yours, and to all eternity You will reign in glory, as it is written in Your Bible: the Lord will reign forever and ever. And it is said: And the Lord will be King over the whole earth; on that day the Lord will be One and His Name One.

The Daily Song

THE DAILY MORNING prayers end with the recitation of one more additional psalm, a different psalm for each day of the week. This custom originated in the Temple in Jerusalem, where the Levites would recite a psalm of the day after the daily morning offering. When the Temple was destroyed, it became customary to recite these psalms after our morning prayers. Though not always immediately obvious, the song of the day reflects the day's significance in creation.

On Sunday

On Sunday we recite Psalm 24. Since this psalm refers to the creation of the world, "For He founded it upon the seas, and established it upon rivers," we recite it on Sunday which corresponds to the first day of creation.

Hayyom yom rishon bashabbat	הַיּוֹם יוֹם רִאשׁוֹן בַּשַּׁבָּת
shebbo hayu halviyyim omerim	שֶׁבּוֹ הָיוּ הַלְוִיִּם אוֹמְרִים
beveit hammikdash:	בְּבֵית הַמִּקְדָּשׁ:
ledavid mizmor ladonai ha'aretz	לְדָוִד מִזְמוֹר לַיהוָה הָאָרֶץ
umelo'ah teivel veyoshvei vah:	וּמְלוֹאָהּ תֵּבֵל וְיֹשְׁבֵי בָהּ:
ki hu al yammim yesadah ve'al	כִּי הוּא עַל יַמִּים יְסָדָהּ וְעַל
neharot yechoneneha: mi ya'aleh	נְהָרוֹת יְכוֹנְנֶהָ: מִי יַעֲלֶה
vehar adonai umi yakum bimkom	בְהַר יְהוָה וּמִי יָקוּם בִּמְקוֹם
kodsho: neki chappayim uvar	קָדְשׁוֹ: נְקִי כַפַּיִם וּבַר
leivav asher lo nasa lashav	לֵבָב אֲשֶׁר לֹא נָשָׂא לַשָּׁוְא
nafshi velo nishba lemirmah:	נַפְשִׁי וְלֹא נִשְׁבַּע לְמִרְמָה:

yissa verachah me'eit adonai	יִשָּׂא בְרָכָה מֵאֵת יְהֹוָה
utzedakah mei'elohei yish'o: zeh	וּצְדָקָה מֵאֱלֹהֵי יִשְׁעוֹ: זֶה
dor doreshav mevakshei fanecha	דּוֹר דּוֹרְשָׁיו מְבַקְשֵׁי פָנֶיךָ
ya'akov selah: se'u she'arim	יַעֲקֹב סֶלָה: שְׂאוּ שְׁעָרִים
rasheichem vehinnase'u pitchei	רָאשֵׁיכֶם וְהִנָּשְׂאוּ פִּתְחֵי
olam veyavo melech hakkavod:	עוֹלָם וְיָבוֹא מֶלֶךְ הַכָּבוֹד:
mi zeh melech hakkavod	מִי זֶה מֶלֶךְ הַכָּבוֹד
adonai izzuz vegibbor adonai	יְהֹוָה עִזּוּז וְגִבּוֹר יְהֹוָה
gibbor milchamah: se'u she'arim	גִּבּוֹר מִלְחָמָה: שְׂאוּ שְׁעָרִים
rasheichem use'u pitchei olam	רָאשֵׁיכֶם וּשְׂאוּ פִּתְחֵי עוֹלָם
veyavo melech hakkavod: mi hu	וְיָבוֹא מֶלֶךְ הַכָּבוֹד: מִי הוּא
zeh melech hakkavod adonai	זֶה מֶלֶךְ הַכָּבוֹד יְהֹוָה
tzeva'ot hu melech hakkavod	צְבָאוֹת הוּא מֶלֶךְ הַכָּבוֹד
selah:	סֶלָה:

Today is the first day of the week, on which the Levites used to recite in the Holy Temple:

A psalm of David: the earth is the Lord's and the fullness thereof, the inhabited world and those who dwell in it. For He founded it upon the seas, and established it upon rivers. Who may ascend the mountain of the Lord, and who may stand in the place of His holiness? The clean of hands and the pure of heart, who has not borne My soul in vain, and has not sworn deceitfully. He will bear the Lord's blessing and righteousness from the God of his deliverance. This is the generation of those who seek Him, the seekers of Your Presence, [God of] Jacob, Selah. Lift up your heads, gates, and be uplifted [you] entrance ways to eternity, so that the King of Glory may enter. Who is this King of Glory? The Lord, strong and mighty; the Lord, the Mighty One in battle. Lift up your heads, gates, and lift, entrance ways to eternity, so that the King of Glory may enter. Who is He, this King of Glory? The Lord of hosts, He is the King of Glory, Selah.

Hayyom yom sheini bashabbat
shebbo hayu halviyyim omerim
beveit hammikdash:

הַיּוֹם יוֹם שֵׁנִי בַּשַּׁבָּת
שֶׁבּוֹ הָיוּ הַלְוִיִּם אוֹמְרִים
בְּבֵית הַמִּקְדָּשׁ:

shir mizmor livnei korach: gadol
adonai umehullal me'od be'ir
eloheinu har kodsho: yefeih nof
mesos kol ha'aretz har tziyyon
yarketei tzafon kiryat melech
rav: elohim be'armenoteha noda
lemisgav: ki hinneih hammelachim
no'adu averu yachdav: heimmah
ra'u kein tamahu nivhalu
nechpazu: re'adah achazatam
sham chil kayyoleidah: beruach
kadim teshabbeir oniyyot tarshish:
ka'asher shama'nu kein ra'inu be'ir
adonai tzeva'ot be'ir eloheinu
elohim yechoneneha ad olam
selah: dimminu elohim chasdecha
bekerev heichalecha: keshimcha
elohim kein tehillatecha al katzvei
eretz tzedek male'ah yeminecha:

שִׁיר מִזְמוֹר לִבְנֵי קֹרַח: גָּדוֹל
יְהֹוָה וּמְהֻלָּל מְאֹד בְּעִיר
אֱלֹהֵינוּ הַר קָדְשׁוֹ: יְפֵה נוֹף
מְשׂוֹשׂ כָּל הָאָרֶץ הַר צִיּוֹן
יַרְכְּתֵי צָפוֹן קִרְיַת מֶלֶךְ
רָב: אֱלֹהִים בְּאַרְמְנוֹתֶיהָ נוֹדַע
לְמִשְׂגָּב: כִּי הִנֵּה הַמְּלָכִים
נוֹעֲדוּ עָבְרוּ יַחְדָּו: הֵמָּה
רָאוּ כֵּן תָּמָהוּ נִבְהֲלוּ
נֶחְפָּזוּ: רְעָדָה אֲחָזָתַם
שָׁם חִיל כַּיּוֹלֵדָה: בְּרוּחַ
קָדִים תְּשַׁבֵּר אֳנִיּוֹת תַּרְשִׁישׁ:
כַּאֲשֶׁר שָׁמַעְנוּ כֵּן רָאִינוּ בְּעִיר
יְהֹוָה צְבָאוֹת בְּעִיר אֱלֹהֵינוּ
אֱלֹהִים יְכוֹנְנֶהָ עַד עוֹלָם
סֶלָה: דִּמִּינוּ אֱלֹהִים חַסְדֶּךָ
בְּקֶרֶב הֵיכָלֶךָ: כְּשִׁמְךָ
אֱלֹהִים כֵּן תְּהִלָּתְךָ עַל קַצְוֵי
אֶרֶץ צֶדֶק מָלְאָה יְמִינֶךָ:

yismach har tziyyon tageilenah	יִשְׂמַח הַר צִיּוֹן תָּגֵלְנָה
benot yehudah lema'an	בְּנוֹת יְהוּדָה לְמַעַן
mishpatecha: sobbu tziyyon	מִשְׁפָּטֶיךָ: סֹבּוּ צִיּוֹן
vehakkifuha sifru migdaleha:	וְהַקִּיפוּהָ סִפְרוּ מִגְדָּלֶיהָ:
shitu libbechem lecheilah	שִׁיתוּ לִבְּכֶם לְחֵילָה
passegu armenoteha lema'an	פַּסְּגוּ אַרְמְנוֹתֶיהָ לְמַעַן
tesapperu ledor acharon: ki zeh	תְּסַפְּרוּ לְדוֹר אַחֲרוֹן: כִּי זֶה
elohim eloheinu olam va'ed hu	אֱלֹהִים אֱלֹהֵינוּ עוֹלָם וָעֶד הוּא
yenahageinu al mut:	יְנַהֲגֵנוּ עַל מוּת:

Today is the second day of the week, on which the Levites used to recite in the Holy Temple:

A song, a psalm by the sons of Korach. The Lord is great and highly extolled in the city of our God, the mountain of His Sanctuary. Beautiful in its panoramic vista, the joy of all the earth is Mount Zion, on the northern extremities (of Jerusalem); the city of the great King. God, in its palaces, has become known as a Stronghold. For behold, the kings assembled, they passed by together. They saw and were astounded, they panicked and fled in haste. Trembling siezed them there, like the pangs of a woman in labor. With an east wind You smashed the ships of Tarshish. As we heard, so we saw in the city of the Lord of hosts, in the city of our God; may God establish it for eternity, Selah. We hoped, God, for Your lovingkindness in the midst of Your Sanctuary. As Your Name, God, so is Your praise— to the ends of the earth; Your right hand is full of righteousness. Let Mount Zion rejoice, let the daughters of Judah exult, because of Your judgments. Rally around Zion and encircle her, count her towers. Consider well her ramparts, raise high her citadels, that you may recount it to future generations. That this is God, our God forever and ever, He will lead us like children.

Hayyom yom shelishi bashabbat

shebbo hayu halviyyim omerim

beveit hammikdash:

הַיּוֹם יוֹם שְׁלִישִׁי בַּשַּׁבָּת שֶׁבּוֹ הָיוּ הַלְוִיִּם אוֹמְרִים בְּבֵית הַמִּקְדָּשׁ:

mizmor le'asaf elohim nitzav

ba'adat el bekerev elohim yishpot:

ad matai tishpetu avel ufenei

resha'im tis'u selah: shiftu dal

veyatom ani varash hatzdiku:

palletu dal ve'evyon miyyad

resha'im hatzilu: lo yade'u velo

yavinu bachasheichah yit'hallachu

yimmotu kol mosedei aretz:

ani amarti elohim attem uvenei

elyon kullechem: achein ke'adam

temutun uche'achad hassarim

tippolu: kumah elohim shafetah

ha'aretz ki attah tinchal bechol

haggoyim:

מִזְמוֹר לְאָסָף אֱלֹהִים נִצָּב בַּעֲדַת אֵל בְּקֶרֶב אֱלֹהִים יִשְׁפֹּט: עַד מָתַי תִּשְׁפְּטוּ עָוֶל וּפְנֵי רְשָׁעִים תִּשְׂאוּ סֶלָה: שִׁפְטוּ דָל וְיָתוֹם עָנִי וָרָשׁ הַצְדִּיקוּ: פַּלְּטוּ דַל וְאֶבְיוֹן מִיַּד רְשָׁעִים הַצִּילוּ: לֹא יָדְעוּ וְלֹא יָבִינוּ בַּחֲשֵׁכָה יִתְהַלָּכוּ יִמּוֹטוּ כָּל מוֹסְדֵי אָרֶץ: אֲנִי אָמַרְתִּי אֱלֹהִים אַתֶּם וּבְנֵי עֶלְיוֹן כֻּלְּכֶם: אָכֵן כְּאָדָם תְּמוּתוּן וּכְאַחַד הַשָּׂרִים תִּפֹּלוּ: קוּמָה אֱלֹהִים שָׁפְטָה הָאָרֶץ כִּי אַתָּה תִנְחַל בְּכָל הַגּוֹיִם:

Today is the third day of the week, on which the Levites used to recite in the Holy Temple:

A psalm of Assaf God stands in the congregation of the Almighty, in the midst of the judges He gives judgment. How long will you judge lawlessly? Will You show partiality to the wicked forever? Render justice to the lowly and the orphan, deal righteously with the poor and destitute. Rescue the lowly and the needy, save them from the hand of the wicked. They neither know nor understand, they walk along in darkness, all the foundations of the earth are shaken. I had said "You are godlike beings, all of you, sons of the Most High." Nevertheless, you shall die like men, and fall like one of the princes. Arise, God, judge the earth, for You will inherit all the nations.

On Wednesday:

On Wednesday, we recite Psalm 94, which builds on the themes of justice from Tuesday's Psalm 82. After examining the justice system, it addresses the abuse of that system through acts of treachery, debauchery, haughtiness, and merciless depravity. The psalmist grapples with the theological response to evil in the world, a question both timeless and timely. To understand the mechanism, parameters, and workings of this divine vengeance, we turn to Psalm 94.

Hayyom yom revi'i bashabbat	הַיּוֹם יוֹם רְבִיעִי בַּשַּׁבָּת
shebbo hayu halviyyim omerim	שֶׁבּוֹ הָיוּ הַלְוִיִּם אוֹמְרִים
beveit hammikdash:	בְּבֵית הַמִּקְדָּשׁ:

el nekamot adonai el nekamot	אֵל נְקָמוֹת יְהֹוָה אֵל נְקָמוֹת
hofia': hinnasei shofeit ha'aretz	הוֹפִיעַ: הִנָּשֵׂא שֹׁפֵט הָאָרֶץ
hasheiv gemul al gei'im: ad matai	הָשֵׁב גְּמוּל עַל גֵּאִים: עַד
resha'im adonai ad matai resha'im	מָתַי רְשָׁעִים יְהֹוָה עַד מָתַי
ya'alozu: yabbi'u	רְשָׁעִים יַעֲלֹזוּ: יַבִּיעוּ

yedabberu atak yit'ammeru kol יְדַבְּרוּ עָתָק יִתְאַמְּרוּ כָּל

po'alei aven: ammecha adonai פֹּעֲלֵי אָוֶן: עַמְּךָ יְהוָה

yedakke'u venachalatecha יְדַכְּאוּ וְנַחֲלָתְךָ

ye'annu: almanah vegeir yaharogu יְעַנּוּ: אַלְמָנָה וְגֵר יַהֲרֹגוּ

vitomim yeratzeichu: vayyomru וִיתוֹמִים יְרַצֵּחוּ: וַיֹּאמְרוּ

lo yir'eh yah velo yavin elohei לֹא יִרְאֶה יָּהּ וְלֹא יָבִין אֱלֹהֵי

ya'akov: binu bo'arim ba'am יַעֲקֹב: בִּינוּ בֹּעֲרִים בָּעָם

uchesilim matai taskilu: hanota וּכְסִילִים מָתַי תַּשְׂכִּילוּ: הֲנֹטַע

ozen halo yishma im yotzer ayin אֹזֶן הֲלֹא יִשְׁמָע אִם יֹצֵר עַיִן

halo yabbit: hayoseir goyim halo הֲלֹא יַבִּיט: הֲיֹסֵר גּוֹיִם הֲלֹא

yochiach hammelammeid adam יוֹכִיחַ הַמְלַמֵּד אָדָם

da'at: adonai yodei'a machshevot דָּעַת: יְהוָה יֹדֵעַ מַחְשְׁבוֹת

adam ki heimmah havel: ashrei אָדָם כִּי הֵמָּה הָבֶל: אַשְׁרֵי

haggever asher teyasserennu הַגֶּבֶר אֲשֶׁר תְּיַסְּרֶנּוּ

yah umittoratecha telammedennu: יָּהּ וּמִתּוֹרָתְךָ תְלַמְּדֶנּוּ:

lehashkit lo mimei ra ad yikkareh לְהַשְׁקִיט לוֹ מִימֵי רָע עַד יִכָּרֶה

larasha shachat: ki lo yittosh לָרָשָׁע שָׁחַת: כִּי לֹא יִטֹּשׁ

adonai ammo venachalato lo יְהוָה עַמּוֹ וְנַחֲלָתוֹ לֹא

ya'azov: ki ad tzedek yashuv יַעֲזֹב: כִּי עַד צֶדֶק יָשׁוּב

mishpat ve'acharav kol yishrei מִשְׁפָּט וְאַחֲרָיו כָּל יִשְׁרֵי

leiv: mi yakum li im merei'im mi לֵב: מִי יָקוּם לִי עִם מְרֵעִים מִי

yityatzeiv li im po'alei aven: lulei יִתְיַצֵּב לִי עִם פֹּעֲלֵי אָוֶן: לוּלֵי

adonai ezratah li kim'at shachenah יְהוָה עֶזְרָתָה לִּי כִּמְעַט שָׁכְנָה

dumah nafshi: Im amarti דוּמָה נַפְשִׁי: אִם אָמַרְתִּי

matah ragli chasdecha adonai מָטָה רַגְלִי חַסְדְּךָ יְהוָה

yis'adeini: berov sar'appai bekirbi יִסְעָדֵנִי: בְּרֹב שַׂרְעַפַּי בְּקִרְבִּי

tanchumecha yesha'ash'u nafshi: תַּנְחוּמֶיךָ יְשַׁעַשְׁעוּ נַפְשִׁי:

hayyechovrecha kissei havvavot הַיְחָבְרְךָ כִּסֵּא הַוּוֹת

yotzeir amal alei chok: yagoddu יֹצֵר עָמָל עֲלֵי חֹק: יָגוֹדּוּ

al nefesh tzaddik vedam naki עַל נֶפֶשׁ צַדִּיק וְדָם נָקִי

yarshi'u: vayhi adonai li lemisgav יַרְשִׁיעוּ: וַיְהִי יְהוָה לִי לְמִשְׂגָּב

veilohai letzur machsi: vayyashev וֵאלֹהַי לְצוּר מַחְסִי: וַיָּשֶׁב

aleihem et onam uvera'atam עֲלֵיהֶם אֶת אוֹנָם וּבְרָעָתָם

yatzmiteim yatzmiteim adonai	יַצְמִיתֵם יַצְמִיתֵם יְהֹוָה
eloheinu: lechu nerannenah	אֱלֹהֵינוּ: לְכוּ נְרַנְּנָה
ladonai nari'ah letzur yish'einu:	לַיהֹוָה נָרִיעָה לְצוּר יִשְׁעֵנוּ:
nekaddemah fanav betodah	נְקַדְּמָה פָנָיו בְּתוֹדָה
bizmirot naria' lo: ki el gadol	בִּזְמִרוֹת נָרִיעַ לוֹ: כִּי אֵל גָּדוֹל
adonai umelech gadol al kol	יְהֹוָה וּמֶלֶךְ גָּדוֹל עַל כָּל
elohim:	אֱלֹהִים:

Today is the fourth day of the week, on which the Levites used to recite in the Holy Temple:

Almighty of vengeance, O Lord, Almighty of vengeance, reveal Yourself. Arise Judge of the earth, repay the arrogant their just reward. How long shall the wicked— O Lord — how long shall the wicked exult? They express, they speak with arrogance; all the evildoers are boastful. O Lord, they crush Your people and Your heritage they oppress. The widow and stranger they kill, and orphans they murder. And they say, "God does not see, the God of Jacob is not concerned." Consider, [you] stupid [ones] among the people,— and you fools when will you become wise? He Who implanted the ear, does He not hear? He Who formed the eye, does He not see? He Who chastises nations, does He not reprove— He that teaches man knowledge? The Lord knows the thoughts of men, that they are vanity. Fortunate is the man whom You chastise, God, and whom You instruct from Your Torah. To grant him tranquility from days of evil, until the pit is dug for the wicked. For the Lord will not abandon His people and His inheritance, He will not forsake. For justice shall return unto righteousness, and all the upright in heart will follow it. Who will rise up for me against the wicked, who will stand up for me against the evildoers? Had the Lord not been my help, in an instant my soul would have dwelt in the silent grave. If [Whenever] I said, my foot has slipped, Your kindliness, O Lord upheld me. When (worrisome) thoughts multiply within me, Your consolations soothe my soul. Can a tribunal of evil have an accord with You— [a tribunal] that makes iniquity into law? They gang up against the life of the righteous, and blood of the innocent they condemn. The Lord has been my stronghold, my God the Rock of my refuge. He turns their violence against them, and with their own wickedness destroys them; O Lord, my God, destroys them. Come let us sing to the Lord; let us shout for joy to the Rock of our Deliverance. Let us greet Him with thanksgiving; with song let us shout for joy to Him. For a great Almighty is the Lord; a great King over all godlike beings.

On Thursday:

Psalm 81 is a joyful call to worship God in which we remember His deliverance of the Israelites from Egypt. It highlights the importance of obedience to God's commandments and the blessings that come from following His ways. This psalm naturally continues the theme of Wednesday's psalm, which discusses the consequences of deviating from God's path.

Hayyom yom chamishi bashabbat	הַיּוֹם יוֹם חֲמִישִׁי בַּשַּׁבָּת
shebbo hayu halviyyim omerim	שֶׁבּוֹ הָיוּ הַלְוִיִּם אוֹמְרִים
beveit hammikdash:	בְּבֵית הַמִּקְדָּשׁ:

lammenatzeach al haggittit le'asaf:	לַמְנַצֵּחַ עַל הַגִּתִּית
harninu leilohim uzzeinu hari'u	לְאָסָף: הַרְנִינוּ לֵאלֹהִים עֻזֵּנוּ
leilohei ya'akov: se'u zimrah	הָרִיעוּ לֵאלֹהֵי יַעֲקֹב: שְׂאוּ
utenu tof kinnor na'im im navel:	זִמְרָה וּתְנוּ תֹף כִּנּוֹר נָעִים עִם
tik'u vachodesh shofar bakkeseh	נָבֶל: תִּקְעוּ בַחֹדֶשׁ שׁוֹפָר
leyom chaggeinu: ki chok	בַּכֶּסֶה לְיוֹם חַגֵּנוּ:
leyisra'el hu mishpat	כִּי חֹק לְיִשְׂרָאֵל הוּא מִשְׁפָּט

leilohei ya'akov: eidut bihoseif   לֵאלֹהֵי יַעֲקֹב: עֵדוּת בִּיהוֹסֵף

samo betzeito al eretz mitzrayim   שָׂמוֹ בְּצֵאתוֹ עַל אֶרֶץ מִצְרָיִם

sefat lo yada'ti eshma: hasiroti   שְׂפַת לֹא יָדַעְתִּי אֶשְׁמָע: הֲסִירוֹתִי

misseivel shichmo kappav   מִסֵּבֶל שִׁכְמוֹ כַּפָּיו

middud ta'avorenah: batzarah   מִדּוּד תַּעֲבֹרְנָה: בַּצָּרָה

karata va'achalletzecha e'encha   קָרָאתָ וָאֲחַלְּצֶךָּ אֶעֶנְךָ

beseiter ra'am evchanecha al   בְּסֵתֶר רַעַם אֶבְחָנְךָ עַל

mei merivah selah: shema ammi   מֵי מְרִיבָה סֶלָה: שְׁמַע עַמִּי

ve'a'idah bach yisra'el im tishma   וְאָעִידָה בָּךְ יִשְׂרָאֵל אִם תִּשְׁמַע

li: lo yihyeh vecha el zar velo   לִי: לֹא יִהְיֶה בְךָ אֵל זָר וְלֹא

tishtachaveh le'el neichar: anochi   תִשְׁתַּחֲוֶה לְאֵל נֵכָר: אָנֹכִי

adonai elohecha hamma'alcha   יְהֹוָה אֱלֹהֶיךָ הַמַּעַלְךָ

mei'eretz mitzrayim harchev   מֵאֶרֶץ מִצְרָיִם הַרְחֶב

picha va'amal'eihu: velo shama   פִּיךָ וַאֲמַלְאֵהוּ: וְלֹא שָׁמַע

ammi lekoli veyisra'el lo avah li: עַמִּי לְקוֹלִי וְיִשְׂרָאֵל לֹא אָבָה לִי:

va'ashallecheihu bishrirut libbam   וָאֲשַׁלְּחֵהוּ בִּשְׁרִירוּת לִבָּם

yeilechu bemo'atzoteihem: lu   יֵלְכוּ בְּמוֹעֲצוֹתֵיהֶם: לוּ

ammi shomei'a li yisra'el bidrachai   עַמִּי שֹׁמֵעַ לִי יִשְׂרָאֵל בִּדְרָכַי

yehalleichu: kim'at oyeveihem   יְהַלֵּכוּ: כִּמְעַט אוֹיְבֵיהֶם

achnia' ve'al tzareihem ashiv yadi: אַכְנִיעַ וְעַל צָרֵיהֶם אָשִׁיב יָדִי:

mesan'ei adonai yechachashu lo   מְשַׂנְאֵי יְהֹוָה יְכַחֲשׁוּ לוֹ

vihi ittam le'olam: vayya'achileihu   וִיהִי עִתָּם לְעוֹלָם: וַיַּאֲכִילֵהוּ

meicheilev chittah umitzur devash   מֵחֵלֶב חִטָּה וּמִצּוּר דְּבַשׁ

asbi'ekka: אַשְׂבִּיעֶךָ:

Today is the fifth day of the week, on which the Levites used to recite in the Holy Temple:

To Him Who grants victory— upon the Gittis, a psalm of Assaf: Sing joyously to God, our strength, shout for joy to the God of Jacob. Take up the hymn, sound the drum, the pleasant harp and the lute. Blow the shofar (ram's horn) on the New Moon, at the appointed time for our festive day. For it is a statute for Israel, a [day of] judgment of the God of Jacob. As a testimony for Yehosef, He ordained it when he went out over the land of Egypt, [where] an unfamiliar language I heard. From the burden, I removed his shoulder, his hands were removed from the cauldron. In distress you called out, and I released you, I answered you [though you called] in secret [I answered you] thunderously; I tested you at the waters of Merivah. Selah. Hear, My people, I will testify about you, Israel, if you would just listen to Me. Let no strange god be within you, nor bow before a foreign god. I am the Lord, your God, Who brought you up from the land of Egypt, open your mouth wide, and I will fill it. But My people did not heed My voice, and Israel did not want Me. So I sent them to follow their heart's desires, let them follow their own devices. If only My people would heed Me, if Israel would walk in My ways. I would immediately subdue their enemies, and turn My hand against their tormentors. Those who cause hate of the Lord deceive [pretend obedience to] Him, but their time (of punishment) will be forever. But He would feed him (Israel) from the cream of the wheat, and from the rock, I would sate you with honey.

On Friday:

On Friday, we read Psalm 93, which celebrates God's sovereignty and majesty, acknowledging His eternal reign and the stability of His creation. According to the sages, we recite this psalm on Friday because that is when God completed the creation of the world and reigned over it all in full glory.

Hayyom yom shishi bashabbat	הַיּוֹם יוֹם שִׁשִּׁי בַּשַּׁבָּת
shebbo hayu halviyyim omerim	שֶׁבּוֹ הָיוּ הַלְוִיִּם אוֹמְרִים
beveit hammikdash:	בְּבֵית הַמִּקְדָּשׁ:

adonai malach gei'ut laveish   יְהֹוָה מָלָךְ גֵּאוּת לָבֵשׁ לָבֵשׁ

laveish adonai oz hit'azzar af   יְהֹוָה עֹז הִתְאַזָּר אַף

tikkon teivel bal timmot: nachon   תִּכּוֹן תֵּבֵל בַּל תִּמּוֹט: נָכוֹן

kis'acha mei'az mei'olam attah: כִּסְאֲךָ מֵאָז מֵעוֹלָם אָתָּה:

nase'u neharot adonai nase'u   נָשְׂאוּ נְהָרוֹת יְהֹוָה נָשְׂאוּ

neharot kolam yis'u neharot   נְהָרוֹת קוֹלָם יִשְׂאוּ נְהָרוֹת

dochyam: mikkolot mayim rabbim   דָּכְיָם: מִקֹּלוֹת מַיִם רַבִּים

addirim mishberei yam addir   אַדִּירִים מִשְׁבְּרֵי יָם אַדִּיר

bammarom adonai: edotecha   בַּמָּרוֹם יְהֹוָה: עֵדֹתֶיךָ

ne'emnu me'od leveitcha na'avah   נֶאֶמְנוּ מְאֹד לְבֵיתְךָ נָאֲוָה

kodesh adonai le'orech yamim: קֹדֶשׁ יְהֹוָה לְאֹרֶךְ יָמִים

Today is the sixth day of the week, on which the Levites used to recite in the Holy Temple:

The Lord has begun His reign, with majesty He has clothed Himself; the Lord clothed Himself, with strength He has girded Himself; He has firmly established the world, so that it cannot be moved. Your throne stands firm from of old, You are from eternity. The rivers have raised—O Lord— the rivers have raised their voice, the rivers raise their raging waves. More than the roar of many waters, mightier than the breakers of the sea, mighty on high are You "O Lord." Your testimonies are extremely faithful; holiness is becoming to Your House, O Lord,—for the length of days.

Notes

____

____

____

____

Prayers before Going to Sleep

The Bedtime Shema

Before going to sleep, we recite a prayer known as The Bedtime *Shema*. It is centered around the *Shema* prayer (see above) with additional prayers added before and after. According to the sages, when one goes to sleep at night, his soul ascends to heaven for a daily accounting leaving the body "unprotected." We therefore recite the Bedtime *Shema* to invoke God's protection.

Forgiveness Prayer

The Bedtime *Shema* begins with a short prayer composed by Rabbi Isaac Luria (c. 1534-1572), declaring our forgiveness for all who may have wronged us throughout the day. Just as we forgive everyone who slighted us, we ask God to forgive us for slighting Him and absolve us of our sins. As the Talmudic sage Rava used to say, "Those who ignore the impulse to get even, all their sins are ignored in the heavenly record."

Ribbono shel olam hareini mocheil	רִבּוֹנוֹ שֶׁל עוֹלָם הֲרֵינִי מוֹחֵל
lechol-mi shehich'is vehiknit oti o	לְכָל־מִי שֶׁהִכְעִיס וְהִקְנִיט אוֹתִי אוֹ
shechata chenegdi bein begufi	שֶׁחָטָא כְּנֶגְדִּי בֵּין בְּגוּפִי
bein bemamoni bein bichvodi	בֵּין בְּמָמוֹנִי בֵּין בִּכְבוֹדִי
bein bechol-asher li bein be'ones	בֵּין בְּכָל־אֲשֶׁר לִי בֵּין בְּאוֹנֶס
bein beratzon bein beshogeig	בֵּין בְּרָצוֹן בֵּין בְּשׁוֹגֵג
bein bemeizid bein	בֵּין בְּמֵזִיד בֵּין

bedibbur bein bema'aseh bein   כִּדְבּוּר בֵּין כְּמַעֲשֶׂה בֵּין

bemachashavah bein beharhor   כְּמַחֲשָׁבָה בֵּין כְּהַרְהוֹר

bein begilgul zeh bein begilgul   בֵּין בְּגִלְגּוּל זֶה בֵּין בְּגִלְגּוּל

acheir lechol-bar yisra'el velo   אַחֵר לְכָל־בַּר יִשְׂרָאֵל וְלֹא

yei'anesh shum adam besibbati.   יֵעָנֵשׁ שׁוּם אָדָם בְּסִבָּתִי.

Yehi ratzon millefanecha adonai   יְהִי רָצוֹן מִלְּפָנֶיךָ יְהוָה

elohai veilohei avotai shelo   אֱלֹהַי וֵאלֹהֵי אֲבוֹתַי שֶׁלֹּא

echeta od umah-shechatati   אֶחֱטָא עוֹד וּמַה־שֶּׁחָטָאתִי

lefanecha mechok berachamecha   לְפָנֶיךָ מְחֹק בְּרַחֲמֶיךָ

harabbim aval lo al-yedei yissurim   הָרַבִּים אֲבָל לֹא עַל־יְדֵי יִסּוּרִים

vocholayim ra'im: yihyu leratzon   וָחֳלָיִים רָעִים: יִהְיוּ לְרָצוֹן

imrei-fi vehegyon libbi lefanecha   אִמְרֵי־פִי וְהֶגְיוֹן לִבִּי לְפָנֶיךָ

adonai tzuri vego'ali.   יְהוָה צוּרִי וְגֹאֲלִי.

Master of the world, I hereby forgive anyone who has angered me, or sinned against me, either physically or financially, against my honor or anything that is mine, whether accidentally or intentionally, inadvertently or deliberately, by speech or by deed, by thought or by speculation, in this incarnation or in any other: any believer [is forgiven], may no man be punished on my account. May it be Your will, O Lord, my God and God of my fathers, that I shall sin no more nor repeat my sins, neither shall I again anger You nor do what is wrong in Your eyes. The sins I have committed, erase in your abounding mercies, but not through suffering or severe illnesses. May the words of my mouth and the thoughts of my heart be acceptable before You, O Lord, my Rock and my Redeemer.

A Prayer for Tranquil Sleep

As part of the Bedtime *Shema*, we recite the *Hamapil* blessing, requesting a peaceful night and entrusting our souls into God's faithful hands. Through this blessing, we seek peace and divine protection as we rest.

Baruch attah adonai eloheinu

melech ha'olam hammappil

chevlei sheinah al einai

utenumah al af'appai: vihi ratzon

millefanecha adonai elohai

veilohei avotai shettashkiveini

leshalom veta'amideini leshalom

ve'al yevahaluni ra'yonai

vachalomot ra'im veharhorim

ra'im utehei mittati sheleimah

lefanecha veha'eir einai pen ishan

hammavet ki attah hammei'ir

le'ishon bat ayin. Baruch attah

adonai hammei'ir la'olam kullo

bichvodo.

בָּרוּךְ אַתָּה יְהֹוָה אֱלֹהֵינוּ
מֶלֶךְ הָעוֹלָם הַמַּפִּיל
חֶבְלֵי שֵׁנָה עַל עֵינָי
וּתְנוּמָה עַל עַפְעַפָּי: וִיהִי רָצוֹן
מִלְּפָנֶיךָ יְהֹוָה אֱלֹהַי וֵאלֹהֵי
אֲבוֹתַי שֶׁתַּשְׁכִּיבֵנִי
לְשָׁלוֹם וְתַעֲמִידֵנִי לְשָׁלוֹם
וְאַל יְבַהֲלוּנִי רַעְיוֹנַי
וַחֲלוֹמוֹת רָעִים וְהַרְהוֹרִים
רָעִים וּתְהֵא מִטָּתִי שְׁלֵמָה
לְפָנֶיךָ וְהָאֵר עֵינַי פֶּן אִישַׁן
הַמָּוֶת כִּי אַתָּה הַמֵּאִיר
לְאִישׁוֹן בַּת עָיִן. בָּרוּךְ אַתָּה
יְהֹוָה הַמֵּאִיר לְעוֹלָם כֻּלּוֹ
בִּכְבוֹדוֹ.

Blessed are You, O Lord, our God, King of the Universe, Who causes the fetters of sleep to fall upon my eyes, and slumber upon my eyelids. May it be Your will, O Lord, my God and God of my fathers to make me lie down in peace, and to raise me (again) to peace. Let my thoughts not terrify me— nor evil dreams or evil fancies (disturb me), and may my bed be perfect before You. And light up my eyes lest I sleep the sleep of death, for You illuminate the pupil of the eye. Blessed are You, O Lord, Who illuminates the whole world with His glory.

Notes

____

____

____

Grace After Meals

AND YOU WILL eat and be sated, and you shall bless the Lord, your God, for the good Land He has given you" (Deuteronomy 8:10). The Bible commands us to bless God after eating a filling meal, to express our appreciation for God's great kindness in giving us food to eat and the blessing of the land of Israel. As a fulfillment of this command, we recite the Grace After Meals after eating a meal containing bread. Below are some of the blessings that make up the Grace After Meals:

Blessing for the Food

In this first blessing, we praise God and acknowledge His kindness and mercy in providing food and sustenance for all living beings. According to the sages, this blessing was composed by Moses in gratitude for the manna that the Children of Israel ate in the wilderness following the Exodus from Egypt.

Baruch attah adonai eloheinu	בָּרוּךְ אַתָּה יְהוָֹה אֱלֹהֵינוּ
melech ha'olam hazzan et-	מֶלֶךְ הָעוֹלָם הַזָּן אֶת־הָעוֹלָם
ha'olam kullo betuvo bechein	כֻּלּוֹ בְּטוּבוֹ בְּחֵן בְּחֶסֶד
bechesed uverachamim hu notein	וּבְרַחֲמִים הוּא נוֹתֵן לֶחֶם
lechem lechol-basar ki le'olam	לְכָל־בָּשָׂר כִּי לְעוֹלָם חַסְדּוֹ
chasdo uvetuvo haggadol tamid	וּבְטוּבוֹ הַגָּדוֹל תָּמִיד לֹא־חָסַר
lo-chasar lanu ve'al-yechsar lanu	לָנוּ וְאַל־יֶחְסַר לָנוּ מָזוֹן
mazon le'olam va'ed ba'avur	לְעוֹלָם וָעֶד בַּעֲבוּר שְׁמוֹ
shemo haggadol ki hu el zan	הַגָּדוֹל כִּי הוּא אֵל זָן וּמְפַרְנֵס
umefarneis lakkol umeitiv lakkol	לַכֹּל וּמֵטִיב לַכֹּל

umeichin mazon lechol-beriyyotav

asher bara. Baruch attah adonai

hazzan et-hakkol.

וּמֵכִין מָזוֹן לְכָל־בְּרִיּוֹתָיו
אֲשֶׁר בָּרָא. בָּרוּךְ אַתָּה יְהֹוָה
הַזָּן אֶת־הַכֹּל.

Blessed are You, O Lord, our God, King of the Universe, Who nourishes the entire world with His goodness, with favor, with kindness, and with mercy. He provides food for all flesh, for His kindness endures forever. And through His great goodness, we have never lacked and we will not lack food forever and ever, for the sake of His great Name. For He is Almighty Who nourishes and maintains all, does good to all, and prepares nourishment for all His creatures which He has created. Blessed are You, O Lord, Who nourishes all.

The Land of Israel

The second blessing was composed by Joshua after the Jewish people ate from the first harvest in the Holy Land. In the following paragraph, we thank God for everything He provides, including the land of Israel.

Ve'al hakkol adonai eloheinu

anachnu modim lach

umevarechim otach yitbarach

shimcha befi kol-chai tamid

le'olam va'ed kakkatuv ve'achalta

vesava'eta uveirachta et-adonai

elohecha al-ha'aretz hattovah

asher natan-lach. Baruch

attah adonai al-ha'aretz ve'al-

hammazon:

וְעַל הַכֹּל יְהֹוָה אֱלֹהֵינוּ
אֲנַחְנוּ מוֹדִים לָךְ
וּמְבָרְכִים אוֹתָךְ יִתְבָּרַךְ
שִׁמְךָ בְּפִי כָל־חַי תָּמִיד
לְעוֹלָם וָעֶד כַּכָּתוּב וְאָכַלְתָּ
וְשָׂבָעְתָּ וּבֵרַכְתָּ אֶת־יְהֹוָה
אֱלֹהֶיךָ עַל־הָאָרֶץ הַטּוֹבָה
אֲשֶׁר נָתַן־לָךְ. בָּרוּךְ
אַתָּה יְהֹוָה עַל־הָאָרֶץ וְעַל־
הַמָּזוֹן.

For everything O Lord, our God, We thank You and bless You. Blessed be Your Name through the mouth of all the living, constantly, forever, as it is written: When You have eaten and are satisfied, You will bless the Lord, your God, for the good land which He has given to you. Blessed are You, O Lord, for the land and for the food.

Jerusalem

The third blessing was written by Kings David and Solomon, who established Jerusalem as the capital of Israel and built the Temple respectively. In this blessing, we ask for God's compassion and support for Israel, Jerusalem, and the house of David. It also expresses our deep desire to rely solely on God's generous provision rather than on the charity of others.

Racheim adonai eloheinu	רַחֵם יְהֹוָה אֱלֹהֵינוּ
al-yisra'el ammecha ve'al	עַל־יִשְׂרָאֵל עַמֶּךָ וְעַל
yerushalayim irecha ve'al tziyyon	יְרוּשָׁלַיִם עִירֶךָ וְעַל צִיּוֹן
mishkan kevodecha ve'al malchut	מִשְׁכַּן כְּבוֹדֶךָ וְעַל מַלְכוּת
beit david meshichecha ve'al-	בֵּית דָּוִד מְשִׁיחֶךָ וְעַל־
habbayit haggadol vehakkadosh	הַבַּיִת הַגָּדוֹל וְהַקָּדוֹשׁ
shennikra shimcha alav eloheinu	שֶׁנִּקְרָא שִׁמְךָ עָלָיו אֱלֹהֵינוּ
avinu re'einu zuneinu parneseinu	אָבִינוּ רְעֵנוּ זוּנֵנוּ פַרְנְסֵנוּ
vechalkeleinu veharvicheinu	וְכַלְכְּלֵנוּ וְהַרְוִיחֵנוּ
veharvach-lanu adonai eloheinu	וְהַרְוַח־לָנוּ יְהֹוָה אֱלֹהֵינוּ
meheirah mikkol-tzaroteinu vena	מְהֵרָה מִכָּל־צָרוֹתֵינוּ וְנָא
al-tatzricheinu adonai eloheinu lo	וְנָא אַל־תַּצְרִיכֵנוּ יְהֹוָה
lidei mattenat basar vadam velo	אֱלֹהֵינוּ לֹא לִידֵי מַתְּנַת בָּשָׂר
lidei halva'atam ki im leyadecha	וָדָם וְלֹא לִידֵי הַלְוָאָתָם
hammelei'ah happetuchah	כִּי אִם לְיָדְךָ הַמְּלֵאָה

hakkedoshah veharechavah

shello neivosh velo nikkaleim

le'olam va'ed:

הַפְּתוּחָה הַקְּדוֹשָׁה
וְהָרְחָבָה שֶׁלֹּא נֵבוֹשׁ וְלֹא
נִכָּלֵם לְעוֹלָם וָעֶד:

Uveneih yerushalayim ir

hakkodesh bimheirah veyameinu:

baruch attah adonai boneih

verachamav yerushalayim, amen.

וּבְנֵה יְרוּשָׁלַיִם עִיר
הַקֹּדֶשׁ בִּמְהֵרָה בְיָמֵינוּ:
בָּרוּךְ אַתָּה יְהֹוָה בּוֹנֵה
בְרַחֲמָיו יְרוּשָׁלָיִם, אָמֵן.

Have compassion, O Lord, our God, on Israel, Your people, on Jerusalem, Your city, on Zion, the dwelling place of Your glory, on the kingship of the house of David, Your anointed; and on the great and holy House upon which Your Name is called. Our God, our Father tend us, nourish us, maintain us, sustain us, relieve us and grant us relief O Lord, our God, speedily from all our troubles. O Lord, our God—may we never be in need of the gifts of men nor of their loans, but only of Your hand which is full, open, holy and generous, so that we may be neither shamed nor humiliated forever and ever. Rebuild Jerusalem, city of the Holy Sanctuary, speedily, in our days. Blessed are You, Lord, Builder of Jerusalem in His mercy. Amen.

God's Goodness

The fourth blessing recognizes God's constant goodness and generosity. Rabbi Shimon Schwab notes that while many people receive life's blessings, not everyone fully appreciates or enjoys them. In this prayer, we first seek God's blessings for all the good things in life and then ask Him to grant us the ability to enjoy them.

Baruch attah adonai eloheinu

בָּרוּךְ אַתָּה יְהֹוָה אֱלֹהֵינוּ

melech ha'olam, ha'el avinu, מֶלֶךְ הָעוֹלָם, הָאֵל אָבִינוּ,

malkeinu, addireinu bore'einu, מַלְכֵּנוּ, אַדִּירֵנוּ בּוֹרְאֵנוּ,

go'aleinu, yotzereinu, kedosheinu גּוֹאֲלֵנוּ, יוֹצְרֵנוּ, קְדוֹשֵׁנוּ

kedosh ya'akov, ro'einu ro'eih קְדוֹשׁ יַעֲקֹב, רוֹעֵנוּ רוֹעֵה

yisra'el, hammelech hattov, יִשְׂרָאֵל, הַמֶּלֶךְ הַטּוֹב,

vehammeitiv lakkol, shebbechol וְהַמֵּטִיב לַכֹּל, שֶׁבְּכָל

yom vayom hu heitiv, hu meitiv, יוֹם וָיוֹם הוּא הֵיטִיב, הוּא מֵטִיב,

hu yeitiv lanu, hu gemalanu, הוּא יֵיטִיב לָנוּ, הוּא גְמָלָנוּ, הוּא

hu gomeleinu, hu yigmeleinu גוֹמְלֵנוּ, הוּא יִגְמְלֵנוּ לָעַד

la'ad lechein ulechesed לְחֵן וּלְחֶסֶד וּלְרַחֲמִים

ulerachamim ulerevach hatzalah וּלְרֶוַח הַצָּלָה וְהַצְלָחָה

vehatzlachah berachah vishu'ah, בְּרָכָה וִישׁוּעָה, נֶחָמָה,

nechamah, parnasah vechalkalah, פַּרְנָסָה וְכַלְכָּלָה,

verachamim, vechayyim וְרַחֲמִים, וְחַיִּים

veshalom, vechol-tov, umikkol-tuv וְשָׁלוֹם, וְכָל־טוֹב, וּמִכָּל־טוֹב

le'olam al yechassereinu. לְעוֹלָם אַל יְחַסְּרֵנוּ.

Blessed are You, Adonoy our God, King of the Universe, the Almighty, our Father, our King, our Mighty One, our Creator, our Redeemer, our Maker, our Holy One, Holy One of Jacob, our Shepherd, Shepherd of Israel, the King, Who is good and beneficent to all. Every single day He has done good, does good, and will do good to us. He has rewarded us, He rewards us, He will reward us forever with favor, kindness, and compassion, relief, rescue, and success, blessing, deliverance, and consolation, maintenance, sustenance, compassion, life, peace, and everything good; and of all good things may He never deprive us.

Notes

Sabbath Prayers

The seventh day of the week is known as the Sabbath, or *Shabbat* in Hebrew. On this holy day, we set aside the worries and business concerns of the week and rest, just as God rested from creating the world on the seventh day. By resting on the Sabbath, we declare our belief in God as the Creator of the world.

Prayer After Lighting the Sabbath Candles

Every Friday evening, just before sundown and the beginning of the Sabbath, we light candles in order to bring peace and light into our homes. While these candles are traditionally lit by women, they may be lit by men as well. After lighting the candles, it is customary to recite the following beautiful prayer for the welfare of one's family.

Yehi ratzon millefanecha,	יְהִי רָצוֹן מִלְּפָנֶיךָ,
adonai elohai elohei yisra'el,	יְיָ אֱלֹהַי אֱלֹהֵי יִשְׂרָאֵל,
shettechonein oti (ve'et ishi) ve'et	שֶׁתְּחוֹנֵן אוֹתִי (וְאֶת אִישִׁי)
kol kerovai, vetittein lanu ulechol	וְאֶת כֹּל קְרוֹבַי, וְתִתֵּן לָנוּ
yisra'el chayyim tovim va'arukkim,	וּלְכָל יִשְׂרָאֵל חַיִּים טוֹבִים
vetizkereinu bezichron tovah	וַאֲרֻכִּים, וְתִזְכְּרֵנוּ בְּזִכְרוֹן
uverachah, vetifkedeinu	טוֹבָה וּבְרָכָה, וְתִפְקְדֵנוּ
bifkuddat yeshu'ah verachamim,	בִּפְקֻדַּת יְשׁוּעָה וְרַחֲמִים,
vetashkein shechinatecha	וְתַשְׁכֵּן שְׁכִינָתְךָ
beineinu, vezakkeinu legaddeil	בֵּינֵינוּ, וְזַכֵּנוּ לְגַדֵּל
banim uvenei vanim chachamim	בָּנִים וּבְנֵי בָנִים חֲכָמִים
unevonim ohavei adonai, yir'ei	וּנְבוֹנִים אוֹהֲבֵי יְיָ, יִרְאֵי
elohim, anshei emet zera kodesh,	אֱלֹהִים, אַנְשֵׁי אֱמֶת זֶרַע קֹדֶשׁ,
badonai deveikim ume'irim et	בַּיְיָ דְּבֵקִים וּמְאִירִים אֶת
ha'olam batorah uvema'asim	הָעוֹלָם בַּתּוֹרָה וּבְמַעֲשִׂים
tovim uvechol melechet avodat	טוֹבִים וּבְכָל מְלֶאכֶת עֲבוֹדַת
habborei. Anna, shema et	הַבּוֹרֵא. אָנָּא, שְׁמַע אֶת
techinnati bizchut sarah verivkah	תְּחִנָּתִי בִּזְכוּת שָׂרָה וְרִבְקָה
rachel velei'ah immoteinu,	רָחֵל וְלֵאָה אִמּוֹתֵינוּ,
veha'eir nereinu shello yichbeh	וְהָאֵר נֵרֵנוּ שֶׁלֹּא יִכְבֶּה

le'olam va'ed, veha'eir panecha

venivvashei'ah. Amen.

לְעוֹלָם וָעֶד, וְהָאֵר פָּנֶיךָ

וְנִוָּשֵׁעָה. אָמֵן.

May it be Your will, O Lord my God and God of Israel, that You be gracious to me (and my spouse) and all my relatives, and grant us and all of Israel good and long lives. Remember us for good and blessing, and consider us for salvation and compassion. May Your Divine Presence dwell among us, and may we merit to raise children and grandchildren who are wise and understanding, who love the Lord and fear God, people of truth, holy offspring, who cling to the Lord and illuminate the world with Torah and good deeds and all the work of serving the Creator. Please, hear my supplication in the merit of Sarah, Rebecca, Rachel, and Leah, our mothers, and illuminate our light so that it never extinguishes forever and ever. May You shine Your face upon us and we shall be saved. Amen.

Notes

Beloved of My Soul

THE *YEDID NEFESH* (beloved of the soul) prayer is tradition-ally recited as the sun sets, ushering in the Sabbath. It is commonly attributed to the sixteenth-century Sephardic Kabbalist, Rabbi Elazar ben Moshe Azikri (1533-1600). It is an intimate prayer of yearning for God's revelation and expresses our deepest longing for spiritual intimacy with our Father in heaven.

Yedid nefesh, av harachman,
meshoch avdach el-retzonach,
yarutz avdach kemo ayyal,
yishtachaveh mul hadarach, ki
ye'erav-lo yedidutach minnofet
tzuf vechol-ta'am.

יְדִיד נֶפֶשׁ, אָב הָרַחְמָן,
מְשׁךְ עַבְדָּךְ אֶל־רְצוֹנָךְ,
יָרוּץ עַבְדָּךְ כְּמוֹ אַיָּל,
יִשְׁתַּחֲוֶה מוּל הֲדָרָךְ, כִּי
יֶעֱרַב־לוֹ יְדִידוּתָךְ מִנֹּפֶת
צוּף וְכָל־טָעַם.

Hadur, na'eh, ziv ha'olam, nafshi
cholat ahavatach, anna, eil, na,
refa-na lah behar'ot lah no'am
zivach, az titchazzeik vetitrappei,
vehayetah lach shifchat olam.

הָדוּר, נָאֶה, זִיו הָעוֹלָם, נַפְשִׁי
חוֹלַת אַהֲבָתָךְ, אָנָּא, אֵל, נָא,
רְפָא־נָא לָהּ בְּהַרְאוֹת לָהּ נֹעַם
זִיוָךְ, אָז תִּתְחַזֵּק וְתִתְרַפֵּא,
וְהָיְתָה לָךְ שִׁפְחַת עוֹלָם.

Vatik, yehemu rachamecha,
vechus-na al-bein ohavach, ki
zeh kammeh nichsof nichsaf
lir'ot betif'eret uzzach, anna, eili,
machmad libbi, chushah-na ve'al
tit'allam.

וָתִיק, יֶהֱמוּ רַחֲמֶיךָ,
וְחוּס־נָא עַל־בֵּן אוֹהֲבָךְ, כִּי
זֶה כַּמֶּה נִכְסֹף נִכְסַף
לִרְאוֹת בְּתִפְאֶרֶת עֻזָּךְ, אָנָּא, אֵלִי,
מַחְמַד לִבִּי, חוּשָׁה־נָּא וְאַל
תִּתְעַלָּם.

Higgaleh-na uferos, chaviv,

הִגָּלֶה־נָא וּפְרֹשׂ, חָבִיב,

alai et-sukkat shelomach, ta'ir עָלַי אֶת־סֻכַּת שְׁלוֹמָךְ, תָּאִיר

eretz mikkevodach, nagilah אֶרֶץ מִכְּבוֹדָךְ, נָגִילָה

venismechah bach, maher, ahuv, וְנִשְׂמְחָה בָּךְ, מַהֵר, אָהוּב,

ki va mo'ed, vechanneini kimei כִּי בָא מוֹעֵד, וְחָנֵּנִי כִּימֵי

olam. עוֹלָם.

Beloved of my soul, compassionate Father, draw me, your servant, to your desire. Would that I could run like a gazelle, and bow before Your beauty, for I find your love sweeter than honey or any delight.

Majestic, Beautiful, Radiance of the world, my soul is sick for your love. God, please heal her by bathing her in your serene light - then she shall surely be strengthened and healed and be Your servant forever.

Ancient One, let Your compassion flow. Have pity on the child whom You love - for I have yearned so long to see your luminescent power. My God, my beloved, hurry; please, do not hide!

Please, my beloved, reveal Yourself. Spread the shelter of your peace over me. May the whole world be illuminated with Your glory; then shall we be glad and rejoice with You. My lover - come quickly, for the time has come - have compassion for me as in days of old.

Notes

____

____

____

____

Come My Beloved

THIS PRAYER, COMPOSED by the kabbalist Rabbi Shlomo HaLevi Alkabetz (1505 – 1584), is recited on Friday at sundown during the service known as *Kabbalat Shabbat*, "Welcoming the Sabbath." This song is based on the Talmud's description of how the Sages would joyously welcome and greet this holy day.

Lechah dodi likrat kallah. Penei shabbat nekabbelah.	לְכָה דוֹדִי לִקְרַאת כַּלָּה. פְּנֵי שַׁבָּת נְקַבְּלָה.
Shamor vezachor bedibbur echad. Hishmi'anu el hammeyuchad. Adonai echad ushmo echad. Lesheim uletif'eret velithillah. Lechah dodi likrat kallah. Penei shabbat nekabbelah.	שָׁמוֹר וְזָכוֹר בְּדִבּוּר אֶחָד. הִשְׁמִיעָנוּ אֵל הַמְיֻחָד. ה׳ אֶחָד וּשְׁמוֹ אֶחָד. לְשֵׁם וּלְתִפְאֶרֶת וְלִתְהִלָּה. לְכָה דוֹדִי לִקְרַאת כַּלָּה. פְּנֵי שַׁבָּת נְקַבְּלָה.
Likrat shabbat lechu veneilechah. Ki hi mekor habberachah. Merosh mikkedem nesuchah. Sof ma'aseh bemachashvah techillah. Lechah dodi likrat kallah. Penei shabbat nekabbelah.	לִקְרַאת שַׁבָּת לְכוּ וְנֵלְכָה. כִּי הִיא מְקוֹר הַבְּרָכָה. מֵרֹאשׁ מִקֶּדֶם נְסוּכָה. סוֹף מַעֲשֶׂה בְּמַחֲשָׁבָה תְּחִלָּה. לְכָה דוֹדִי לִקְרַאת כַּלָּה. פְּנֵי שַׁבָּת נְקַבְּלָה.
Mikdash melech ir meluchah. Kumi tze'i mittoch hahafeichah. Rav lach shevet be'eimek habbacha. Vehu yachamol alayich chemlah. Lechah dodi likrat kallah. Penei	מִקְדַשׁ מֶלֶךְ עִיר מְלוּכָה. קוּמִי צְאִי מִתּוֹךְ הַהֲפֵכָה. רַב לָךְ שֶׁבֶת בְּעֵמֶק הַבָּכָא. וְהוּא יַחֲמוֹל עָלַיִךְ חֶמְלָה. לְכָה דוֹדִי לִקְרַאת כַּלָּה. פְּנֵי

shabbat nekabbelah.

שַׁבָּת נְקַבְּלָה.

Hitna'ari mei'afar kumi. Livshi bigdei tif'arteich ammi. Al yad ben yishai beit hallachmi. Karevah el nafshi ge'alah. Lechah dodi likrat kallah. Penei shabbat nekabbelah.

הִתְנַעֲרִי מֵעָפָר קוּמִי. לִבְשִׁי בִּגְדֵי תִפְאַרְתֵּךְ עַמִּי. עַל יַד בֶּן יִשַׁי בֵּית הַלַּחְמִי. קָרְבָה אֶל נַפְשִׁי גְאָלָהּ. לְכָה דוֹדִי לִקְרַאת כַּלָּה. פְּנֵי שַׁבָּת נְקַבְּלָה.

Hit'or'ri Hit'or'ri. Ki va orech kumi ori. Uri uri shir dabbeiri. Kevod adonai alayich niglah. Lechah dodi likrat kallah. Penei shabbat nekabbelah.

הִתְעוֹרְרִי הִתְעוֹרְרִי. כִּי בָא אוֹרֵךְ קוּמִי אוֹרִי. עוּרִי עוּרִי שִׁיר דַּבֵּרִי. כְּבוֹד ה' עָלַיִךְ נִגְלָה. לְכָה דוֹדִי לִקְרַאת כַּלָּה. פְּנֵי שַׁבָּת נְקַבְּלָה.

Lo teivoshi velo tikkalemi. Mah tishtochachi umah tehemi. Bach yechesu aniyyei ammi. Venivnetah ir al tillah. Lechah dodi likrat kallah. Penei shabbat nekabbelah.

לֹא תֵבוֹשִׁי וְלֹא תִכָּלְמִי. מַה תִּשְׁתּוֹחֲחִי וּמַה תֶּהֱמִי. בָּךְ יֶחֱסוּ עֲנִיֵּי עַמִּי. וְנִבְנְתָה עִיר עַל תִּלָּהּ. לְכָה דוֹדִי לִקְרַאת כַּלָּה. פְּנֵי שַׁבָּת נְקַבְּלָה.

Vehayu limshisah shosayich. Verachaku kol mevalle'ayich. Yasis alayich elohayich. Kimsos chatan al kallah. Lechah dodi likrat kallah. Penei shabbat nekabbelah.

וְהָיוּ לִמְשִׁסָּה שֹׁאסָיִךְ. וְרָחֲקוּ כָּל מְבַלְּעָיִךְ. יָשִׂישׂ עָלַיִךְ אֱלֹהָיִךְ. כִּמְשׂוֹשׂ חָתָן עַל כַּלָּה. לְכָה דוֹדִי לִקְרַאת כַּלָּה. פְּנֵי שַׁבָּת נְקַבְּלָה.

Yamin us'mol tifrotzi. Ve'et adonai ta'aritzi. Al yad ish ben partzi. Venismechah venagilah. Lechah dodi likrat kallah. Penei shabbat nekabbelah.

יָמִין וּשְׂמֹאל תִּפְרוֹצִי. וְאֶת ה' תַּעֲרִיצִי. עַל יַד אִישׁ בֶּן פַּרְצִי. וְנִשְׂמְחָה וְנָגִילָה. לְכָה דוֹדִי לִקְרַאת כַּלָּה. פְּנֵי שַׁבָּת נְקַבְּלָה.

Bo'i veshalom ateret ba'lah. Gam

בּוֹאִי בְשָׁלוֹם עֲטֶרֶת בַּעְלָהּ. גַּם

besimchah uvetzoholah. Toch
emunei am segullah. Bo'i challah.
Bo'i challah. Lechah dodi likrat
kallah. Penei shabbat nekabbelah.

כְּשִׂמְחָה וּבְצָהֳלָה. תּוֹךְ
אֱמוּנֵי עַם סְגֻלָּה. בּוֹאִי כַלָּה.
בּוֹאִי כַלָּה. לְכָה דוֹדִי לִקְרַאת כַּלָּה.
פְּנֵי שַׁבָּת נְקַבְּלָה.

Come, beloved to greet the bride! Let us welcome the Sabbath.

"Observe" and "Remember" in one utterance. The One and Only God allowed us to hear. God is one and His name is one. For renown and for splendor and for praise. Come, beloved to greet the bride! Let us welcome the Sabbath.

Let us go to welcome the Sabbath. For she is the source of blessing. From the very start, from the beginning she was designated. Last in creation and first in thought. Come, beloved to greet the bride! Let us welcome the Sabbath.

Sanctuary of the King, city of royalty. Rise and go forth from the ruins. Too long have you sat in the valley sorrow. And He will shower you with compassion. Come, beloved to greet the bride! Let us welcome the Sabbath.

Shake it off, rise from the ashes. Wear the garments of the glory of My people. Through the son of Jesse of Bethlehem. Draw close to my soul and redeem it. Come, beloved to greet the bride! Let us welcome the Sabbath.

Wake up, wake up. For your light has come, rise and illuminate. Awaken, awaken, speak a song. The honor of God is revealed upon you. Come, beloved to greet the bride! Let us welcome the Sabbath.

Do not be ashamed or humiliated. Why should you be downcast and why should you be dejected? Within you the afflicted of My people will seek refuge. And the city will be rebuilt on its former site. Come, beloved to greet the bride! Let us welcome the Sabbath.

And your oppressors will be destroyed. And those who would devour you will be cast far away. Your God will rejoice over you. Like a bridegroom rejoices over his bride. Come, beloved to greet the bride! Let us welcome the Sabbath.

Right and left you will proliferate. And you will extol God. Through the man who descends from Peretz. And we shall celebrate and rejoice. Come, beloved to greet the bride! Let us welcome the Sabbath.

Come in peace, crown of her husband. With both joy and fanfare. Among the faithful, the virtuous people. Come O bride. Come O bride. Come, beloved to greet the bride! Let us welcome the Sabbath.

Notes

Blessing One's Children

I T IS CUSTOMARY to bless our children on Friday night before the first Sabbath meal. Since the Sabbath is a source of blessing, it is a particularly auspicious time for blessing our children.

In Genesis 48:20, Jacob told his two grandchildren: "By you shall Israel invoke blessings, saying: God make you like Ephraim and Manasseh." Why do we bless our sons to be like Ephraim and Manasseh as opposed to the forefathers or any one of Jacob's children?

Rabbi Ovadia Hadiah explained that Joseph's sons were raised in Egypt, in a household visited by Egyptian officials, and received an Egyptian education. Though Egyptian society was deeply corrupt and suffused with idolatry, injustice, and immorality, Joseph's sons held fast to their religious beliefs and identity. They resisted outside influences and remained true to their father's teachings. Ephraim and Manasseh were strong, confident, and secure in their mission in life. We bless our children to have the inner conviction and courage to remain strong in their beliefs and family traditions despite all the dangerous influences and societal pressures that surround them. For the people of Israel, this blessing gained great importance during the 2,000-year exile following the destruction of the Temple in Jerusalem.

Ephraim and Manasseh are also the first siblings in the Bible who live together in peace and harmony. Unlike other siblings in the Bible who view each other as rivals, such as Cain and Abel, Jacob and Esau, and Joseph and his brothers, Ephraim and Manasseh demonstrate brotherly love and harmony. Even when Jacob placed the younger Ephraim before the older Manasseh, brotherly love prevailed and Manasseh did not become jealous of his brother. We bless our children to follow in their footsteps.

For a boy:
Yesimcha elohim ke'efrayim
vechimnasheh.

For a girl:
Yesimeich elohim kesarah, rivkah,
rachel velei'ah.

Continue:
Yevarech'cha adonai
veyishmerecha. Ya'eir adonai
panav eilecha vichunnekka. Yissa
adonai panav eilecha veyaseim
lecha shalom.

For a boy: יְשִׂימְךָ אֱלֹהִים כְּאֶפְרַיִם וְכִמְנַשֶּׁה.

For girl: יְשִׂימֵךְ אֱלֹהִים כְּשָׂרָה, רִבְקָה, רָחֵל וְלֵאָה.

Continue: יְבָרֶכְךָ אֲדֹנָי וְיִשְׁמְרֶךָ. יָאֵר אֲדֹנָי פָּנָיו אֵלֶיךָ וִיחֻנֶּךָּ. יִשָּׂא אֲדֹנָי פָּנָיו אֵלֶיךָ וְיָשֵׂם לְךָ שָׁלוֹם.

For a boy: May God make you like Ephraim and Manasseh.

For a girl: May God make you like Sarah, Rebecca, Rachel, and Leah.

Continue: May the Lord bless you and protect you. May the Lord shine His countenance upon you and give you grace. May the Lord lift His countenance upon you and give you peace.

Notes

____

____

____

____

____

Peace Be Upon You

The sages teach that two ministering angels accompany us home from the synagogue every Friday night. This four-stanza song is traditionally sung at the beginning of the Friday night meal to welcome these angels, request their blessing, and then bid them farewell. The theme of this song is peace - the vessel that contains all other blessings. May God grant us peace speedily in our time.

Shalom aleichem mal'achei
hashareit mal'achei elyon

שָׁלוֹם עֲלֵיכֶם מַלְאֲכֵי
הַשָּׁרֵת מַלְאֲכֵי עֶלְיוֹן

mimmelech malchei hammelachim
hakkadosh baruch hu.

מִמֶּלֶךְ מַלְכֵי הַמְּלָכִים
הַקָּדוֹשׁ בָּרוּךְ הוּא.

Bo'achem leshalom mal'achei
hashalom mal'achei elyon

בּוֹאֲכֶם לְשָׁלוֹם מַלְאֲכֵי
הַשָּׁלוֹם מַלְאֲכֵי עֶלְיוֹן

mimmelech malchei hammelachim
hakkadosh baruch hu.

מִמֶּלֶךְ מַלְכֵי הַמְּלָכִים
הַקָּדוֹשׁ בָּרוּךְ הוּא.

Barechuni leshalom mal'achei
hashalom mal'achei elyon

בָּרְכוּנִי לְשָׁלוֹם מַלְאֲכֵי
הַשָּׁלוֹם מַלְאֲכֵי עֶלְיוֹן

mimmelech malchei hammelachim
hakkadosh baruch hu.

מִמֶּלֶךְ מַלְכֵי הַמְּלָכִים
הַקָּדוֹשׁ בָּרוּךְ הוּא.

Tzeitchem leshalom mal'achei
hashalom mal'achei elyon

צֵאתְכֶם לְשָׁלוֹם מַלְאֲכֵי
הַשָּׁלוֹם מַלְאֲכֵי עֶלְיוֹן

mimmelech malchei hammelachim
hakkadosh baruch hu.

מִמֶּלֶךְ מַלְכֵי הַמְּלָכִים
הַקָּדוֹשׁ בָּרוּךְ הוּא.

Peace be upon you, ministering angels, angels of the Most High,

from the King of kings, the Holy One, blessed be He.

May your coming be in peace, angels of peace, angels of the Most High,

from the King of kings, the Holy One, blessed be He.

Bless me with peace, angels of peace, angels of the Most High,

from the King of kings, the Holy One, blessed be He.

May your departure be in peace, angels of peace, angels of the Most High,

from the King of kings, the Holy One, blessed be He.

Notes

____

____

____

____

____

____

Woman of Valor

❝ WOMAN OF VALOR," is taken from the concluding passage of the book of Proverbs (Proverbs 31:10-31), in which King Solomon sings the praises of his beloved mother Bathsheba. These verses are traditionally sung at the beginning of the Friday night meal.

According to popular understanding, this song is sung to honor the matriarch of the family who tirelessly cares for the household and its members throughout the week. However, some interpret it metaphorically, suggesting that the verses refer to the Sabbath itself. In Jewish liturgy, the Sabbath is often personified with feminine qualities, such as the Sabbath Queen or Bride. From this perspective, "Woman of Valor" is a song of love and appreciation for the Sabbath and the blessings it brings each week.

Eishet-chayil mi yimtza verachok mippeninim michrah:

אֵשֶׁת־חַיִל מִי יִמְצָא וְרָחֹק מִפְּנִינִים מִכְרָהּ׃

Batach bah leiv ba'lah veshalal lo yechsar:

בָּטַח בָּהּ לֵב בַּעְלָהּ וְשָׁלָל לֹא יֶחְסָר׃

Gemalat'hu tov velo-ra kol yemei chayyeha:

גְּמָלַתְהוּ טוֹב וְלֹא־רָע כֹּל יְמֵי חַיֶּיהָ׃

Dareshah tzemer ufishtim vatta'as becheifetz kappeha:

דָּרְשָׁה צֶמֶר וּפִשְׁתִּים וַתַּעַשׂ בְּחֵפֶץ כַּפֶּיהָ׃

Hayetah ko'oniyyot socher mimmerchak tavi lachmah:

הָיְתָה כָּאֳנִיּוֹת סוֹחֵר מִמֶּרְחָק תָּבִיא לַחְמָהּ׃

Vattakom be'od layyelah
vattittein teref leveitah vechok
lena'aroteha:

וַתָּקָם בְּעוֹד לַיְלָה וַתִּתֵּן
טֶרֶף לְבֵיתָהּ וְחֹק
לְנַעֲרֹתֶיהָ:

Zamemah sadeh vattikkacheihu
mipperi chappeha nate'ah karem:

זָמְמָה שָׂדֶה וַתִּקָּחֵהוּ
מִפְּרִי כַפֶּיהָ נָטְעָה כָּרֶם:

Chagerah ve'oz motneha
vatte'ammeitz zero'oteha:

חָגְרָה בְעוֹז מָתְנֶיהָ
וַתְּאַמֵּץ זְרוֹעֹתֶיהָ:

Ta'amah ki-tov sachrah lo-yichbeh
vallai'lah neirah:

טָעֲמָה כִּי־טוֹב סַחְרָהּ לֹא־יִכְבֶּה
בַלַּיְלָה נֵרָהּ:

Yadeha shillechah vakkishor
vechappeha tamechu falech:

יָדֶיהָ שִׁלְּחָה בַכִּישׁוֹר
וְכַפֶּיהָ תָּמְכוּ פָלֶךְ:

Kappah paresah le'ani veyadeha
shillechah la'evyon:

כַּפָּהּ פָּרְשָׂה לֶעָנִי וְיָדֶיהָ
שִׁלְּחָה לָאֶבְיוֹן:

Lo-tira leveitah mishaleg ki chol-
beitah lavush shanim:

לֹא־תִירָא לְבֵיתָהּ מִשָּׁלֶג כִּי כָל־
בֵּיתָהּ לָבֻשׁ שָׁנִים:

Marvaddim asetah-lah sheish
ve'argaman levushah:

מַרְבַדִּים עָשְׂתָה־לָּהּ שֵׁשׁ
וְאַרְגָּמָן לְבוּשָׁהּ:

Noda bashe'arim ba'lah beshivto
im-ziknei-aretz:

נוֹדָע בַּשְּׁעָרִים בַּעְלָהּ בְּשִׁבְתּוֹ
עִם־זִקְנֵי־אָרֶץ:

Sadin asetah vattimkor vachagor
natenah lakkena'ani:

סָדִין עָשְׂתָה וַתִּמְכֹּר וַחֲגוֹר
נָתְנָה לַכְּנַעֲנִי:

Oz-vehadar levushah vattischak
leyom acharon:

עֹז־וְהָדָר לְבוּשָׁהּ וַתִּשְׂחַק
לְיוֹם אַחֲרוֹן:

Piha patechah vechochmah
vetorat chesed al-leshonah:

פִּיהָ פָּתְחָה בְחָכְמָה
וְתוֹרַת חֶסֶד עַל־לְשׁוֹנָה:

Tzofiyyah halichot beitah
velechem atzlut lo tocheil:

צוֹפִיָּה הֲלִיכוֹת בֵּיתָהּ
וְלֶחֶם עַצְלוּת לֹא תֹאכֵל:

Kamu vaneha vay'asheruha ba'lah
vayehallah:

קָמוּ בָנֶיהָ וַיְאַשְּׁרוּהָ בַּעְלָהּ
וַיְהַלְלָהּ:

Rabbot banot asu chayil ve'at alit
al-kullanah:

רַבּוֹת בָּנוֹת עָשׂוּ חָיִל וְאַתְּ עָלִית
עַל־כֻּלָּנָה:

Sheker hachein vehevel hayyofi
ishah yir'at-adonai hi tithallal:

שֶׁקֶר הַחֵן וְהֶבֶל הַיֹּפִי
אִשָּׁה יִרְאַת־יְהֹוָה הִיא תִתְהַלָּל:

Tenu-lah mipperi yadeha vihalluha
vashe'arim ma'aseha:

תְּנוּ־לָהּ מִפְּרִי יָדֶיהָ וִיהַלְלוּהָ
בַשְּׁעָרִים מַעֲשֶׂיהָ:

A woman of valor, who can find? Her worth is far beyond that of rubies.

Her husband puts his confidence in her, And lacks no good thing.

She is good to him, never bad, All the days of her life.

She looks for wool and flax, And sets her hand to them with a will.

She is like a merchant fleet, Bringing her food from afar.

She rises while it is still night, And supplies provisions for her household, The daily fare of her maids.

She sets her mind on an estate and acquires it; She plants a vineyard by her own labors.

She girds herself with strength, And performs her tasks with vigor.

She sees that her business thrives; Her lamp never goes out at night.

She sets her hand to the distaff; Her fingers work the spindle.

She gives generously to the poor; Her hands are stretched out to the needy.

She is not worried for her household because of snow, For her whole household is dressed in crimson.

She makes covers for herself; Her clothing is linen and purple.

Her husband is prominent in the gates, As he sits among the elders of the land.

She makes cloth and sells it, And offers a girdle to the merchant.

She is clothed with strength and splendor; She looks to the future cheerfully.

Her mouth is full of wisdom, Her tongue with kindly teaching.

She oversees the activities of her household And never eats the bread of idleness.

Her children declare her happy; Her husband praises her,

"Many women have done well, But you surpass them all."

Grace is deceptive, Beauty is illusory; It is for her fear of the Lord that a woman is to be praised.

Extol her for the fruit of her hand, And let her works praise her in the gates.

Notes

____

____

____

____

____

____

____

____

____

____

____

____

Kiddush: Sanctifying the Sabbath

The Sabbath is the holiest day of the week. Because God created the world in six days and rested on the seventh, we work for six days and rest on the seventh. And just as God sanctified the Sabbath day, we begin the first Sabbath meal by sanctifying the day with the following words, taken from Genesis 2:1-3, recited over a cup of wine.

וַיְכֻלּוּ הַשָּׁמַיִם וְהָאָרֶץ
וְכָל צְבָאָם: וַיְכַל אֱלֹהִים
בַּיּוֹם הַשְּׁבִיעִי מְלַאכְתּוֹ אֲשֶׁר
עָשָׂה. וַיִּשְׁבֹּת בַּיּוֹם הַשְּׁבִיעִי
מִכָּל מְלַאכְתּוֹ אֲשֶׁר עָשָׂה:
וַיְבָרֶךְ אֱלֹהִים אֶת יוֹם הַשְּׁבִיעִי
וַיְקַדֵּשׁ אֹתוֹ. כִּי בוֹ שָׁבַת
מִכָּל מְלַאכְתּוֹ אֲשֶׁר בָּרָא
אֱלֹהִים לַעֲשׂוֹת:

Vayechulu hashmayim veha'aretz vechol tzeva'am: vayechal elohim bayom hashvi'i melachto asher asah. Vayyishbot bayom hashvi'i mikkol melachto asher asah: vayevarech elohim et yom hashvi'i vayekaddeish oto. Ki vo shavat mikkol melachto asher bara elohim la'asot:

And He completed the heavens and the earth and all their hosts. And God completed on the seventh day His work which He had done; and He rested on the seventh day from all His work which He had done. And God blessed the seventh day, and He sanctified it; for on it He had rested from all the work which He had created to do.

The Soul of Every Living Being Shall Bless You

ON THE SABBATH and holidays, we incorporate additional paragraphs of praise into the morning prayers. One of the most revered and beautiful of these supplementary prayers is "The Soul of Every Living Being Shall Bless You," a powerful expression of praise and gratitude. It highlights our complete dependence on God's mercy, our inability to fully praise His greatness and our passionate commitment to dedicating ourselves to His service. This prayer is also recited during the Passover seder on the first night of Passover.

<table>
<tr><td>

Nishmat kol chai tevareich et
shimcha adonai elheinu. Veruach
kol basar tefa'eir uteromeim
zichrecha malkeinu tamid: min
ha'olam ve'ad ha'olam attah eil.
Umibbal'adecha ein lanu melech
goel umoshia'. Podeh umatzil
umefarneis umeracheim bechol eit
tzarah vetzukah. Ein lanu melech
ozer vesomeich ella attah: elohei
harishonim veha'acharonim.
Elo'ah kol beriot. Adon kol toladot.
Hammehullal berov hattishbachot.
Hammenaheig olamo bechesed
uveriotav berachamim: va'donai lo
yanum velo yishan. Ham'oreir

</td><td dir="rtl">

נִשְׁמַת כָּל חַי תְּבָרֵךְ אֶת
שְׁמְךָ ה' אֱלֹהֵינוּ. וְרוּחַ
כָּל בָּשָׂר תְּפָאֵר וּתְרוֹמֵם
זִכְרְךָ מַלְכֵּנוּ תָּמִיד: מִן
הָעוֹלָם וְעַד הָעוֹלָם אַתָּה אֵל.
וּמִבַּלְעָדֶיךָ אֵין לָנוּ מֶלֶךְ
גּוֹאֵל וּמוֹשִׁיעַ. פּוֹדֶה וּמַצִּיל
וּמְפַרְנֵס וּמְרַחֵם בְּכָל עֵת
צָרָה וְצוּקָה. אֵין לָנוּ מֶלֶךְ
עוֹזֵר וְסוֹמֵךְ אֶלָּא אַתָּה: אֱלֹהֵי
הָרִאשׁוֹנִים וְהָאַחֲרוֹנִים.
אֱלוֹהַּ כָּל בְּרִיּוֹת. אֲדוֹן כָּל תּוֹלָדוֹת.
הַמְּהֻלָּל בְּרוֹב הַתִּשְׁבָּחוֹת.
הַמְּנַהֵג עוֹלָמוֹ בְּחֶסֶד
וּבְרִיּוֹתָיו בְּרַחֲמִים: וַה'
לֹא יָנוּם וְלֹא יִישָׁן. הַמְּעוֹרֵר

</td></tr>
</table>

yesheinim. Vehammeikitz
nirdamim. Vehammeisiach
ilmim. Vehammattir asurim.
Vehassomech noflim.
Vehazzokef kefufim. Lecha
levaddecha anachnu
modim: illu finu malei shirah
kayyam. Uleshoneinu rinnah
kahamon gallav. Veshftoteinu
shevach kemerchavei rakia'.
Ve'eineinu me'irot kashemesh
vechayyarei'ach. Veyadeinu
ferusot kenishrei shamayim.
Veragleinu kallot ka'ayyalot. Ein
anachnu maspikim lehodot lecha
adonai eloheinu veilohei avoteinu.
Ulevareich et shemecha al achat
me'elef alfei alafim veribbei
revavot pe'amim. Hattovot
she'asita im avoteinu ve'immanu:
mimmitzrayim ge'altanu adonai
eloheinu. Umibbeit avadim
peditanu. Bera'av zantanu.
Uvesava kilkaltanu. Meicherev
hitzaltanu. Umiddever millat'tanu.
Umeicholayim ra'im vene'emanim
dillitanu: ad heinnah azarunu
rachamecha. Velo azavunu
chasadecha ve'al tittesheinu
adonai eloheinu lanetzach: al
kein eivarim sheppillagta banu.
Veruach uneshamah shennafachta
be'appeinu. Velashon asher samta

יְשֵׁנִים. וְהַמֵּקִיץ
נִרְדָּמִים. וְהַמֵּשִׂיחַ
אִלְמִים. וְהַמַּתִּיר אֲסוּרִים.
וְהַסּוֹמֵךְ נוֹפְלִים.
וְהַזּוֹקֵף כְּפוּפִים. לְךָ
לְבַדְּךָ אֲנַחְנוּ
מוֹדִים: אִלּוּ פִינוּ מָלֵא שִׁירָה
כַיָּם. וּלְשׁוֹנֵנוּ רִנָּה
כַּהֲמוֹן גַּלָּיו. וְשִׂפְתוֹתֵינוּ
שֶׁבַח כְּמֶרְחֲבֵי רָקִיעַ.
וְעֵינֵינוּ מְאִירוֹת כַּשֶּׁמֶשׁ
וְכַיָּרֵחַ. וְיָדֵינוּ
פְרוּשׂוֹת כְּנִשְׁרֵי שָׁמָיִם.
וְרַגְלֵינוּ קַלּוֹת כָּאַיָּלוֹת. אֵין
אֲנַחְנוּ מַסְפִּיקִים לְהוֹדוֹת לְךָ
ה׳ אֱלֹהֵינוּ וֵאלֹהֵי אֲבוֹתֵינוּ.
וּלְבָרֵךְ אֶת שְׁמֶךָ עַל אַחַת
מֵאֶלֶף אַלְפֵי אֲלָפִים וְרִבֵּי
רְבָבוֹת פְּעָמִים. הַטּוֹבוֹת
שֶׁעָשִׂיתָ עִם אֲבוֹתֵינוּ וְעִמָּנוּ:
מִמִּצְרַיִם גְּאַלְתָּנוּ ה׳
אֱלֹהֵינוּ. וּמִבֵּית עֲבָדִים
פְּדִיתָנוּ. בְּרָעָב זַנְתָּנוּ.
וּבְשָׂבָע כִּלְכַּלְתָּנוּ. מֵחֶרֶב
הִצַּלְתָּנוּ. וּמִדֶּבֶר מִלַּטְתָּנוּ.
וּמֵחֳלָיִם רָעִים וְנֶאֱמָנִים
דִּלִּיתָנוּ: עַד הֵנָּה עֲזָרוּנוּ
רַחֲמֶיךָ. וְלֹא עֲזָבוּנוּ
חֲסָדֶיךָ וְאַל תִּטְּשֵׁנוּ
ה׳ אֱלֹהֵינוּ לָנֶצַח: עַל
כֵּן אֵבָרִים שֶׁפִּלַּגְתָּ בָּנוּ.
וְרוּחַ וּנְשָׁמָה שֶׁנָּפַחְתָּ
בְּאַפֵּינוּ. וְלָשׁוֹן אֲשֶׁר שַׂמְתָּ

befinu. Hein heim. Yodu vivarechu
vishabbechu vifa'aru virom'mu
veya'aritzu veyakdishu veyamlichu
et shimcha malkeinu: ki chol peh
lecha yodeh. Vechol lashon lecha
tishava. Vechol berech lecha
tichra. Vechol komah lefanecha
tishtachaveh. Vechol levavot
yira'ucha. Vechol kerev uchelayot
yezammeru lishmecha. Kaddavar
shekkatuv. Kol atzmotai tomarnah
adonai mi chamocha. Matzil ani
meichazak mimmennu. Ve'ani
ve'evyon miggozlo. Mi yidmeh
lach. Umi yishveh lach. Umi
ya'arach lach. Ha'el haggadol
haggibbor vehannora el elyon.
Koneh shamayim va'aretz:
nehallelcha uneshabbeichacha
unefa'ercha unevareich et shem
kodshecha. Ka'amur, ledavid,
barechi nafshi et adonai. Vechol
kerovai et shem kadesho:

Ha'el beta'atzumot uzzecha.
Haggadol bichvod shemecha.
Haggibbor lanetzach vehannora
benorotecha: hammelech
hayosheiv al kissei ram venisa:

Shochein ad marom vekadosh
shemo. Vechatuv rannenu
tzaddikim badonai. Layyesharim

בְּפִינוּ. הֵן הֵם. יוֹדוּ וִיבָרְכוּ
וִישַׁבְּחוּ וִיפָאֲרוּ וִירוֹמְמוּ
וְיַעֲרִיצוּ וְיַקְדִּישׁוּ וְיַמְלִיכוּ
אֶת שִׁמְךָ מַלְכֵּנוּ: כִּי כָל פֶּה
לְךָ יוֹדֶה. וְכָל לָשׁוֹן לְךָ
תִשָּׁבַע. וְכָל בֶּרֶךְ לְךָ
תִכְרַע. וְכָל קוֹמָה לְפָנֶיךָ
תִשְׁתַּחֲוֶה. וְכָל לְבָבוֹת
יִירָאוּךָ. וְכָל קֶרֶב וּכְלָיוֹת
יְזַמְּרוּ לִשְׁמֶךָ. כַּדָּבָר
שֶׁכָּתוּב. כָּל עַצְמוֹתַי תֹּאמַרְנָה
ה' מִי כָמוֹךָ. מַצִּיל עָנִי
מֵחָזָק מִמֶּנּוּ. וְעָנִי
וְאֶבְיוֹן מִגֹּזְלוֹ. מִי יִדְמֶה
לָּךְ. וּמִי יִשְׁוֶה לָּךְ. וּמִי
יַעֲרָךְ לָךְ. הָאֵל הַגָּדוֹל
הַגִּבּוֹר וְהַנּוֹרָא אֵל עֶלְיוֹן.
קוֹנֵה שָׁמַיִם וָאָרֶץ:
נְהַלֶּלְךָ וּנְשַׁבֵּחֲךָ
וּנְפָאֶרְךָ וּנְבָרֵךְ אֶת שֵׁם
קָדְשֶׁךָ. כָּאָמוּר, לְדָוִד,
בָּרְכִי נַפְשִׁי אֶת ה'. וְכָל
קְרָבַי אֶת שֵׁם קָדְשׁוֹ:

הָאֵל בְּתַעֲצֻמוֹת עֻזֶּךָ.
הַגָּדוֹל בִּכְבוֹד שְׁמֶךָ.
הַגִּבּוֹר לָנֶצַח וְהַנּוֹרָא
בְּנוֹרְאוֹתֶיךָ: הַמֶּלֶךְ
הַיּוֹשֵׁב עַל כִּסֵּא רָם וְנִשָּׂא:

שׁוֹכֵן עַד מָרוֹם וְקָדוֹשׁ
שְׁמוֹ. וְכָתוּב רַנְּנוּ
צַדִּיקִים בַּה'. לַיְשָׁרִים

navah tehillah: נָאוָה תְהִלָּה:

Befi yesharim tithallal. Uvedivrei   בְּפִי יְשָׁרִים תִּתְהַלָּל.
tzaddikim titbarach. Uvilshon   וּבְדִבְרֵי צַדִּיקִים תִּתְבָּרַךְ.
chasidim titromam. Uvekerev   וּבִלְשׁוֹן חֲסִידִים תִּתְרוֹמָם.
kedoshim titkaddash: וּבְקֶרֶב קְדוֹשִׁים תִּתְקַדָּשׁ:

Uvemakhalot rivevot ammecha   וּבְמַקְהֲלוֹת רִבְבוֹת עַמְּךָ
beit yisrael. Berinnah yitpa'ar   בֵּית יִשְׂרָאֵל. בְּרִנָּה יִתְפָּאַר
shimcha malkeinu bechol dor   שִׁמְךָ מַלְכֵּנוּ בְּכָל דּוֹר
vador. Shekkein chovat kol   וָדוֹר. שֶׁכֵּן חוֹבַת כָּל
hayyetzurim. Lefanecha adonai   הַיְצוּרִים. לְפָנֶיךָ ה'
eloheinu veilohei avoteinu.   אֱלֹהֵינוּ וֵאלֹהֵי אֲבוֹתֵינוּ.
Lehodot lehalleil leshabbei'ach   לְהוֹדוֹת לְהַלֵּל לְשַׁבֵּחַ
lefa'eir leromeim lehaddeir   לְפָאֵר לְרוֹמֵם לְהַדֵּר
levareich le'alleih ulekalleis. Al kol   לְבָרֵךְ לְעַלֵּה וּלְקַלֵּס. עַל כָּל
divrei shirot vetishbechot david   דִּבְרֵי שִׁירוֹת וְתִשְׁבְּחוֹת דָּוִד
ben yishai avdecha meshichecha: בֶּן יִשַׁי עַבְדְּךָ מְשִׁיחֶךָ:

The soul of every living being shall bless Your Name, O Lord, our God, the spirit of all flesh shall always glorify and exalt Your remembrance, our King. From this world to the World to Come, You are God and other than You we have no king, redeemer, or savior. He who liberates, rescues and sustains, answers and is merciful in every time of distress and anguish, we have no king, helper or supporter but You!

God of the first and the last, God of all creatures, Master of all Generations, Who is extolled through a multitude of praises, Who guides His world with kindness and His creatures with mercy. The Lord is truth; He neither slumbers nor sleeps. He Who rouses the sleepers and awakens the slumberers. Who raises the dead and heals the sick, causes the blind to see and straightens the bent. Who makes the mute speak and reveals what is hidden. To You alone we give thanks!

Were our mouth as full of song as the sea, and our tongue as full of joyous song as its multitude of waves, and our lips as full of praise as the breadth of the heavens, and our eyes as brilliant as the sun and the moon, and our hands as outspread as the eagles of the sky and our feet as swift as hinds – we still could not thank You sufficiently, O Lord, our God and God of our forefathers, and to bless Your Name for even one of the thousand and thousands of thousands and myriad myriads of favors, miracles and wonders that you performed for our ancestors and for us.

At first You redeemed us from Egypt, O Lord, our God, and liberated us from the house of bondage. In famine You nourished us, and in plenty you sustained us. From sword you saved us; from plague you let us escape; and from severe and enduring diseases you spared us. Until now Your mercy has helped us, and Your kindness has not forsaken us. Do not abandon us, O Lord, our God, forever.

Therefore, the organs that you set within us and the spirit and soul that you breathed into our nostrils, and the tongue that you placed in our mouth - all of them shall thank and bless and praise and glorify, exalt and revere, be devoted, sanctify and declare the sovereignty of Your Name, our King. For every mouth shall offer thanks to You; every tongue shall vow allegiance to You; every knee shall bend to You; every erect spine shall prostrate itself before You; all hearts shall fear You; and all innermost feelings and thoughts shall sing praises to Your name, as it is written: "All my bones shall say, O Lord, who is like You? You save the poor man from one who is stronger than he, the poor and destitute from the one who would rob him."

The outcry of the poor You hear, the screams of the destitute You listen to, and You save. And it is written: "Sing joyfully, O righteous, before the Lord; for the upright praise is fitting."

By the mouth of the upright You shall be exalted;
By the lips of the righteous shall You be blessed;
By the tongue of the devout shall You be sanctified;
And amid the holy shall You be lauded.

And in the assemblies of the myriads of Your people, the House of Israel, it is the duty of all creatures, before you O Lord, our God and God of our forefathers to thank, laud, praise, glorify, exalt, adore, render triumphant, bless, raise high, and sing praises - even beyond all expressions of the songs and praises of David, the son of Jesse, Your servant, Your anointed.

Notes

____

____

____

____

____

____

____

____

____

The Splendor of the Seventh Day

IN THIS PRAYER we state that all of the praises we mention in our prayers are directed at the God Who rested from the six days of creation on the Sabbath. Though His presence is not always obvious on earth, the Sabbath is an eternal testimony to God's creation of the world.

<table>
<tr><td>

La'el asher shavat mikkol
hamma'asim. Bayyom hashevi'i
hit'allah veyashav al kissei
chevodo. Tif'eret atah leyom
hammenuchah. oneg kara leyom
hashabbat. Zeh shevach shel
yom hashevi'i. Shebbo shavat el
mikkol melachto: veyom hashevi'i
meshabbei'ach ve'omier. Mizmor
shir leyom hashabbat. Tov lehodot
ladonai: lefichach yefa'aru
vivarechu la'el kol yetzurav.
shevach yekar ugedullah.
Yittenu la'el melech yotzeir kol.
Hammanchil menuchah le'ammo
yisra'el bikdushato beyom
shabbat kodesh: shimcha adonai
eloheinu yitkaddash. Vezichrecha
malkeinu yitpa'ar. Bashamayim
mimma'al ve'al ha'aretz mittachat:
titbarach moshi'einnu al shevach

</td><td dir="rtl">

לָאֵל אֲשֶׁר שָׁבַת מִכָּל
הַמַּעֲשִׂים. בַּיּוֹם הַשְּׁבִיעִי
הִתְעַלָּה וְיָשַׁב עַל כִּסֵּא
כְבוֹדוֹ. תִּפְאֶרֶת עָטָה לְיוֹם
הַמְּנוּחָה. עֹנֶג קָרָא לְיוֹם
הַשַּׁבָּת. זֶה שֶׁבַח שֶׁל
יוֹם הַשְּׁבִיעִי. שֶׁבּוֹ שָׁבַת אֵל
מִכָּל מְלַאכְתּוֹ: וְיוֹם הַשְּׁבִיעִי
מְשַׁבֵּחַ וְאוֹמֵר. מִזְמוֹר
שִׁיר לְיוֹם הַשַּׁבָּת. טוֹב
לְהוֹדוֹת לַה': לְפִיכָךְ יְפָאֲרוּ
וִיבָרְכוּ לָאֵל כָּל יְצוּרָיו.
שֶׁבַח יְקָר וּגְדֻלָּה.
יִתְּנוּ לָאֵל מֶלֶךְ יוֹצֵר כָּל.
הַמַּנְחִיל מְנוּחָה לְעַמּוֹ
יִשְׂרָאֵל בִּקְדֻשָׁתוֹ בְּיוֹם
שַׁבַּת קֹדֶשׁ: שִׁמְךָ ה'
אֱלֹהֵינוּ יִתְקַדַּשׁ. וְזִכְרְךָ
מַלְכֵּנוּ יִתְפָּאַר. בַּשָּׁמַיִם
מִמַּעַל וְעַל הָאָרֶץ מִתָּחַת:
תִּתְבָּרַךְ מוֹשִׁיעֵנוּ עַל שֶׁבַח

</td></tr>
</table>

ma'asei yadecha. Ve'al me'orei or
she'asita yefa'arucha selah.

מַעֲשֵׂי יָדֶיךָ. וְעַל מְאוֹרֵי אוֹר
שֶׁעָשִׂיתָ יְפָאֲרוּךְ סֶלָה.

To the God who rested from all His works. On the seventh day, He ascended and sat on His throne of glory. He adorned the day of rest with splendor and called the Sabbath a delight. This is the praise of the seventh day: on this day He rested from all His labors. And the seventh day gives praises and says, "A psalm, a song for the Sabbath day. It is good to give thanks to the Lord." Therefore, all His creations shall glorify and bless God. Praise, honor, and greatness they shall give to the God, the King, Creator of all, who grants rest to His people Israel in His holiness on the holy Sabbath day. Your name, O Lord our God, shall be sanctified, and Your remembrance, our King, shall be glorified in the heavens above and on the earth below. You shall be blessed, our Savior, for the work of Your hands, and for the luminous lights You have made, they shall glorify You forever.

Notes

Song of the Day for Sabbath

P SALM 92 IS a song of praise to God. It is recited as part of the prayers at the start of the Sabbath, and is also recited as the "Song of the Day" for the Sabbath. The psalm is introduced as "A song with musical accompaniment for the Sabbath day. It is good to give thanks to the Lord…" Rabbi David Kimchi explains that the Sabbath is the perfect time to sing praises to God because we are free from the burdens of the rest of the week. On this day, we have time to focus on our relationship with the Almighty. Free time doesn't mean a vacation from worship; rather, it is an opportunity to reflect on and strengthen our connection with Him.

הַיּוֹם יוֹם שַׁבָּת קוֹדֶשׁ
שֶׁבּוֹ הָיוּ הַלְוִיִּם אוֹמְרִים
בְּבֵית הַמִּקְדָּשׁ:

Hayom yom shabbat kodesh
shebbo hayu haleviyyim omrim
beveit hammikdash:

מִזְמוֹר שִׁיר לְיוֹם הַשַּׁבָּת:
טוֹב לְהוֹדוֹת לַה'. וּלְזַמֵּר
לְשִׁמְךָ עֶלְיוֹן: לְהַגִּיד
בַּבֹּקֶר חַסְדֶּךָ.
וֶאֱמוּנָתְךָ בַּלֵּילוֹת: עֲלֵי
עָשׂוֹר וַעֲלֵי נָבֶל. עֲלֵי הִגָּיוֹן
בְּכִנּוֹר: כִּי שִׂמַּחְתַּנִי
ה' בְּפָעֳלֶךָ. בְּמַעֲשֵׂי
יָדֶיךָ אֲרַנֵּן: מַה גָּדְלוּ
מַעֲשֶׂיךָ ה'. מְאֹד עָמְקוּ
מַחְשְׁבֹתֶיךָ: אִישׁ בַּעַר לֹא
יֵדָע. וּכְסִיל לֹא יָבִין אֶת זֹאת:
בִּפְרֹחַ רְשָׁעִים כְּמוֹ עֵשֶׂב.

Mizmor shir leyom hashabbat:
tov lehodot ladonai, ulezammeir
leshimcha elyon: lehaggid
babboker chasdecha,
ve'emunatecha balleilot: alei
asor va'alei navel, alei higgaiyon
bechinnor: ki simachtani
adonai befo'olecha, bema'asei
yadecha arannein: mah gadelu
ma'asecha adonai, meod ameku
machshevotecha: ish ba'ar lo
yeida, uchesil lo yavin et zot:
bifro'ach resha'im kemo eisev,

vayyatzitzu kol po'alei aven,   וַיָּצִיצוּ כָּל פֹּעֲלֵי אָוֶן.

lehishomdam adei ad: ve'attah   לְהִשָּׁמְדָם עֲדֵי עַד: וְאַתָּה

marom le'olam adonai: ki   מָרוֹם לְעוֹלָם ה': כִּי הִנֵּה

hinneih oyvecha adonai, ki   אֹיְבֶיךָ ה'. כִּי הִנֵּה

hinneih oyvecha yoveidu,   אֹיְבֶיךָ יֹאבֵדוּ. יִתְפָּרְדוּ

yitparedu kol po'alei aven: כָּל פֹּעֲלֵי אָוֶן: וַתָּרֶם

vattarem kir'eim karni, balloti   כִּרְאֵים קַרְנִי. בַּלֹּתִי בְּשֶׁמֶן

beshemen ra'anan: vattabbeit   רַעֲנָן. וַתַּבֵּט עֵינִי בְּשׁוּרָי.

eini beshurai, bakkamim alai   בַּקָּמִים עָלַי מְרֵעִים תִּשְׁמַעְנָה

merei'im tishma'nah azenai: אָזְנָי: צַדִּיק כַּתָּמָר יִפְרָח.

tzaddik kattamar yifrach, ke'erez   כְּאֶרֶז בַּלְּבָנוֹן יִשְׂגֶּה:

ballevanon yisgeh: shetulim beveit   שְׁתוּלִים בְּבֵית ה'. בְּחַצְרוֹת

adonai, bechatzrot eloheinu   אֱלֹהֵינוּ יַפְרִיחוּ: עוֹד יְנוּבוּן

yafrichu: od yenuvun beseivah,   בְּשֵׂיבָה. דְּשֵׁנִים וְרַעֲנַנִּים

desheinim vera'anannim yihyu: יִהְיוּ: לְהַגִּיד כִּי יָשָׁר ה'.

lehaggid ki yashar adonai, tzuri   צוּרִי וְלֹא עַוְלָתָה בּוֹ:

velo avlatah bo:

*Today is the holy Sabbath day, on which the Levites would sing in
the Temple:*

*A song with musical accompaniment for the Sabbath day. It is good
to give thanks to the Lord, and to sing to Your name, O Most High.
To declare in the morning Your kindness and Your faith at night.
Upon a ten-stringed harp and upon a psaltery, with speech upon a
harp. For You have made me happy O Lord, with Your work; with
the work of Your hands I shall exult. How great are Your works, O
Lord! Your thoughts are very deep. A boorish man does not know;
neither does a fool understand this. When the wicked flourish like
grass, and all workers of violence blossom, only to be destroyed to
eternity. But You remain on high forever, O Lord. For behold Your
enemies, O Lord, for behold Your enemies will perish; all workers
of violence will scatter. But You have raised my horn like that of a*

wild ox; to soak me with fresh oil. My eye has gazed upon those who stare at me [with envy]; when evildoers rise up against me, my ears hear [them]. The righteous one flourishes like the palm; as a cedar in Lebanon he grows. Planted in the house of the Lord, in the courts of our God they will flourish. They will yet grow in old age; fat and fresh will they be. To declare that the Lord is upright, my rock in Whom there is no injustice.

Notes

Sabbath Songs

THERE IS A beautiful tradition in Judaism to sing songs during the Sabbath meals. Many of the traditional Sabbath songs are hymns or poems written by various rabbis and sages during the early Middle Ages that were later set to music. We eat three festive meals over the course of the Sabbath, at night, in the late morning and in the late afternoon, and there are different songs that are customarily sung at each of these three meals.

Friday Night Dinner

Rest and Joy

This song celebrates the rewards that await those who observe and honor the holy Sabbath: "Rest, joy, and light." The Sabbath offers rest from the week's physical struggles and full engagement in spiritual pursuits. It is also a day of joy, as there is no greater happiness than serving the Lord without obstacles.

Menuchah vesimchah or	מְנוּחָה וְשִׂמְחָה אוֹר
layyehudim, yom shabbaton	לַיְּהוּדִים, יוֹם שַׁבָּתוֹן
yom machamaddim Shomerav	יוֹם מַחֲמַדִּים שׁוֹמְרָיו
vezocherav heimmah me'idim, ki	וְזוֹכְרָיו הֵמָּה מְעִידִים, כִּי
leshishah kol beru'im ve'omedim.	לְשִׁשָּׁה כֹּל בְּרוּאִים וְעוֹמְדִים.
Shemei shamayim eretz	שְׁמֵי שָׁמַיִם אֶרֶץ
veyammim, kol tzeva marom	וְיַמִּים, כָּל צְבָא מָרוֹם

gevohim veramim. Tannin
ve'adam vechayyat re'eimim, ki
beyah adonai tzur olamim.

גְּבוֹהִים וְרָמִים. תַּנִּין וְאָדָם
וְחַיַּת רְאֵמִים, כִּי בְיָהּ יְיָ צוּר
עוֹלָמִים.

Hu asher dibbeir le'am segullato,
shamor lekaddesho mibbo'o
ve'ad tzeito. Shabbat kodesh yom
chemdato, ki vo shavat el mikkol
melachto.

הוּא אֲשֶׁר דִּבֶּר לְעַם סְגֻלָּתוֹ,
שָׁמוֹר לְקַדְּשׁוֹ מִבֹּאוֹ וְעַד
צֵאתוֹ. שַׁבַּת קֹדֶשׁ יוֹם
חֶמְדָּתוֹ, כִּי בוֹ שָׁבַת אֵל מִכָּל
מְלַאכְתּוֹ.

Bemitzvat shabbat el yachalitzach,
kum kera eilav yachish
le'ammetzach nishmat kol
chai vegam na'aritzach, echol
besimchah ki kevar ratzach.

בְּמִצְוַת שַׁבָּת אֵל יַחֲלִיצָךְ,
קוּם קְרָא אֵלָיו יָחִישׁ
לְאַמְּצָךְ נִשְׁמַת כָּל חַי וְגַם
נַעֲרִיצָךְ, אֱכוֹל בְּשִׂמְחָה כִּי
כְבָר רָצָךְ.

Bemishneh lechem vekiddush
rabbah, berov mat'ammim
veruach nedivah yizku lerav tuv
hammit'annegim bah, bevi'at
go'eil lechayyei ha'olam habba.

בְּמִשְׁנֶה לֶחֶם וְקִדּוּשׁ
רַבָּה, בְּרוֹב מַטְעַמִּים
וְרוּחַ נְדִיבָה יִזְכּוּ לְרַב טוּב
הַמִּתְעַנְּגִים בָּהּ, בְּבִיאַת גּוֹאֵל
לְחַיֵּי הָעוֹלָם הַבָּא.

Rest and joy, light for the Jews, The Sabbath day, a day of delight

Those who observe and remember it testify that all creations were made in six days and still endure.

The exalted heavens, the earth, and the seas, All the hosts of the high and lofty realms,

The serpent, humanity, and the wild beasts, For the Lord, God is the Rock of the Universe.

He is the One who spoke to His treasured people, To observe it and sanctify it from its arrival until its departure, the holy Sabbath, His day of desire, For on it, God rested from all His work.

With the commandment of the Sabbath, God will strengthen you, Rise and call to Him, He will hasten to fortify you. Recite "the soul of every living thing" and "we will exalt you," Eat with joy, for He already favors you.

With double bread and the great Kiddush, With abundant delicacies and a generous spirit,

May those who delight in it merit great goodness, With the coming of the Redeemer, eternal life in the world to come.

O Lord, Master of the Universe

This song was written in Aramiac by Rabbi Israel Najara of Gaza, one of the great rabbis and poets of the 16th century. It speaks of the greatness of God and how all of His creations sing His praises. We ask God to save His people, return them from the exile and rebuild the Temple in Jerusalem, where all people will rejoice together as one.

Yah ribbon olam ve'alemayya, ant hu malka melech malchayya, ovad gevureteich vetimhayya, shefar kodamach lehachavayya.

יָהּ רִבּוֹן עָלַם וְעָלְמַיָּא, אַנְתְּ הוּא מַלְכָּא מֶלֶךְ מַלְכַיָּא, עוֹבַד גְּבוּרְתֵּךְ וְתִמְהַיָּא, שְׁפַר קֳדָמָךְ לְהַחֲוַיָּא.

Shevachin asadder tzafra veramsha, lach elaha kaddisha di vera kol nafsha,

שְׁבָחִין אֲסַדֵּר צַפְרָא וְרַמְשָׁא, לָךְ אֱלָהָא קַדִּישָׁא דִּי בְרָא כָּל נַפְשָׁא,

irin kaddishin uvenei enasha,
cheivat bera ve'ofei shemayya.

עִירִין קַדִּישִׁין וּבְנֵי אֱנָשָׁא,
חֵיוַת בָּרָא וְעוֹפֵי שְׁמַיָּא.

Ravrevin ovedeich vetakkifin,
machich remayya vezakkif kefifin,
lu yichyeh gevar shenin
alfin, la yei'ol gevureteich
bechushbenayya.

רַבְרְבִין עוֹבְדֵיךְ וְתַקִּיפִין,
מָכִיךְ רְמַיָּא וְזַקִּיף כְּפִיפִין,
לוּ יִחְיֶה גְבַר שְׁנִין
אַלְפִּין, לָא יֵעוֹל גְּבוּרְתֵּךְ
בְּחֻשְׁבְּנַיָּא.

Elaha di leih yekar urevuta, perok
yat anach mippum aryevata,
ve'appeik yat ammeich miggo
galuta, ammeich di vechart mikkol
ummayya.

אֱלָהָא דִּי לֵהּ יְקַר וּרְבוּתָא, פְּרוֹק
יַת עָנָךְ מִפֻּם אַרְיְוָתָא,
וְאַפֵּיק יַת עַמֵּךְ מִגּוֹ
גָּלוּתָא, עַמֵּךְ דִּי בְחַרְתְּ מִכָּל
אֻמַּיָּא.

Lemikdasheich tuv ulekodesh
kudshin, atar di veih yechedun
ruchin venafshin, vizammerun lach
shirin verachashin, birusheleim
karta deshuferayya.

לְמִקְדָּשֵׁךְ תּוּב וּלְקֹדֶשׁ
קֻדְשִׁין, אֲתַר דִּי בֵהּ יֶחֱדוּן
רוּחִין וְנַפְשִׁין, וִיזַמְּרוּן לָךְ
שִׁירִין וְרַחֲשִׁין, בִּירוּשְׁלֵם
קַרְתָּא דְשׁוּפְרַיָּא.

O Lord, Master of the universe and all worlds, You are the King, the King of kings, The work of Your might and wonders, Are beautiful to declare before You.

I arrange praises morning and evening, To You, Holy God, who created every soul, Holy beings and the children of men, Living creatures and the birds of the sky.

Great and mighty are Your deeds, You humble the proud and straighten the bent, Even if a man lived a thousand years ago, He could not comprehend Your might.

God to whom belongs honor and greatness, Save Your sheep from the mouth of the lions, And bring forth Your people from exile, Your people whom You chose from all nations.

Return to Your sanctuary and to the Holy of Holies, The place where spirits and souls rejoice, And they will sing to You songs and hymns, In Jerusalem, the city of beauty.

Rock from Whose Food We Have Eaten

This song is an introduction to the Grace After Meals. It includes the same themes as the Grace After Meals, expressing gratitude for the abundant food that God provides, appreciation for the land of Israel and the hope that He will bring the Messiah and rebuild Jerusalem and the Temple.

Tzur mishello achalnu, barechu
emunai. Sava'nu vehotarnu
kidvar adonai.

צוּר מִשֶּׁלּוֹ אָכַלְנוּ, בָּרְכוּ
אֱמוּנַי. שָׂבַעְנוּ וְהוֹתַרְנוּ
כִּדְבַר יְיָ.

Hazzan et olamo, ro'einu avinu,
achalnu et lachmo, veyeino
shatinu, al ken nodeh lishmo,
unehallelo befinu, amarnu
ve'aninu, ein kadosh kadonai.

הַזָּן אֶת עוֹלָמוֹ, רוֹעֵנוּ אָבִינוּ,
אָכַלְנוּ אֶת לַחְמוֹ, וְיֵינוֹ
שָׁתִינוּ, עַל כֵּן נוֹדֶה לִשְׁמוֹ,
וּנְהַלְלוֹ בְּפִינוּ, אָמַרְנוּ
וְעָנִינוּ, אֵין קָדוֹשׁ כַּיְיָ.

Beshir vekol todah nevareich
le'eloheinu, al eretz chemdah
tovah shehinchil la'avoteinu.
Mazon vetzeidah hisbia'
lenafsheinu, chasdo gavar aleinu,
ve'emet adonai.

בְּשִׁיר וְקוֹל תּוֹדָה נְבָרֵךְ
לֵאלֹהֵינוּ, עַל אֶרֶץ חֶמְדָּה
טוֹבָה שֶׁהִנְחִיל לַאֲבוֹתֵינוּ.
מָזוֹן וְצֵדָה הִשְׂבִּיעַ
לְנַפְשֵׁנוּ, חַסְדּוֹ גָּבַר עָלֵינוּ,
וֶאֱמֶת יְיָ.

Racheim bechasdecha al
ammecha tzureinu, al tziyyon
mishkan kevodecha, zevul beit
tif'artenu, ben david avdecha
yavo veyig'aleinu, ruach appeinu
meshiach adonai.

רַחֵם בְּחַסְדֶּךָ עַל
עַמְּךָ צוּרֵנוּ, עַל צִיּוֹן
מִשְׁכַּן כְּבוֹדֶךָ, זְבוּל בֵּית
תִּפְאַרְתֵּנוּ, בֶּן דָּוִד עַבְדֶּךָ
יָבֹא וְיִגְאָלֵנוּ, רוּחַ אַפֵּינוּ
מְשִׁיחַ יְיָ.

Yibbaneh hammikdash, ir tziyyon
temallei, vesham nashir shir
chadash, uvirnanah na'aleh,
harachaman hannikdash yitbarach
veyit'alleh, al kos yayin malei,
kevirkat adonai.

יִבָּנֶה הַמִּקְדָּשׁ, עִיר צִיּוֹן
תְּמַלֵּא, וְשָׁם נָשִׁיר שִׁיר
חָדָשׁ, וּבִרְנָנָה נַעֲלֶה,
הָרַחֲמָן הַנִּקְדָּשׁ יִתְבָּרַךְ
וְיִתְעַלֶּה, עַל כּוֹס יַיִן מָלֵא,
כְּבִרְכַּת יְיָ.

Rock from whose food we have eaten, bless [Him], my faithful ones. We have eaten and left over, like the word of God.

The One who sustains His world, our Shepherd and our Father. We have eaten His bread and drunk His wine, Therefore we will thank His name and praise Him with our mouths. We said and answered, "There is none as holy as God."

With song and a voice of thanksgiving, we will bless our God for the precious, good land that He has bequeathed to our ancestors. He has satisfied our souls with food and provisions. His kindness has prevailed over us, and truth is God.

Have mercy in Your kindness on Your people, our Rock, on Zion, the abode of Your glory, the cherished house of our splendor. May the son of David, Your servant, come and redeem us, the breath of our nostrils, the anointed of God.

May the Temple be rebuilt, the city of Zion be filled, and there we will sing a new song, and with joyous song ascend. May the merciful One, who is sanctified, be blessed and exalted, over a full cup of wine, worthy of the blessing of God.

Sabbath Day Lunch

Blessed is the Most Exalted God

The poem praises God for giving us a day of complete rest. It highlights the great rewards for those who honor the Sabbath, and its deep importance to man and to God.

Baruch el elyon asher natan menuchah, lenafshenu pidyon mishe'eit va'anachah. Vhu yidrosh letziyyon ir hanniddachah, ad-anah tugeyon nefesh ne'enachah?	בָּרוּךְ אֵל עֶלְיוֹן אֲשֶׁר נָתַן מְנוּחָה, לְנַכְשֵׁנוּ פִּדְיוֹן מִשְׂאֵת וַאֲנָחָה.וְהוּא יִדְרשׁ לְצִיּוֹן עִיר הַנִּדָּחָה, עַד-אָנָה תּוּגְיוֹן נֶכֶשׁ נֶאֱנָחָה?
Hashomer shabbat, habbein im habbat, la'eil yeiratzu keminchah al-machavat	הַשּׁוֹמֵר שַׁבָּת, הַבֵּן עִם הַבַּת, לָאֵל יֵרָצוּ כְּמִנְחָה עַל-מַחֲבַת
Rocheiv ba'aravot melech olamim, et-amo lishbot izzein banne'imim. Bema'achalei areivot, beminei mat'amim, bemalbushei chavod zevach mishpachah	רוֹכֵב בָּעֲרָבוֹת מֶלֶךְ עוֹלָמִים, אֶת-עַמּוֹ לִשְׁבֹּת אִזֵּן בַּנְּעִימִים. בְּמַאֲכָלֵי עֲרֵבוֹת, בְּמִינֵי מַטְעַמִּים, בְּמַלְבּוּשֵׁי כָבוֹד זֶבַח מִשְׁפָּחָה
Hashomer shabbat...	הַשּׁוֹמֵר שַׁבָּת...

Ve'ashrei kol-chocheh letashlumei cheifel, mei'et kol socheh shochein ba'arafel. Nachalah lo yizkeh bahar uvashafel, nachalah umenuchah, kashemesh lo zarechah.

Hashomer shabbat...

Kol-shomer shabbat kaddat mechalalo, hein hachsher chibbat kodesh goralo. Vim yatza chovat hayyom ashrei lo, le'el adon mecholelo minchah hi sheluchah.

Hashomer shabbat...

Chemdat hayyamim kera'o eli tzur, vashrei litmimim im-yihyeh natzur. keter hillumim al-rosham yatzur, tzur ha'olamim rucho bam nachah.

Hashomer shabbat...

Zachor et-yom hashabbat lekaddesho, karno ki gavehah neizer al-rosho. Al-kein yittein ha'adam lenafsho oneg vegam-simchah bahem lemoshchah.

Hashomer shabbat...

Kodesh hi lachem shabbat

וְאַשְׁרֵי כָּל-חוֹכֶה לְתַשְׁלוּמֵי כֶּפֶל, מֵאֵת כָּל סוֹכֶה שׁוֹכֵן בָּעֲרָפֶל. נַחֲלָה לוֹ יִזְכֶּה בָּהָר וּבַשָּׁפֶל, נַחֲלָה וּמְנוּחָה, כַּשֶּׁמֶשׁ לוֹ זָרֲחָה.

הַשּׁוֹמֵר שַׁבָּת...

כָּל-שׁוֹמֵר שַׁבָּת כַּדָּת מֵחַלְלוֹ, הֵן הַכְשֵׁר חִבַּת קֹדֶשׁ גּוֹרָלוֹ. וְאִם יָצָא חוֹבַת הַיּוֹם אַשְׁרֵי לוֹ, לְאֵל אָדוֹן מְחוֹלְלוֹ מִנְחָה הִיא שְׁלוּחָה.

הַשּׁוֹמֵר שַׁבָּת...

חֶמְדַּת הַיָּמִים קְרָאוֹ אֵלִי צוּר, וְאַשְׁרֵי לִתְמִימִים אִם-יִהְיֶה נָצוּר. כֶּתֶר הִלּוּמִים עַל-רֹאשָׁם יָצוּר, צוּר הָעוֹלָמִים רוּחוֹ בָּם נָחָה.

הַשּׁוֹמֵר שַׁבָּת...

זָכוֹר אֶת-יוֹם הַשַּׁבָּת לְקַדְּשׁוֹ, קַרְנוֹ כִּי גָבְהָה נֵזֶר עַל-רֹאשׁוֹ. עַל-כֵּן יִתֵּן הָאָדָם לְנַפְשׁוֹ עֹנֶג וְגַם-שִׂמְחָה בָּהֶם לְמָשְׁחָה.

הַשּׁוֹמֵר שַׁבָּת...

קֹדֶשׁ הִיא לָכֶם שַׁבָּת

hammalkah, el-toch bateichem
lehaniach berachah. Bechol-
moshevoteichem lo ta'asu
melachah, beneichem
uvenoteichem, eved vegam-
shifchah.

הַמַּלְכָּה, אֶל-תּוֹךְ בָּתֵּיכֶם
לְהָנִיחַ בְּרָכָה. בְּכָל-
מוֹשְׁבוֹתֵיכֶם לֹא תַעֲשׂוּ
מְלָאכָה, בְּנֵיכֶם
וּבְנוֹתֵיכֶם, עֶבֶד וְגַם-
שִׁפְחָה.

Hashomer shabbat...

הַשּׁוֹמֵר שַׁבָּת...

Blessed is the Most Exalted God who gave rest, To our souls it is a relief from toil and sighing. May He seek out Zion, the forsaken city, How long will the soul's lament and sighing endure?

Whoever keeps the Sabbath, man and woman alike, Will be pleasing to God as a meal offering on a sacred pan.

He who rides on the heavens, the King of the universe, that His people rest on the Sabbath He made them hear in pleasantness. With delightful foods, with various delicacies, In garments of honor, a family feast.

Whoever keeps the Sabbath...

And praiseworthy are all who await double reward, From the one Who sees all but dwells in the clouds. He will grant him an inheritance in the mountain and valley, An inheritance and resting place, like the one upon whom the sun shines.

Whoever keeps the Sabbath...

Whoever safeguards the Sabbath properly from desecration, Behold, the sanctity of holiness is his destiny. And if he fulfills the obligation of the day, praiseworthy is he, To God, the Lord who created him, it is sent as a gift.

Whoever keeps the Sabbath...

'The most beloved of days' is what my God and Rock it, And praises are due to the upright if it is guarded. A crown of gems will be upon their heads, The Rock of the worlds, His spirit will be content with them.

Whoever keeps the Sabbath...

He who remembers the Sabbath day to sanctify it, His honor will rise like a crown upon its head. Therefore, a person should give to himself joy and also gladness, with which to exalt himself.

Whoever keeps the Sabbath...

The Sabbath, the queen, is holy to you, To bring blessing into your homes. In all your dwellings, do not do work, Your sons and daughters, servant and also maidservant.

Whoever keeps the Sabbath...

This Day is Honored

This song encourages us to honor the Sabbath, promising that God will generously reward our efforts to observe it properly.

Yom zeh mechubbad mikkol yamim, ki vo shavat tzur olamim.

יוֹם זֶה מְכֻבָּד מִכָּל יָמִים, כִּי בוֹ שָׁבַת צוּר עוֹלָמִים.

Sheishet yamim ta'aseh
melachtecha, veyom hashevi'i
lelohecha, shabbat lo ta'aseh vo
melachah, ki chol asah sheishet
yamim.

Yom zeh...

Rishon hu lemikra'ei kodesh, yom
shabbaton yom shabbat kodesh,
al kein kol ish beyeino yekaddesh,
al shetei lechem yivtze'u temimim.

Yom zeh...

Echol mashmannim sheteih
mamtakkim, ki el yittein lechol bo
deveikim, beeged lilbosh lechem
chukkim, basar vedagim vechol
mat'ammim.

Yom zeh...

Lo techsar kol bo ve'achalta
vesava'eta uveirachta et adonai
elohecha asher ahavta, ki
veirachcha mikkol ha'ammim.

Yom zeh...

Hashamayim mesapperim
kevodo, vegam ha'aretz male'ah
chasdo, re'u ki chol eilleh asetah

שֵׁשֶׁת יָמִים תַּעֲשֶׂה
מְלַאכְתֶּךָ, וְיוֹם הַשְּׁבִיעִי
לֵאלֹהֶיךָ, שַׁבָּת לֹא תַעֲשֶׂה בּוֹ
מְלָאכָה, כִּי כֹל עָשָׂה שֵׁשֶׁת
יָמִים.

יוֹם זֶה....

רִאשׁוֹן הוּא לְמִקְרָאֵי קֹדֶשׁ, יוֹם
שַׁבָּתוֹן יוֹם שַׁבָּת קֹדֶשׁ,
עַל כֵּן כָּל אִישׁ בְּיֵינוֹ יְקַדֵּשׁ,
עַל שְׁתֵּי לֶחֶם יִבְצְעוּ תְמִימִים.

יוֹם זֶה....

אֱכוֹל מַשְׁמַנִּים שְׁתֵה
מַמְתַּקִּים, כִּי אֵל יִתֵּן לְכָל בּוֹ
דְבֵקִים, בֶּגֶד לִלְבּוֹשׁ לֶחֶם
חֻקִּים, בָּשָׂר וְדָגִים וְכָל
מַטְעַמִּים.

יוֹם זֶה....

לֹא תֶחְסַר כֹּל בּוֹ וְאָכַלְתָּ
וְשָׂבָעְתָּ וּבֵרַכְתָּ אֶת יְיָ
אֱלֹהֶיךָ אֲשֶׁר אָהַבְתָּ, כִּי
בֵרַכְךָ מִכָּל הָעַמִּים.

יוֹם זֶה....

הַשָּׁמַיִם מְסַפְּרִים
כְּבוֹדוֹ, וְגַם הָאָרֶץ מָלְאָה
חַסְדּוֹ, רְאוּ כִּי כָל אֵלֶה עָשְׂתָה

yado, ki hu hatzur po'olo tamim.   יָדוֹ, כִּי הוּא הַצּוּר פָּעֳלוֹ תָמִים.

Yom zeh...   ...יוֹם זֶה

This day is honored above all days, for on it the Creator of the world rested.

For six days you may do your work, but the seventh day is for your God. On the Sabbath do not do any work on it, for all was made in six days.

This day...

It is the first of the holy convocations, a day of rest, the holy Sabbath day. Therefore, every man shall sanctify it with wine, and break complete loaves of bread.

This day...

Eat rich foods and drink sweet beverages, for God provides for all who cling to Him garments to wear and bread in abundance, meat, fish, and all delicacies.

This day...

You will lack nothing on it, you shall eat and be satisfied and bless the Lord your God whom you love, for He has blessed you more than all nations.

This day...

The heavens declare His glory, and the earth is filled with His kindness. See that all these were made by His hand, for He is the Rock; His work is perfect.

This day...

Proclaim Freedom!

This song is a plea to God to protect Israel, destroy her oppressors and bring peace and redemption to God's children.

Deror yikra levein im bat,
veyintzarechem kemo vavat,
ne'im shimchem velo yushbat,
shevu venuchu beyom shabbat.

דְּרוֹר יִקְרָא לְבֵן עִם בַּת,
וְיִנְצָרְכֶם כְּמוֹ בָבַת,
נְעִים שִׁמְכֶם וְלֹא יֻשְׁבַּת,
שְׁבוּ וְנוּחוּ בְּיוֹם שַׁבָּת.

Derosh navi ve'ulami, ve'ot yesha
aseih immi, neta sorek betoch
karmi, she'eih shav'at benei ammi.

דְּרוֹשׁ נָוִי וְאוּלָמִי, וְאוֹת יֶשַׁע
עֲשֵׂה עִמִּי, נְטַע שׂוֹרֵק בְּתוֹךְ
כַּרְמִי, שְׁעֵה שַׁוְעַת בְּנֵי עַמִּי.

Deroch purah betoch batzerah,
vegam bavel asher gaverah,
netotz tzarai be'af ve'evrah,
shema koli beyom ekra.

דְּרוֹךְ פּוּרָה בְּתוֹךְ בָּצְרָה,
וְגַם בָּבֶל אֲשֶׁר גָּבְרָה,
נְתוֹץ צָרַי בְּאַף וְעֶבְרָה,
שְׁמַע קוֹלִי בְּיוֹם אֶקְרָא.

Elohim tein bammidbar har, hadas
shittah berosh tidhar, velammazhir
velannizhar, shelomim tein kemei
nahar.

אֱלֹהִים תֵּן בַּמִּדְבָּר הַר, הֲדַס
שִׁטָּה בְּרוֹשׁ תִּדְהָר, וְלַמַּזְהִיר
וְלַנִּזְהָר, שְׁלוֹמִים תֵּן כְּמֵי
נָהָר.

Hadoch kamai el kanna, bemog
leivav uvammeginnah, venarchiv
peh unemallenah, leshoneinu
lecha rinnah.

הֲדוֹךְ קָמַי אֵל קַנָּא, בְּמוֹג
לֵבָב וּבַמְּגִנָּה, וְנַרְחִיב
פֶּה וּנְמַלְּאֶנָּה, לְשׁוֹנֵנוּ
לְךָ רִנָּה.

De'eih chochmah lenafshecha,
vehi cheter leroshecha, netzor
mitzvat kedoshecha, shemor
shabbat kodshecha.

דְּעֵה חָכְמָה לְנַפְשֶׁךָ,
וְהִיא כֶתֶר לְרֹאשֶׁךָ, נְצוֹר
מִצְוַת קְדוֹשֶׁךָ, שְׁמוֹר
שַׁבַּת קָדְשֶׁךָ.

He shall proclaim freedom for man and woman, and protect them as the apple of the eye. Your reputation will be pleasant and will not cease, Rest and be content on the Sabbath day.

Seek my Temple and my Hall, and perform a sign of salvation for me. Plant a choice vine in my vineyard, Hear the cry of my people.

Tread the winepress in Bozrah, and also in Babylon, which had prevailed. Shatter my adversaries in anger and wrath, hear my voice on the day I call.

O God, let bloom on the desert-like mountain, myrtle, acacia, cypress, and box tree. And to the one who warns and is careful, grant peace like flowing water.

Trample my foes, O zealous God, with faint-heartedness and grief. We will widen our mouths and fill them, our tongues will sing songs of joy for You.

Let your soul know wisdom, for it is a crown for your head. Keep the commandments of your Holy One, observe your holy Sabbath.

The Third Meal

Wishing the Sabbath Farewell

The third Sabbath meal is traditionally eaten towards the end of the Sabbath day as the sun begins to set. It is customary to sing Psalm 23, a beautiful prayer of unwavering faith and trust in God, as we prepare to leave the Sabbath and reenter the struggles of the week.

Mizmor ledavid adonai ro'i lo
echsar: Bin'ot deshe yarbitzeini
al-mei menuchot yenahaleini:
Nafshi yeshoveiv yancheini
vema'gelei-tzedek lema'an
shemo: Gam ki-eilech begei
tzalmavet lo-ira ra ki-attah immadi
shivt'cha umish'antecha heimmah
yenachamuni: Ta'aroch lefanai
shulchan neged tzorerai dishanta
vashemen roshi kosi revayah:
Ach tov vachesed yirdefuni kol-
yemei chayyai veshavti beveit-
adonai le'orech yamim.

מִזְמוֹר לְדָוִד יְהֹוָה רֹעִי לֹא
אֶחְסָר: בִּנְאוֹת דֶּשֶׁא יַרְבִּיצֵנִי
עַל־מֵי מְנֻחוֹת יְנַהֲלֵנִי:
נַפְשִׁי יְשׁוֹבֵב יַנְחֵנִי
בְמַעְגְּלֵי־צֶדֶק לְמַעַן
שְׁמוֹ: גַּם כִּי־אֵלֵךְ בְּגֵיא
צַלְמָוֶת לֹא־אִירָא רָע כִּי־אַתָּה עִמָּדִי
שִׁבְטְךָ וּמִשְׁעַנְתֶּךָ הֵמָּה
יְנַחֲמֻנִי: תַּעֲרֹךְ לְפָנַי
שֻׁלְחָן נֶגֶד צֹרְרָי דִּשַּׁנְתָּ
בַשֶּׁמֶן רֹאשִׁי כּוֹסִי רְוָיָה:
אַךְ טוֹב וָחֶסֶד יִרְדְּפוּנִי כָּל־
יְמֵי חַיָּי וְשַׁבְתִּי בְּבֵית־
יְהֹוָה לְאֹרֶךְ יָמִים:

A psalm of David. The Lord is my shepherd; I lack nothing. He makes me lie down in green pastures; He leads me to water in places of repose; He renews my life; He guides me in right paths as befits His name. Though I walk through a valley of deepest darkness, I fear no harm, for You are with me; Your rod and Your staff—they comfort me. You spread a table for me in full view of my enemies; You anoint my head with oil; my drink is abundant. Only goodness and steadfast love shall pursue me all the days of my life, and I shall dwell in the house of the Lord for many long years.

The *Yedid Nefesh*, Beloved of the Soul, prayer, which expresses a deep yearning for spiritual closeness with God, is traditionally recited at sunset to welcome the Sabbath (page 88). It is also sung during the third meal, just before the Sabbath draws to a close.

Conclusion of the Sabbath

Havdalah: The Separation Prayer

The fourth of the Ten Commandments instructs us to "Remember the Sabbath day to make it holy" (Exodus 20:8). The sages explain that this means we should declare the Sabbath's holiness when it begins and when it ends. As we end the Sabbath after a day of Divine rest, we again declare its holiness over a cup of wine in a prayer called *Havdalah*, or Separation. This prayer not only marks the transition from the sacred Sabbath to the ordinary week but also reminds us to carry the spirituality of the Sabbath into the days ahead.

In addition to a cup of wine, this prayer also includes blessings over spices and a lit candle. The sages explain that on the Sabbath we are given an "extra soul," and as the Sabbath departs, so does this extra spirit. To console ourselves over the loss of this special level of spirituality, we smell pleasant fragrances that "restore the soul."

As a result of Adam and Eve's sin, God chose to hide the primordial light He created at the beginning of the world. At the conclusion of the first Sabbath, the sun set, and darkness appeared for the first time. Adam was terrified, but God inspired him to strike two stones together and create fire. In response, Adam praised God for creating fire using the very same blessing we recite as part of the *Havdalah* prayer. Reciting this blessing over fire reminds us that just as Adam created light from a rock to combat the darkness, we too can find clarity and illumination in challenging times, sometimes from the most unexpected sources.

Hinneih el yeshu'ati evtach velo
efchad ki azzi vezimrat yah adonai
vai'hi li lishu'ah: ushe'avtem
mayim besason mimma'ai'nei
hayyeshu'ah: ladonai hayyeshu'ah
al ammecha virchatecha selah:
adonai tzeva'ot immanu misgav
lanu elohei ya'akov selah:
adonai tzeva'ot, ashrei adam
botei'ach bach: adonai hoshi'ah,
hammelech ya'aneinu veyom
kare'einu: layyehudim hayetah
orah vesimchah vesason vikar:
kayn tih'yeh lanu: kos yeshu'ot
essa uvesheim adonai ekra:
baruch attah adonai eloheinu
melech ha'olam, borei peri
haggafen:

הִנֵּה אֵל יְשׁוּעָתִי אֶבְטַח וְלֹא
אֶפְחָד כִּי עָזִּי וְזִמְרָת יָהּ יי
וַיְהִי לִי לִישׁוּעָה: וּשְׁאַבְתֶּם
מַיִם בְּשָׂשׂוֹן מִמַּעַיְנֵי
הַיְשׁוּעָה: לַיי הַיְשׁוּעָה
עַל עַמְּךָ בִרְכָתֶךָ סֶּלָה:
יי צְבָאוֹת עִמָּנוּ מִשְׂגָּב
לָנוּ אֱלֹהֵי יַעֲקֹב סֶלָה: יי
צְבָאוֹת, אַשְׁרֵי אָדָם בֹּטֵחַ
בָּךְ: יי הוֹשִׁיעָה, הַמֶּלֶךְ
יַעֲנֵנוּ בְיוֹם קָרְאֵנוּ:
לַיְּהוּדִים הָיְתָה אוֹרָה
וְשִׂמְחָה וְשָׂשֹׂן וִיקָר: כֵּן
תִּהְיֶה לָנוּ: כּוֹס יְשׁוּעוֹת אֶשָּׂא
וּבְשֵׁם יי אֶקְרָא: בָּרוּךְ
אַתָּה יי אֱלֹהֵינוּ מֶלֶךְ
הָעוֹלָם, בּוֹרֵא פְּרִי הַגָּפֶן:

*Behold, God is my salvation; I will trust and not be afraid, for the Lord
God is my strength and song, and He has been my salvation. You shall
draw water with joy from the springs of salvation. Salvation belongs to
the Lord; may Your blessing be upon Your people forever. The Lord of
Hosts is with us; the God of Jacob is our everlasting fortress. The Lord
of Hosts, happy is the person who trusts in You. Lord, save us; may the
King answer us on the day we call. For the Jews there was light and joy,
gladness and honor; so may it be for us. I will lift the cup of salvation
and call upon the name of the Lord. Blessed are You, Lord our God, King
of the universe, Who creates the fruit of the vine.*

Baruch attah adonai eloheinu
melech ha'olam, borei minei
vesamim.

בָּרוּךְ אַתָּה יי אֱלֹהֵינוּ
מֶלֶךְ הָעוֹלָם, בּוֹרֵא מִינֵי
בְשָׂמִים.

Blessed are You, Lord our God, King of the universe, who creates various kinds of spices.

Baruch attah adonai eloheinu
melech ha'olam, borei me'orei
ha'eish.

בָּרוּךְ אַתָּה יי אֱלֹהֵינוּ
מֶלֶךְ הָעוֹלָם, בּוֹרֵא מְאוֹרֵי
הָאֵשׁ.

Blessed are You, L-rd our G-d, King of the universe, who creates the lights of the fire.

Baruch attah adonai eloheinu
melech ha'olam, hammavdil
bein kodesh lechol, bein or
lechoshech, bein yisra'el
la'ammim, bein yom hashevi'i
lesheishet yemei hamma'aseh,

בָּרוּךְ אַתָּה יי אֱלֹהֵינוּ
מֶלֶךְ הָעוֹלָם, הַמַּבְדִּיל
בֵּין קֹדֶשׁ לְחוֹל, בֵּין אוֹר
לְחֹשֶׁךְ, בֵּין יִשְׂרָאֵל
לָעַמִּים, בֵּין יוֹם הַשְּׁבִיעִי
לְשֵׁשֶׁת יְמֵי הַמַּעֲשֶׂה,

baruch attah adonai, hammavdil
bein kodesh lechol.

בָּרוּךְ אַתָּה יי, הַמַּבְדִּיל
בֵּין קֹדֶשׁ לְחוֹל.

Blessed are You, Lord our God, King of the universe, who distinguishes between the holy and the profane, between light and darkness, between Israel and the nations, between the seventh day and the six working days. Blessed are You, O Lord, who distinguishes between the holy and the profane.

Who Separates Between Holy and Profane

The following song, traditionally sung after the *Havdalah* ceremony, is based on the blessing above which recognizes that God separates between holy and profane. It asks for forgiveness, blessings, and protection as we enter a new week.

Hammavdil bein kodesh lechol.
Chatoteinu hu yimchol. Zar'einu
vechaspeinu yarbeh kachol.
Vechakkochavim balla'yelah.

הַמַּבְדִּיל בֵּין קֹדֶשׁ לְחוֹל.
חַטֹּאתֵינוּ הוּא יִמְחוֹל. זַרְעֵנוּ
וְכַסְפֵּנוּ יַרְבֶּה כַּחוֹל.
וְכַכּוֹכָבִים בַּלָּיְלָה.

Yom panah ketzeil tomer. Ekra
la'eil alai gomer. Amar shomer. Ata
voker vegam la'yelah.

יוֹם פָּנָה כְּצֵל תֹּמֶר. אֶקְרָא
לָאֵל עָלַי גּוֹמֵר. אָמַר שׁוֹמֵר. אָתָא
בֹקֶר וְגַם לָיְלָה.

Tzidkatecha kehar tavor. Al
chata'ai avor ta'avor. Keyom
etmol ki ya'avor. Ve'ashmurah
balla'yelah.

צִדְקָתְךָ כְּהַר תָּבוֹר. עַל
חֲטָאַי עָבֹר תַּעֲבוֹר. כְּיוֹם
אֶתְמוֹל כִּי יַעֲבוֹר. וְאַשְׁמוּרָה
בַּלָּיְלָה.

Chalefah onat minchati. Mi yittein
menuchati. Yaga'ti be'anchati.
Ascheh bechol la'yelah.

חָלְפָה עוֹנַת מִנְחָתִי. מִי יִתֵּן
מְנוּחָתִי. יָגַעְתִּי בְּאַנְחָתִי.
אַשְׂחֶה בְּכָל לָיְלָה.

Koli bal yuntal. Petach li sha'ar
hammenutal. Sheroshi nimla tal.
Kevutzotai resisei la'yelah.

קוֹלִי בַּל יֻנְטָל. פְּתַח לִי שַׁעַר
הַמְּנוּטָל. שֶׁרֹאשִׁי נִמְלָא טָל.
קְוֻצּוֹתַי רְסִיסֵי לָיְלָה.

Hei'ater nora ve'ayom. Ashaveia'
tenah fidyom. Beneshef be'erev
yom. Be'ishon la'yelah.

הֵעָתֵר נוֹרָא וְאָיֹם. אֲשַׁוֵּעַ
תְּנָה פִדְיֹם. בְּנֶשֶׁף בְּעֶרֶב
יוֹם. בְּאִישׁוֹן לָיְלָה.

Keraticha yah hoshi'eini. Orach
chayyim todi'eini. Middallut
tevatze'eini. Miyom ve'ad la'yelah.

קְרָאתִיךָ יָהּ הוֹשִׁיעֵנִי. אֹרַח
חַיִּים תּוֹדִיעֵנִי. מִדַּלּוּת
תְּבַצְּעֵנִי. מִיּוֹם וְעַד לָיְלָה.

Taher tinnuf ma'asai. Pen yomru
mach'isai. Ayyeh na elo'ah osai.
Notein zemirot balla'yelah.

טַהֵר טִנּוּף מַעֲשַׂי. פֶּן יֹאמְרוּ
מַכְעִיסַי. אַיֵּה נָא אֱלוֹהַּ עֹשָׂי.
נוֹתֵן זְמִירוֹת בַּלָּיְלָה.

Nachnu veyadecha kachomer.
Selach na al kal vachomer. Yom
leyom yabbia' omer. Vela'yelah
lelay'lah.

נַחְנוּ בְיָדְךָ כַּחוֹמֶר.
סְלַח נָא עַל קַל וָחוֹמֶר. יוֹם
לְיוֹם יַבִּיעַ אוֹמֶר. וְלַיְלָה
לְלָיְלָה.

Hammavdil bein kodesh lechol.
Chatoteinu yimchol. Zar'einu
vechaspeinu yarbeh kachol.
Vechakochavim balla'yelah

הַמַּבְדִּיל בֵּין קֹדֶשׁ לְחוֹל.
חַטֹּאתֵינוּ יִמְחוֹל. זַרְעֵנוּ
וְכַסְפֵּנוּ יַרְבֶּה כַּחוֹל.
וְכַכּוֹכָבִים בַּלָּיְלָה

*He Who separates between the sacred and the profane. May He
forgive our sins. May our offspring and our wealth increase like
[the sand on] the seashore. And like the stars at night.*

*The day has moved on like the shadow of a palm tree, I will call
upon God that He fulfill for me what the Watchman said: Morning
has come and also night.*

Your righteousness is lofty like Mount Tabor. As for my sins, may You overlook them like yesterday that has passed on, and like a watch of the night.

The time of my afternoon offering has passed, who will give me rest? I am tired of sighing. I am drenched with tears each night.

My voice shall not be withdrawn. Open for me the lofty gate. For my head is filled with dew. My locks with the drops of the night.

Be receptive, Awesome and Fearsome One. When I cry out, grant redemption. At night, when daylight wanes, and in the darkness of the night.

I have called upon you, O God, save me. Show me the path of life. You shall rescue me from my poverty as quickly as from day to night.

Purify the filth of my actions, lest my provokers say, 'Where is now the God who made me? Who gives cause for songs at night?'

We are in Your hand like clay, please forgive sins both small and great. Day after day, night after night, brings expressions of praise.

He Who separates between the sacred and the profane. May He forgive our sins. May our offspring and our money increase like [the sand on] the seashore. And like the stars at night.

Eliyyahu hannavi eliyyahu hattishbi eliyyahu haggil'adi bimemheirah yavo eileinu im mashiach ben david.

אֵלִיָּהוּ הַנָּבִיא אֵלִיָּהוּ הַתִּשְׁבִּי אֵלִיָּהוּ הַגִּלְעָדִי בִּמְהֵרָה יָבוֹא אֵלֵינוּ עִם מָשִׁיחַ בֶּן דָּוִד.

Elijah the prophet, Elijah the Tishbite, Elijah the Gileadite, may he come to us soon with the Messiah, son of David.

Notes

Holiday Prayers

Hallel: A Prayer of Praise

ON ROSH CHODESH (the monthly New Moon celebration) and on most holidays we recite the *Hallel* prayer. *Hallel* means praise, and this prayer is an extended expression of praise and thanks to God for the many kindnesses He has bestowed upon us. *Hallel* is made up of Psalms 113-118, and is generally sung joyously.

Psalm 113

Psalm 113 is the introductory psalm of the *Hallel* prayer. It calls upon the "servants of the Lord" to praise His name from sunrise to sunset. When we admire, love, or appreciate someone, we talk about them all the time. For those who dedicate their lives to God, the natural result of this love and admiration is to praise Him "from the rising of the sun in the East to its setting." Even though God "sits on high," He lowers Himself to care for every person on earth. This recognition inspires our continuous praise.

Halleluyah hallelu avdei adonai.	הַלְלוּיָהּ הַלְלוּ עַבְדֵי יְהֹוָה.
Halelu et sheim adonai: yehi	הַלְלוּ אֶת שֵׁם יְהֹוָה: יְהִי
sheim adonai mevorach. Mei'attah	שֵׁם יְהֹוָה מְבֹרָךְ. מֵעַתָּה
ve'ad olam: mimmizrach shemesh	וְעַד עוֹלָם: מִמִּזְרַח שֶׁמֶשׁ
ad mevo'o. Mehullal shem adonai:	עַד מְבוֹאוֹ. מְהֻלָּל שֵׁם יְהֹוָה:
ram al kol goyim adonai. Al	רָם עַל כָּל גּוֹיִם יְהֹוָה. עַל
hashamayim kevodo: mi kadonai	הַשָּׁמַיִם כְּבוֹדוֹ: מִי כַּיהֹוָה
eloheinu hammagbihi lashavet:	אֱלֹהֵינוּ הַמַּגְבִּיהִי לָשָׁבֶת:

hammashpili lir'ot bashamayim
uva'aretz: mekimi mei'afar dal.
Mei'ashpot yarim evyon: lehoshivi
im nedivim. Im nedivei ammo:
moshivi akeret habbayit. Eim
habbanim semeichah. Halleluyah:

הַמַּשְׁפִּילִי לִרְאוֹת בַּשָּׁמַיִם
וּבָאָרֶץ: מְקִימִי מֵעָפָר דָּל.
מֵאַשְׁפֹּת יָרִים אֶבְיוֹן: לְהוֹשִׁיבִי
עִם נְדִיבִים. עִם נְדִיבֵי עַמּוֹ:
מוֹשִׁיבִי עֲקֶרֶת הַבַּיִת. אֵם
הַבָּנִים שְׂמֵחָה. הַלְלוּיָהּ:

Halleluyah! Praise, servants of the Lord, praise the name of the Lord. May the Name of the Lord be blessed from now and forever. From the rising of the sun in the East to its setting, the name of the Lord is praised. Above all nations is the Lord, His honor is above the heavens. Who is like the Lord, our God, Who sits on high; Who looks down upon the heavens and the earth? He brings up the poor out of the dirt; from the refuse piles, He raises the destitute. To seat him with the nobles, with the nobles of his people. He seats a barren woman in a home, a happy mother of children. Halleluyah!

Psalm 114

This psalm celebrates the miracles God performed for the Jewish people when He took them out of Egypt. It vividly recounts the miraculous changes to the natural order of the world, such as the sea parting, the Jordan reversing, and mountains and hills dancing (a hint to the giving of the Bible at Mount Sinai). The redemption from Egypt demonstrated God's complete mastery over the world—He created nature and only He can change it.

Betzeit yisra'el mimmitzrayim, beit
ya'akov mei'am lo'eiz: hayetah
yehudah lekodsho, yisra'el
mamshelotav: hayyam

בְּצֵאת יִשְׂרָאֵל מִמִּצְרָיִם, בֵּית
יַעֲקֹב מֵעַם לֹעֵז: הָיְתָה
יְהוּדָה לְקָדְשׁוֹ, יִשְׂרָאֵל
מַמְשְׁלוֹתָיו: הַיָּם

ra'ah vayyanos, hayyarden

yissov le'achor: heharim rakedu

che'eilim, geva'ot kivnei tzon: mah

lecha hayyam ki tanus, hayyardein

tissov le'achor: heharim tirkedu

che'eilim, geva'ot kivnei tzon:

millifnei adon chuli aretz, millifnei

eloah ya'akov: hahofechi hatzur

agam mayim, challamish lema'y'no

mayim:

רָאָה וַיָּנֹס, הַיַּרְדֵּן

יִסֹּב לְאָחוֹר: הֶהָרִים רָקְדוּ

כְאֵילִים, גְּבָעוֹת כִּבְנֵי צֹאן: מַה

לְּךָ הַיָּם כִּי תָנוּס, הַיַּרְדֵּן

תִּסֹּב לְאָחוֹר: הֶהָרִים תִּרְקְדוּ

כְאֵילִים, גְּבָעוֹת כִּבְנֵי צֹאן:

מִלִּפְנֵי אָדוֹן חוּלִי אָרֶץ, מִלִּפְנֵי

אֱלוֹהַּ יַעֲקֹב: הַהֹפְכִי הַצּוּר

אֲגַם מָיִם, חַלָּמִישׁ לְמַעְיְנוֹ

מָיִם:

In Israel's going out from Egypt, the house of Jacob from a people of foreign speech. Judah was his sanctuary, and Israel, his dominion. The Sea saw and fled, the Jordan turned to the rear. The mountains danced like rams, the hills like young sheep. What is happening to you, O Sea, that you are fleeing, O Jordan that you turn to the rear; O mountains that you dance like rams, O hills like young sheep? From before the Master, tremble O earth, from before the Lord of Jacob. He who turns the boulder into a pond of water, the flint into a spring of water.

Psalm 115:1-11

Psalm 115 contrasts the futility of idols and false gods with the glory of the God of Israel.

Lo lanu adonai lo lanu. Ki

leshimcha tein kavod. Al

chasdecha al amittecha:

lammah yomru haggoyim.

Ayeih na eloheihem: veiloheinu

vashamayim. Kol asher chafeitz

לֹא לָנוּ יְהוָה לֹא לָנוּ. כִּי

לְשִׁמְךָ תֵּן כָּבוֹד. עַל

חַסְדְּךָ עַל אֲמִתֶּךָ:

לָמָה יֹאמְרוּ הַגּוֹיִם.

אַיֵּה נָא אֱלֹהֵיהֶם: וֵאלֹהֵינוּ

בַשָּׁמָיִם. כֹּל אֲשֶׁר חָפֵץ

asah: atzabbeihem kesef vezahav. עָשָׂה: עֲצַבֵּיהֶם כֶּסֶף וְזָהָב.

Ma'aseih yedei adam: peh lahem מַעֲשֵׂה יְדֵי אָדָם: פֶּה לָהֶם

velo yedabbeiru. Einayim lahem וְלֹא יְדַבֵּרוּ. עֵינַיִם לָהֶם

velo yir'u: oznayim lahem velo וְלֹא יִרְאוּ: אָזְנַיִם לָהֶם וְלֹא

yishma'u. Af lahem velo yerichun: יִשְׁמָעוּ. אַף לָהֶם וְלֹא יְרִיחוּן:

yedeihem velo yemishun. יְדֵיהֶם וְלֹא יְמִישׁוּן.

Ragleihem velo yehalleichu. Lo רַגְלֵיהֶם וְלֹא יְהַלֵּכוּ. לֹא

yehgu bigronam: kemohem yihyu יֶהְגּוּ בִּגְרוֹנָם: כְּמוֹהֶם יִהְיוּ

oseihem. Kol asher botei'ach עֹשֵׂיהֶם. כֹּל אֲשֶׁר בֹּטֵחַ

bahem: yisra'el betach badonai. בָּהֶם: יִשְׂרָאֵל בְּטַח בַּיהֹוָה.

Ezram umaginnam hu: beit aharon עֶזְרָם וּמָגִנָּם הוּא: בֵּית אַהֲרֹן

bitchu badonai. Ezram umaginnam בִּטְחוּ בַּיהֹוָה. עֶזְרָם וּמָגִנָּם

hu: yir'ei adonai bitchu badonai. הוּא: יִרְאֵי יְהֹוָה בִּטְחוּ בַּיהֹוָה.

Ezram umaginnam hu: עֶזְרָם וּמָגִנָּם הוּא:

Not to us, not to us, but rather to Your name, give glory for your kindness and for your truth. Why should the nations say, "Say, where is their God?" But our God is in the heavens, all that He wanted, He has done. Their idols are silver and gold, the work of men's hands. They have a mouth but do not speak; they have eyes but do not see. They have ears but do not hear; they have a nose but do not smell. Hands, but they do not feel; feet, but do not walk; they do not make a peep from their throat. Like them will be their makers, all those that trust in them. Israel, trust in the Lord; their help and shield is He. House of Aharon, trust in the Lord; their help and shield is He. Those that fear the Lord, trust in the Lord; their help and shield is He.

Psalm 115:12-18

The concluding verses of Psalm 115 celebrate God's blessings and faithfulness to those who fear Him. The Lord blesses His people, and we have the privilege and duty to praise Him forever.

Adonai zecharanu yevareich,　יְהֹוָה זְכָרָנוּ יְבָרֵךְ,

yevareich et beit yisra'el,　יְבָרֵךְ אֶת בֵּית יִשְׂרָאֵל,

yevareich et beit aharon:　יְבָרֵךְ אֶת בֵּית אַהֲרֹן:

yevareich yir'ei adonai,　יְבָרֵךְ יִרְאֵי יְהֹוָה,

hakketannim im haggedolim:　הַקְּטַנִּים עִם הַגְּדֹלִים:

yosef adonai aleichem, aleichem　יֹסֵף יְהֹוָה עֲלֵיכֶם, עֲלֵיכֶם

ve'al beneichem: beruchim attem　וְעַל בְּנֵיכֶם: בְּרוּכִים אַתֶּם

ladonai, oseh shamayim va'aretz:　לַיהֹוָה, עֹשֵׂה שָׁמַיִם וָאָרֶץ:

hashamayim shamayim ladonai,　הַשָּׁמַיִם שָׁמַיִם לַיהֹוָה,

veha'aretz natan livnei adam:　וְהָאָרֶץ נָתַן לִבְנֵי אָדָם:

lo hammeitim yehallu yah, velo　לֹא הַמֵּתִים יְהַלְלוּ יָהּ, וְלֹא

kol yoredei dumah: va'anachnu　כָּל יֹרְדֵי דוּמָה: וַאֲנַחְנוּ

nevareich yah, mei'attah ve'ad　נְבָרֵךְ יָהּ, מֵעַתָּה וְעַד

olam, halluyah:　עוֹלָם, הַלְלוּיָהּ:

The Lord who remembers us, will bless; He will bless the House of Israel; He will bless the House of Aharon. He will bless those that fear the Lord, the small ones with the great ones. May the Lord bring increase to you, to you and to your children. Blessed are you to the Lord, the maker of the heavens and the earth. The heavens are the Lord's heavens, but the earth He has given to the children of man. It is not the dead that will praise the Lord, and not those that go down to silence. But we will bless the Lord from now and forever. Halleluyah!

Psalm 116:1-11

The first 11 verses of Psalm 116 express gratitude and love for the Lord, who hears and responds to our cries for help.

Ahavti ki yishma adonai et koli　אָהַבְתִּי כִּי יִשְׁמַע יְהֹוָה אֶת קוֹלִי

tachanunai: ki hittah ozno li.　תַּחֲנוּנָי: כִּי הִטָּה אָזְנוֹ לִי.

Uveyamai ekra: afafuni chevlei
mavet. Umetzarei she'ol
metza'uni. Tzarah veyagon emtza:
uvesheim adonai ekra. annah
adonai malletah nafshi: channun
adonai vetzaddik. Veiloheinu
merachem: shomer petayim
adonai. Dalloti veli yehoshia':
shuvi nafshi limnucha'yechi.
Ki adonai gamal ala'yechi: ki
chillatzta nafshi mimmavet. Et
eini min dim'ah. Et ragli middechi:
ethaleich lifnei adonai. Be'artzot
hachayyim: he'emanti ki adabber.
Ani aniti me'od: ani amarti
vechafezi. Kol ha'adam kozeiv:

וּבְיָמַי אֶקְרָא: אֲפָפוּנִי חֶבְלֵי
מָוֶת. וּמְצָרֵי שְׁאוֹל
מְצָאוּנִי. צָרָה וְיָגוֹן אֶמְצָא:
וּבְשֵׁם יְהֹוָה אֶקְרָא. אָנָּה
יְהֹוָה מַלְּטָה נַפְשִׁי: חַנּוּן
יְהֹוָה וְצַדִּיק. וֵאלֹהֵינוּ
מְרַחֵם: שֹׁמֵר פְּתָאיִם
יְהֹוָה. דַּלֹּתִי וְלִי יְהוֹשִׁיעַ:
שׁוּבִי נַפְשִׁי לִמְנוּחָיְכִי.
כִּי יְהֹוָה גָּמַל עָלָיְכִי: כִּי
חִלַּצְתָּ נַפְשִׁי מִמָּוֶת. אֶת
עֵינִי מִן דִּמְעָה. אֶת רַגְלִי מִדֶּחִי:
אֶתְהַלֵּךְ לִפְנֵי יְהֹוָה. בְּאַרְצוֹת
הַחַיִּים: הֶאֱמַנְתִּי כִּי אֲדַבֵּר.
אֲנִי עָנִיתִי מְאֹד: אֲנִי אָמַרְתִּי
בְחָפְזִי. כָּל הָאָדָם כֹּזֵב:

*I have loved the Lord - since He hears my voice, my supplications.
Since He inclined His ear to me - and in my days, I will call out.
The pangs of death have encircled me and the straits of the Pit
have found me and I found grief. And in the name of the Lord I
called, "Please Lord, Spare my soul." Gracious is the Lord and
righteous, and our God acts mercifully. The Lord watches over
the silly; I was poor and He has saved me. Return, my soul to your
tranquility, since the Lord has favored you. Since You have rescued
my soul from death, my eyes from tears, my feet from stumbling. I
will walk before the Lord in the lands of the living. I have trusted,
when I speak - I am very afflicted. I said in my haste, all men are
hypocritical.*

Psalm 116:12-19

We can never repay God for all the kindness He shows us.
After all, what can we give the Lord? All we can do is praise
and thank Him, acknowledging His endless generosity and
expressing our gratitude for His boundless blessings.

Mah ashiv ladonai, kol tagmulohi
alai: kos yeshu'ot essa, uvesheim
adonai ekra: nedarai ladonai
ashalleim, negdah na lechol
ammo: yakar be'einei adonai
hammavetah lachasidav: annah
adonai ki ani avdecha, ani
avdecha ben amatecha, pittachta
lemoserai: lecha ezbach zevach
todah, uvesheim adonai ekra:
nedarai ladonai ashalleim, negdah
na lechol ammo: bechatzrot beit
adonai betocheichi yerushalayim,
halluyah:

מָה אָשִׁיב לַיהֹוָה, כָּל תַּגְמוּלוֹהִי
עָלָי: כּוֹס יְשׁוּעוֹת אֶשָּׂא, וּבְשֵׁם
יְהֹוָה אֶקְרָא: נְדָרַי לַיהֹוָה
אֲשַׁלֵּם, נֶגְדָה נָּא לְכָל
עַמּוֹ: יָקָר בְּעֵינֵי יְהֹוָה
הַמָּוְתָה לַחֲסִידָיו: אָנָּה
יְהֹוָה כִּי אֲנִי עַבְדֶּךָ, אֲנִי
עַבְדְּךָ בֶּן אֲמָתֶךָ, פִּתַּחְתָּ
לְמוֹסֵרָי: לְךָ אֶזְבַּח זֶבַח
תּוֹדָה, וּבְשֵׁם יְהֹוָה אֶקְרָא:
נְדָרַי לַיהֹוָה אֲשַׁלֵּם, נֶגְדָה
נָּא לְכָל עַמּוֹ: בְּחַצְרוֹת בֵּית
יְהֹוָה בְּתוֹכֵכִי יְרוּשָׁלָיִם,
הַלְלוּיָהּ:

*What can I give back to the Lord for all that He has favored me?
A cup of salvations I will raise up and I will call out in the name
of the Lord. My vows to the Lord I will pay, now in front of His
entire people. Precious in the eyes of the Lord is the death of His
pious ones. Please Lord, since I am Your servant, the son of Your
maidservant; You have opened my chains. To You will I offer a
thanksgiving offering and I will call out in the name of the Lord.
My vows to the Lord I will pay, now in front of His entire people. In
the courtyards of the house of the Lord, in your midst, Jerusalem.
Halleluyah!*

Psalm 117

This short chapter describes how, in the times of the Messiah, all the nations of the world will recognize and praise God. In those times it will finally be clear to everyone that the God of Israel is the one true God.

הַלְלוּ אֶת יְהֹוָה כָּל גּוֹיִם,
שַׁבְּחוּהוּ כָּל הָאֻמִּים: כִּי
גָבַר עָלֵינוּ חַסְדּוֹ, וֶאֱמֶת
יְהֹוָה לְעוֹלָם, הַלְלוּיָהּ:

Hallelu et adonai kol goyim, shabbechuhu kol ha'ummim: ki gavar aleinu chasdo, ve'emet adonai le'olam, halleluyah:

Praise the name of the Lord, all nations; extol Him all peoples. Since His kindness has overwhelmed us and the truth of the Lord is forever. Halleluyah!

Psalm 118

The rest of the *Hallel* prayer consists of Psalm 118. In this section, it says that those who fear the Lord will declare, "His kindness is forever." Someone who fears the Lord has nothing else to fear, because he recognizes that everything comes from God and places his trust completely in Him. When you "take refuge with the Lord," you no longer have anything to worry about, as it says: "The Lord is for me, I will not fear; what can man do to me?" With this perspective, you also recognize that all salvation and success come from the Lord. He is the one to call out to when we need help, and He is the one we praise when help is granted.

Psalm 118:1-4

hodu ladonai ki tov - ki le'olam
chasdo: yomar na yisra'el - ki
le'olam chasdo: yomru na veit
aharon - ki le'olam chasdo:
yomru na yir'ei adonai - ki le'olam
chasdo:

הוֹדוּ לַיהֹוָה כִּי טוֹב - כִּי לְעוֹלָם
חַסְדּוֹ: יֹאמַר נָא יִשְׂרָאֵל - כִּי
לְעוֹלָם חַסְדּוֹ: יֹאמְרוּ נָא בֵית
אַהֲרֹן - כִּי לְעוֹלָם חַסְדּוֹ:
יֹאמְרוּ נָא יִרְאֵי יְהֹוָה - כִּי לְעוֹלָם
חַסְדּוֹ:

*Thank the Lord, since He is good, since His kindness is forever. Let
Israel now say, "His kindness is forever." Let the House of Aharon
now say, "His kindness is forever." Let those that fear the Lord now
say, "His kindness is forever."*

Psalm 118:5-20

Min hammeitzar karati yah. Anani
bammerchav yah: adonai li lo ira.
Mah ya'aseh li adam: adonai li
be'ozerai. Va'ani er'eh veson'ai:
tov lachasot badonai. Mibbetoach
ba'adam: tov lachasot badonai.
Mibbetoach bindivim: kol goyim
sevavuni. Besheim adonai ki
amilam: sabbuni gam sevavuni.
Besheim adonai ki amilam:
sabbuni chidvorim. Do'achu
ke'esih kotzim. Besheim adonai ki
amilam: dachoh dechitani linpol.
Vadonai azarani: azzi vezimrat
yah. Va'yhi li lishu'ah: kol rinnah
vishu'ah be'oholei tzaddikim.

מִן הַמֵּצַר קָרָאתִי יָּה. עֲנָנִי
בַמֶּרְחָב יָּה: יְהֹוָה לִי לֹא אִירָא.
מַה יַּעֲשֶׂה לִי אָדָם: יְהֹוָה לִי
בְּעֹזְרָי. וַאֲנִי אֶרְאֶה בְשֹׂנְאָי:
טוֹב לַחֲסוֹת בַּיהֹוָה. מִבְּטֹחַ
בָּאָדָם: טוֹב לַחֲסוֹת בַּיהֹוָה.
מִבְּטֹחַ בִּנְדִיבִים: כָּל גּוֹיִם
סְבָבוּנִי. בְּשֵׁם יְהֹוָה כִּי
אֲמִילַם: סַבּוּנִי גַם סְבָבוּנִי.
בְּשֵׁם יְהֹוָה כִּי אֲמִילַם:
סַבּוּנִי כִדְבוֹרִים. דֹּעֲכוּ
כְּאֵשׁ קוֹצִים. בְּשֵׁם יְהֹוָה כִּי
אֲמִילַם: דָּחֹה דְחִיתַנִי לִנְפֹּל.
וַיהֹוָה עֲזָרָנִי: עָזִּי וְזִמְרָת
יָּה. וַיְהִי לִי לִישׁוּעָה: קוֹל רִנָּה
וִישׁוּעָה בְּאָהֳלֵי צַדִּיקִים.

Yemin adonai osah chayil: yemin adonai romeimah. Yemin adonai osah chayil: lo amut ki echyeh. Va'asappeir ma'asei yah: yassor yisseranni yah. Velammavet lo netanani: pitchu li sha'arei tzedek. Avo vam odeh yah: zeh hasha'ar ladonai. Tzaddikim yavo'u vo:

יְמִין יְהֹוָה עֹשָׂה חָיִל: יְמִין יְהֹוָה רוֹמֵמָה. יְמִין יְהֹוָה עֹשָׂה חָיִל: לֹא אָמוּת כִּי אֶחְיֶה. וַאֲסַפֵּר מַעֲשֵׂי יָהּ: יַסּוֹר יִסְּרַנִּי יָהּ. וְלַמָּוֶת לֹא נְתָנָנִי: פִּתְחוּ לִי שַׁעֲרֵי צֶדֶק. אָבֹא בָם אוֹדֶה יָהּ: זֶה הַשַּׁעַר לַיהֹוָה. צַדִּיקִים יָבֹאוּ בוֹ:

From the strait I have called, Lord; He answered me from the wide space, the Lord. The Lord is for me, I will not fear, what will man do to me? The Lord is for me with my helpers, and I shall glare at those that hate me. It is better to take refuge with the Lord than to trust in man. It is better to take refuge with the Lord than to trust in nobles. All the nations surrounded me - in the name of the Lord, as I will chop them off. They surrounded me, they also encircled me - in the name of the Lord, as I will chop them off. They surrounded me like bees, they were extinguished like a fire of thorns - in the name of the Lord, as I will chop them off. You have surely pushed me to fall, but the Lord helped me. My boldness and song is the Lord, and He has become my salvation. The sound of happy song and salvation is in the tents of the righteous, the right hand of the Lord acts powerfully. I will not die but rather I will live and tell over the acts of the Lord. The Lord has surely chastised me, but He has not given me over to death. Open up for me the gates of righteousness; I will enter them, thank the Lord. This is the gate of the Lord, the righteous will enter it.

Psalm 118:21-24 (each line is said twice)

Odecha ki anitani, vattehi li lishu'ah.

אוֹדְךָ כִּי עֲנִיתָנִי, וַתְּהִי לִי לִישׁוּעָה.

Even ma'asu habbonim, hayetah lerosh pinnah.

אֶבֶן מָאֲסוּ הַבּוֹנִים, הָיְתָה לְרֹאשׁ פִּנָּה.

Mei'eit adonai hayetah zot, hi niflat be'eineinu.

מֵאֵת יְהֹוָה הָיְתָה זֹּאת, הִיא נִפְלָאת בְּעֵינֵינוּ.

Zeh hayyom asah adonai, nagilah venismechah vo:

זֶה הַיּוֹם עָשָׂה יְהֹוָה, נָגִילָה וְנִשְׂמְחָה בוֹ:

I will thank You, since You answered me and You have become my salvation.

The stone that was left by the builders has become the main cornerstone.

From the Lord was this, it is wondrous in our eyes.

This is the day of the Lord, let us exult and rejoice upon it.

Pslam 118:25 (Each phrase is said twice)

Anna adonai hoshi'ah na:

אָנָּא יְהֹוָה הוֹשִׁיעָה נָּא:

Anna adonai hatzlichah na:

אָנָּא יְהֹוָה הַצְלִיחָה נָּא:

Please, Lord, save us now! Please, Lord, give us success now!

Psalms 118:26-29 (each line is said twice)

Baruch habba besheim adonai, beirachnuchem mibbeit adonai:

בָּרוּךְ הַבָּא בְּשֵׁם יְהֹוָה, בֵּרַכְנוּכֶם מִבֵּית יְהֹוָה:

El adonai vayya'er lanu, isru
chag ba'avotim, ad karnot
hammizbeach:

אֵל יְהֹוָה וַיָּאֶר לָנוּ, אִסְרוּ
חַג בַּעֲבוֹתִים, עַד קַרְנוֹת
הַמִּזְבֵּחַ:

Eili attah ve'odekka, elohai
aromemekka:

אֵלִי אַתָּה וְאוֹדֶךָ, אֱלֹהַי
אֲרוֹמְמֶךָ:

Hodu ladonai ki tov, ki le'olam
chasdo:

הוֹדוּ לַיהֹוָה כִּי טוֹב, כִּי לְעוֹלָם
חַסְדּוֹ:

*Blessed be the one who comes in the name of the Lord, we have
blessed you from the house of the Lord. God is the Lord, and He
has illuminated us; tie up the festival offering with ropes until it
reaches the corners of the altar. You are my Power and I will Thank
You; my God and I will exalt You. Thank the Lord, since He is good,
since His kindness is forever.*

Notes

May Our Prayers Ascend to You

THE FOLLOWING PRAYER is added into both the *Amida* prayer as well as the Grace After Meals on *Rosh Chodesh* (New Moon) and Jewish holidays. It expresses the hope that our prayers will ascend to God and receive a divine response.

Eloheinu veilohei avoteinu	אֱלֹהֵינוּ וֵאלֹהֵי אֲבוֹתֵינוּ
ya'aleh veyavo veyaggia'	יַעֲלֶה וְיָבוֹא וְיַגִּיעַ
veyeira'eh veyeiratzeh veyishama	וְיֵרָאֶה וְיֵרָצֶה וְיִשָּׁמַע
veyippakeid veyizzacheir	וְיִפָּקֵד וְיִזָּכֵר
zichroneinu ufikdoneinu vezichron	זִכְרוֹנֵנוּ וּפִקְדוֹנֵנוּ וְזִכְרוֹן
avoteinu vezichron mashiach	אֲבוֹתֵינוּ וְזִכְרוֹן מָשִׁיחַ
ben david avdecha. Vezichron	בֶּן דָּוִד עַבְדֶּךָ. וְזִכְרוֹן
yerushalayim ir kodshecha	יְרוּשָׁלַיִם עִיר קָדְשֶׁךָ
vezichron kol ammecha beit	וְזִכְרוֹן כָּל עַמְּךָ בֵּית
yisra'el lefanecha lifleitah letvoah	יִשְׂרָאֵל לְפָנֶיךָ לִפְלֵיטָה לְטוֹבָה
lechein ulechesed ulerachamim	לְחֵן וּלְחֶסֶד וּלְרַחֲמִים
lechayyim uleshalom beyom:	לְחַיִּים וּלְשָׁלוֹם בְּיוֹם:
(New Moon) -	ראש חודש –
rosh hachodesh hazzeh:	רֹאשׁ הַחֹדֶשׁ הַזֶּה:
(Passover) -	לפסח –
chag hammatzot hazzeh:	חַג הַמַּצּוֹת הַזֶּה:
(Feast of Weeks) -	לשבועות –
chag hashavu'ot hazzeh:	חַג הַשָּׁבוּעוֹת הַזֶּה:
(Feast of Tabernacles) -	סוכות –
chag hassukkot hazzeh:	חַג הַסֻּכּוֹת הַזֶּה:
(Eighth Day of Assembly) -	לשמיני עצרת ולשמחת תורה –
hashmini chag ha'atzeret hazzeh:	הַשְּׁמִינִי חַג הָעֲצֶרֶת הַזֶּה:

zachereinu adonai elheinu bo
letovah. Ufakedenu bo livrachah.
Vehvoshi'einu bo lechayyim.
Uvidvar yeshu'ah verachamim
chus vechonnenu veracheim
aleinu vehvoshi'einu ki elecha
eineinu ki el melech channun
verachum attah:

זָכְרֵנוּ ה' אֱלֹהֵינוּ בּוֹ
לְטוֹבָה. וּפָקְדֵנוּ בּוֹ לִבְרָכָה.
וְהוֹשִׁיעֵנוּ בּוֹ לְחַיִּים.
וּבִדְבַר יְשׁוּעָה וְרַחֲמִים
חוּס וְחָנֵּנוּ וְרַחֵם
עָלֵינוּ וְהוֹשִׁיעֵנוּ כִּי אֵלֶיךָ
עֵינֵינוּ כִּי אֵל מֶלֶךְ חַנּוּן
וְרַחוּם אָתָּה:

Our God and God of our fathers, may there ascend, come, and reach, appear, be desired, and heard, counted and recalled our remembrance and reckoning; the remembrance of our fathers; the remembrance of the Messiah the son of David, Your servant; the remembrance of Jerusalem, city of Your Sanctuary and the remembrance of Your entire people, the House of Israel, before You for survival, for well-being, for favor, kindliness, compassion, for life and peace on this day of:

For Rosh Chodesh - This new moon:
For Passover - This festival of Matzot (Unleavened Bread):
For Shavuot - This festival of Weeks:
For Sukkot - This festival of Booths:
For Shemini Atzeret and Simchat Torah - This eighth day festival of assembly:

Remember us O Lord, our God, on this day for well-being; be mindful of us on this day for blessing, and deliver us for life. In accord with the promise of deliverance and compassion, spare us and favor us, have compassion on us and deliver us; for our eyes are directed to You, because You are the Almighty Who is King, Gracious, and Merciful.

Rosh Chodesh (New Moon)

Rosh Chodesh (New Moon) literally means "the head of the month," and it is celebrated for a day or two at the beginning of each new lunar month. Jewish months follow the cycle of the moon, and each new month begins when the new moon appears in the sky.

The people of Israel are often compared to the moon. Just as the moon waxes and wanes but never really disappears, the light and strength of Israel has fluctuated throughout history, growing stronger at times and dimmer at others. However, even in the darkest periods of our history, our light has never been completely extinguished. This is one reason why we celebrate when the new moon appears in the night sky each month.

Blessing the New Moon

The following prayer is recited on the Sabbath before *Rosh Chodesh* (New Moon). As we announce the date of the New Moon, we beseech God, asking for a new month that is both good and blessed. What is the difference between these two qualities? Our lives can be good without necessarily feeling blessed. At the start of the month, we pray that God grants us a month that is evidently good and also feels like a true blessing.

Yehi ratzon millefanecha adonai	יְהִי רָצוֹן מִלְפָנֶיךָ ה'
eloheinu veilohei avoteinu.	אֱלֹהֵינוּ וֵאלֹהֵי אֲבוֹתֵינוּ.
Shettechaddeish aleinu et	שֶׁתְּחַדֵּשׁ עָלֵינוּ אֶת

hachodesh hazzeh letovah
velivrachah. Vetitten lanu chayyim
arukkim. Chayyim shel shalom.
Chayyim shel tovah. Chayyim shel
berachah. Chayyim shel parnasah.
Chayyim shel chillutz atzamot.
Chayyim sheyeish bahem
yir'at shamayim veyir'at cheit.
Chayyim she'ein bahem bushah
uchelimmah. Chayyim shel osher
vechavod. Chayyim shettehei
vanu ahavat torah veyir'at
shamayim. Chayyim sheyyimale'u
mish'alot libbeinu letvoah amen
selah.

Yechaddesheihu hakkadosh
baruch hu aleinu ve'al kol ammo
beit yisra'el bechol makom
sheheim. Letvoah velivrachah.
Lesason ulesimchah. Lishu'ah
ulenechamah. Lefarnasah
tovah ulechalkalah. Lechayyim
uleshalom. Lishmu'ot tovot.
Velivsorot tovot. (in the winter -
veligshamim be'ittam). Velirfu'ah
sheleimah. Velig'ulah kerovah
venomar amen.

הַחֹדֶשׁ הַזֶּה לְטוֹבָה
וְלִבְרָכָה. וְתִתֶּן לָנוּ חַיִּים
אֲרֻכִּים. חַיִּים שֶׁל שָׁלוֹם.
חַיִּים שֶׁל טוֹבָה. חַיִּים שֶׁל
בְּרָכָה. חַיִּים שֶׁל פַּרְנָסָה.
חַיִּים שֶׁל חִלּוּץ עֲצָמוֹת.
חַיִּים שֶׁיֵּשׁ בָּהֶם
יִרְאַת שָׁמַיִם וְיִרְאַת חֵטְא.
חַיִּים שֶׁאֵין בָּהֶם בּוּשָׁה
וּכְלִמָּה. חַיִּים שֶׁל עֹשֶׁר
וְכָבוֹד. חַיִּים שֶׁתְּהֵא
בָנוּ אַהֲבַת תּוֹרָה וְיִרְאַת
שָׁמַיִם. חַיִּים שֶׁיִּמָּלְאוּ
מִשְׁאֲלוֹת לִבֵּנוּ לְטוֹבָה אָמֵן
סֶלָה.

יְחַדְּשֵׁהוּ הַקָּדוֹשׁ
בָּרוּךְ הוּא עָלֵינוּ וְעַל כָּל עַמּוֹ
בֵּית יִשְׂרָאֵל בְּכָל מָקוֹם
שֶׁהֵם. לְטוֹבָה וְלִבְרָכָה.
לְשָׂשׂוֹן וּלְשִׂמְחָה. לִישׁוּעָה
וּלְנֶחָמָה. לְפַרְנָסָה
טוֹבָה וּלְכַלְכָּלָה. לְחַיִּים
וּלְשָׁלוֹם. לִשְׁמוּעוֹת טוֹבוֹת.
וְלִבְשׂוֹרוֹת טוֹבוֹת. (בַּחוֹרֶף -
וְלִגְשָׁמִים בְּעִתָּם). וְלִרְפוּאָה
שְׁלֵמָה. וְלִגְאֻלָּה קְרוֹבָה
וְנֹאמַר אָמֵן.

*May it be Your will, Lord our God and God of our fathers, that You
renew for us this month for good and blessing. Grant us long life, a
life of peace, a life of goodness, a life of blessing, a life of sustenance,
a life of physical health, a life in which there is fear of heaven and*

fear of sin, a life without shame or disgrace, a life of wealth and honor, a life in which we have love of Torah and fear of heaven, a life in which our heartfelt requests are fulfilled for the good. Amen Selah.

May the Holy One, blessed be He, renew it upon us and upon all His people, the house of Israel, in every place where they are, for good and for blessing, for joy and for happiness, for salvation and for comfort, for good sustenance and for adequate sustenance, for life and for peace, for good tidings and for good news. In winter - for rain in its time, for complete healing, and for near redemption, and let us say, Amen.

My Soul Blesses the Lord - Psalm 104

At the end of the morning prayers on *Rosh Chodesh*, it is customary to recite Psalm 104, known as "My Soul Blesses the Lord." Psalm 104 is a poetic celebration of God's creation and His majesty. It is recited on *Rosh Chodesh* because of its reference to the cycle of the moon and the setting of the calendar, "He made the moon to fix seasons."

Barechi nafshi et-adonai adonai	בָּרְכִי נַפְשִׁי אֶת־יְהֹוָה יְהֹוָה
elohai gadalta me'od, hod	אֱלֹהַי גָּדַלְתָּ מְּאֹד, הוֹד
vehadar lavasheta: oteh or	וְהָדָר לָבָשְׁתָּ: עֹטֶה אוֹר
kassalmah, noteh shamayim	כַּשַּׂלְמָה, נוֹטֶה שָׁמַיִם
kayyeri'ah: hamkareh vammayim	כַּיְרִיעָה: הַמְקָרֶה בַמַּיִם
aliyyotav hassam-avim rechuvo,	עֲלִיּוֹתָיו הַשָּׂם־עָבִים רְכוּבוֹ,
hammehalleich al-kanfei-	הַמְהַלֵּךְ עַל־כַּנְפֵי־
ruach: oseh mal'achav ruchot,	רוּחַ: עֹשֶׂה מַלְאָכָיו רוּחוֹת,
mesharetav eish loheit: yasad	מְשָׁרְתָיו אֵשׁ לֹהֵט: יָסַד
eretz al-mechoneha, bal-timmot	אֶרֶץ עַל־מְכוֹנֶיהָ, בַּל־תִּמּוֹט

olam va'ed: tehom kallevush
kissito, al-harim ya'amdu mayim:
min-ga'aratecha yenusun,
min-kol ra'amcha yeichafeizun:
ya'alu harim yeredu veka'ot,
el-mekom zeh yasadta lahem:
gevul-samta bal-ya'avorun, bal-
yeshuvun lechassot ha'aretz:
hammeshallei'ach ma'yanim
bannechalim, bein harim
yehalleichun: yashku kol-chayto
sadai, yishberu fera'im tzema'am:
aleihem of-hashamayim yishkon,
mibbein ofa'im yittenu-kol:
mashkeh harim mei'aliyyotav,
mipperi ma'asecha tisba ha'aretz:
matzmiach chatzir labbeheimah
ve'eisev la'avodat ha'adam,
lehotzi lechem min-ha'aretz:
veyayin yesammach levav-enosh
lehatzhil panim mishamen,
velechem levav-enosh yis'ad:
yisbe'u atzei adonai arzei levanon
asher nata: asher-sham tzipporim
yekanneinu, chasidah beroshim
beitah: harim haggevohim
layye'eilim, sela'im machseh
lashefannim: Asah yarei'ach
lemo'adim shemesh yada mevo'o:
tashet choshech vihi la'yelah, bo-
tirmos kol-chayto-ya'ar: hakkefirim
sho'agim lattaref, ulevakkeish
mei'el ochlam: tizrach hashemesh

עוֹלָם וָעֶד: תְּהוֹם כַּלְּבוּשׁ
כִּסִּיתוֹ, עַל־הָרִים יַעַמְדוּ מָיִם:
מִן־גַּעֲרָתְךָ יְנוּסוּן,
מִן־קוֹל רַעַמְךָ יֵחָפֵזוּן:
יַעֲלוּ הָרִים יֵרְדוּ בְקָעוֹת,
אֶל־מְקוֹם זֶה יָסַדְתָּ לָהֶם:
גְּבוּל־שַׂמְתָּ בַּל־יַעֲבֹרוּן, בַּל־
יְשֻׁבוּן לְכַסּוֹת הָאָרֶץ:
הַמְשַׁלֵּחַ מַעְיָנִים
בַּנְּחָלִים, בֵּין הָרִים
יְהַלֵּכוּן: יַשְׁקוּ כָּל־חַיְתוֹ
שָׂדָי, יִשְׁבְּרוּ פְרָאִים צְמָאָם:
עֲלֵיהֶם עוֹף־הַשָּׁמַיִם יִשְׁכּוֹן,
מִבֵּין עֳפָאִים יִתְּנוּ־קוֹל:
מַשְׁקֶה הָרִים מֵעֲלִיּוֹתָיו,
מִפְּרִי מַעֲשֶׂיךָ תִּשְׂבַּע הָאָרֶץ:
מַצְמִיחַ חָצִיר לַבְּהֵמָה
וְעֵשֶׂב לַעֲבֹדַת הָאָדָם,
לְהוֹצִיא לֶחֶם מִן־הָאָרֶץ:
וְיַיִן יְשַׂמַּח לְבַב־אֱנוֹשׁ
לְהַצְהִיל פָּנִים מִשָּׁמֶן,
וְלֶחֶם לְבַב־אֱנוֹשׁ יִסְעָד:
יִשְׂבְּעוּ עֲצֵי יְהוָה אַרְזֵי לְבָנוֹן
אֲשֶׁר נָטָע: אֲשֶׁר־שָׁם צִפֳּרִים
יְקַנֵּנוּ, חֲסִידָה בְּרוֹשִׁים
בֵּיתָהּ: הָרִים הַגְּבֹהִים
לַיְּעֵלִים, סְלָעִים מַחְסֶה
לַשְׁפַנִּים: עָשָׂה יָרֵחַ
לְמוֹעֲדִים שֶׁמֶשׁ יָדַע מְבוֹאוֹ:
תָּשֶׁת חֹשֶׁךְ וִיהִי לָיְלָה, בּוֹ־
תִרְמֹשׂ כָּל־חַיְתוֹ־יָעַר: הַכְּפִירִים
שֹׁאֲגִים לַטָּרֶף, וּלְבַקֵּשׁ
מֵאֵל אָכְלָם: תִּזְרַח הַשֶּׁמֶשׁ

yei'aseifun, ve'el-me'onotam	יֵאָסֵפוּן, וְאֶל־מְעוֹנֹתָם
yirbatzun: yeitzei adam lefo'olo,	יִרְבָּצוּן: יֵצֵא אָדָם לְפָעֳלוֹ,
vela'avodato adei-arev: mah-	וְלַעֲבֹדָתוֹ עֲדֵי־עָרֶב: מָה־
rabbu ma'asecha adonai kullam	רַבּוּ מַעֲשֶׂיךָ יְהוָה כֻּלָּם
bechochmah asita, male'ah	בְּחָכְמָה עָשִׂיתָ, מָלְאָה
ha'aretz kinyanecha: zeh hayyam	הָאָרֶץ קִנְיָנֶךָ: זֶה הַיָּם
gadol urechav yadayim sham-	גָּדוֹל וּרְחַב יָדָיִם שָׁם־
remes ve'ein mispar, chayyot	רֶמֶשׂ וְאֵין מִסְפָּר, חַיּוֹת
ketannot im-gedolot: sham	קְטַנּוֹת עִם־גְּדֹלוֹת: שָׁם
oniyyot yehalleichun, livyatan	אֳנִיּוֹת יְהַלֵּכוּן, לִוְיָתָן
zeh yatzarta lesachek-bo: kullam	זֶה יָצַרְתָּ לְשַׂחֶק־בּוֹ: כֻּלָּם
eleicha yesabbeirun, lateit ochlam	אֵלֶיךָ יְשַׂבֵּרוּן, לָתֵת אָכְלָם
be'itto: tittein lahem yilkotun,	בְּעִתּוֹ: תִּתֵּן לָהֶם יִלְקֹטוּן,
tiftach yadecha yisbe'un tov:	תִּפְתַּח יָדְךָ יִשְׂבְּעוּן טוֹב:
tastir panecha yibbaheilun toseif	תַּסְתִּיר פָּנֶיךָ יִבָּהֵלוּן תֹּסֵף
rucham yigva'un, ve'el-afaram	רוּחָם יִגְוָעוּן, וְאֶל־עֲפָרָם
yeshuvun: teshallach ruchacha	יְשׁוּבוּן: תְּשַׁלַּח רוּחֲךָ
yibbarei'un, utechaddeish	יִבָּרֵאוּן, וּתְחַדֵּשׁ
penei adamah: yehi chevod	פְּנֵי אֲדָמָה: יְהִי כְבוֹד
adonai le'olam, yismach	יְהוָה לְעוֹלָם, יִשְׂמַח
adonai bema'asav: hammabbit	יְהוָה בְּמַעֲשָׂיו: הַמַּבִּיט
la'aretz vattir'ad, yigga beharim	לָאָרֶץ וַתִּרְעָד, יִגַּע בֶּהָרִים
veye'eshanu: ashirah ladonai	וְיֶעֱשָׁנוּ: אָשִׁירָה לַיהוָה
bechayyai, azammerah leilohai	בְּחַיָּי, אֲזַמְּרָה לֵאלֹהַי
be'odi: ye'erav alav sichi, anochi	בְּעוֹדִי: יֶעֱרַב עָלָיו שִׂיחִי, אָנֹכִי
esmach badonai: yittammu	אֶשְׂמַח בַּיהוָה: יִתַּמּוּ
chatta'im min-ha'aretz uresha'im	חַטָּאִים מִן־הָאָרֶץ וּרְשָׁעִים
od einam barechi nafshi et-adonai	עוֹד אֵינָם בָּרְכִי נַפְשִׁי אֶת־יְהוָה
hallelujah:	הַלְלוּיָהּ:

*My soul, bless the Lord; the Lord, my God, You are greatly exalted;
with beauty and splendor are You clothed. Enwrapped in light,
garment-like, He spreads out the heavens like a curtain. He Who*

covers His upper chambers with water, He Who makes clouds His chariot, He Who walks upon wings of wind. He Who makes winds His messengers, flaming fires His servants. He Who established the earth upon its foundations, [so] that it shall never be moved. The deep, He covered it with a garment; the waters remain on mountains. At Your shout they retreated, at Your thunderous voice they hastened away. They go up mountains, down into valleys, to the specific place You founded for them. You set a boundary [which] they may not cross, lest they return to cover the earth. He Who sends springs into streams to flow between the mountains; to water all the beasts of the fields; the wild ones quench their thirst. Over them dwell the birds of the sky, from among the branches, they give voice. [You] Who waters the mountains from His upper chambers, from the fruit of Your works the earth is sated. [You] Who causes grass to sprout for cattle, and vegetation for the labor of man, to bring forth bread from the earth; wine to cheer the heart of man, to make [his] face shine from oil, and bread to sustain the heart of man. The Lord's trees are sated, the cedars of Lebanon that He planted; where birds make their nests, the stork—the firs are her home. The high mountains [are] for the wild goats, the rocks a refuge for the rabbits. He made the moon to fix seasons the sun knows its place to set. You make darkness and night comes, in which move about all the beasts of the forest. —The young lions roar for prey, and seek their food from the Almighty. [When] the sun rises, they gather and come into their dens to lie. Man goes out to his work, to his labor until evening. How many are Your works, the Lord! You made them all with wisdom; the earth is full of Your possessions! This sea, great and wide— therein are innumerable creeping things, animals small and great. There ships travel; this Leviathan You formed to frolic with. They all look to You expectantly, to provide their food in its time. [When] You give it to them, they gather it in; [when] You open Your hand, they are sated with goodness. When You hide Your face, they are panic-

stricken; When You gather in their breath, they perish, and to their dust they return. When You send Your spirit, they will be created [anew]; and You will renew the face of the earth. The glory of the Lord will endure forever, the Lord will rejoice in His works— Who gazes upon the earth and it trembles; Who touches the mountains and they erupt. I will sing to the Lord with my life; I will offer hymns to my God as long as I am alive. May my words be pleasant to Him; I will rejoice in the Lord. Sin will be excised from the earth, and the wicked will be no more; My soul bless the Lord, Praise God.

Notes

Pesach (Passover)

PASSOVER CELEBRATES THE Exodus from Egypt. In Temple times, the highlight of the Passover observance was eating the Paschal lamb that was offered on the eve of the holiday. Since the Temple's destruction, this practice has been discontinued. Nevertheless, the holiday commences with a ceremonial meal known as the Passover *Seder*, during which participants vividly recount the Exodus story. This narrative is traditionally told through the reading of the *Haggadah*, which aptly means "telling." We include here selected passages from the Passover *Haggadah*. For the full text, see The Israel Bible Passover Haggadah.

The Four Questions

The section of the Haggadah recounting the story of the Exodus begins with a set of four questions which are designed to spark curiosity and engage participants, especially the children. Encouraging questions also helps us celebrate our freedom, since only those who are free have the liberty to ask questions.

Mah nishtannah halla'ylah hazzeh mikkol halleilot?	מַה נִּשְׁתַּנָּה הַלַּיְלָה הַזֶּה מִכָּל הַלֵּילוֹת?
Shebbechol halleilot anu ochelin chameitz umatzah, halla'ylah hazzeh – kullo matzah.	שֶׁבְּכָל הַלֵּילוֹת אָנוּ אוֹכְלִין חָמֵץ וּמַצָּה, הַלַּיְלָה הַזֶּה - כֻּלּוֹ מַצָּה.
Shebbechol halleilot anu ochelin	שֶׁבְּכָל הַלֵּילוֹת אָנוּ אוֹכְלִין

she'ar yerakot – halla'ylah hazzeh
maror.

שְׁאָר יְרָקוֹת - הַלַּיְלָה הַזֶּה
מָרוֹר.

Shebbechol halleilot ein anu
matbilin afilu pa'am echat –
halla'ylah hazzeh shetei fe'amim.

שֶׁבְּכָל הַלֵּילוֹת אֵין אָנוּ
מַטְבִּילִין אֲפִילוּ פַּעַם אֶחָת -
הַלַּיְלָה הַזֶּה שְׁתֵּי פְעָמִים.

Shebbechol halleilot anu ochelin
bein yoshevin uvein mesubbin –
halla'ylah hazzeh kullanu
mesubbin.

שֶׁבְּכָל הַלֵּילוֹת אָנוּ אוֹכְלִין
בֵּין יוֹשְׁבִין וּבֵין מְסֻבִּין -
הַלַּיְלָה הַזֶּה כֻּלָּנוּ
מְסֻבִּין.

What makes this night different from all other nights?
On every other night we eat either bread or matza, but tonight there is only matza?
On every other night we eat many different greens, but tonight we will eat bitter herbs?
On every other night we do not dip [our food] at all, but tonight we will dip it twice?
On every other night some sit to eat and some recline, but tonight we are all reclining?

The Four Sons

In four different verses, the Bible commands us to tell the story of the Exodus to our children. The sages interpret this to mean that we must tell the story in four different ways, corresponding to four different types of children. When it comes to teaching our children, we do not believe that one size fits all. Instead, each child has their own needs, personality, and learning style, and we must engage each one in the way that works best for them.

Keneged arba'ah vanim dibberah
torah: echad chacham, ve'echad
rasha, ve'echad tam, ve'echad
she'eino yodel'a lish'ol.

Chacham mah hu omer?
Mah ha'eidot vehachukkim
vehammishpatim asher tzivvah
adonai eloheinu etchem.
Ve'af attah emor lo kehilchot
happesach: ein maftirin achar
happesach afikoman:

Rasha mah hu omer? Mah
ha'avodah hazzot lachem. Lachem
– velo lo. Ulefi shehotzi et atzmo
min hakkelal kafar be'ikkar. Ve'af
attah hakheh et shinnav ve'emor
lo: "ba'avur zeh asah adonai li
betzeti mimmitzrayim". Li velo-lo.
Illu hayah sham, lo hayah nig'al:

Tam mah hu omer? Mah zot.
Ve'amarta eilav "bechozek yad
hotzi'anu adonai mimmitzrayim
mibbeit avadim".

Veshe'eino yodel'a lish'ol –
at petach lo, shenne'emar,
vehiggadta levincha bayyom hahu
leimor, ba'avur zeh asah adonai li
betzeiti mimmitzrayim.

כְּנֶגֶד אַרְבָּעָה בָנִים דִּבְּרָה
תוֹרָה: אֶחָד חָכָם, וְאֶחָד
רָשָׁע, וְאֶחָד תָּם, וְאֶחָד
שֶׁאֵינוֹ יוֹדֵעַ לִשְׁאוֹל.

חָכָם מָה הוּא אוֹמֵר?
מָה הָעֵדֹת וְהַחֻקִּים
וְהַמִּשְׁפָּטִים אֲשֶׁר צִוָּה
יְיָ אֱלֹהֵינוּ אֶתְכֶם.
וְאַף אַתָּה אֱמוֹר לוֹ כְּהִלְכוֹת
הַפֶּסַח: אֵין מַפְטִירִין אַחַר
הַפֶּסַח אֲפִיקוֹמָן:

רָשָׁע מָה הוּא אוֹמֵר? מָה
הָעֲבוֹדָה הַזֹּאת לָכֶם. לָכֶם
– וְלֹא לוֹ. וּלְפִי שֶׁהוֹצִיא אֶת עַצְמוֹ
מִן הַכְּלָל כָּפַר בְּעִקָּר. וְאַף
אַתָּה הַקְהֵה אֶת שִׁנָּיו וֶאֱמוֹר
לוֹ: "בַּעֲבוּר זֶה עָשָׂה יְיָ לִי
בְּצֵאתִי מִמִּצְרָיִם". לִי וְלֹא-לוֹ.
אִלּוּ הָיָה שָׁם, לֹא הָיָה נִגְאָל:

תָּם מָה הוּא אוֹמֵר? מַה זֹּאת.
וְאָמַרְתָּ אֵלָיו "בְּחוֹזֶק יָד
הוֹצִיאָנוּ יְיָ מִמִּצְרַיִם
מִבֵּית עֲבָדִים".

וְשֶׁאֵינוֹ יוֹדֵעַ לִשְׁאוֹל –
אַתְּ פְּתַח לוֹ, שֶׁנֶּאֱמַר,
וְהִגַּדְתָּ לְבִנְךָ בַּיּוֹם הַהוּא
לֵאמֹר, בַּעֲבוּר זֶה עָשָׂה יְיָ לִי
בְּצֵאתִי מִמִּצְרָיִם.

The Torah relates to four types of sons – one who is wise, one who is wicked, one with a simple nature, and one who does not know how to ask.

The WISE SON - what does he say?
"What are the testimonies, the statutes and laws, that the Lord our God commanded you?" And you must tell him the laws of Passover: "After eating the Passover offering one does not eat anything more".

The WICKED SON - what does he say?
"What is this service to you?" "To you," he says, not to him. When he sets himself apart from the community, he denies the very core of our beliefs. And you must set his teeth on edge and tell him, "Because of this the Lord acted for me when I came out of Egypt." "For me," and not for him; had he been there he would not have been redeemed.

The SIMPLE-NATURED SON - what does he say?
"What is this?" And you must tell him, "With a strong hand the Lord brought us out of Egypt, from the grip of slavery."

And the ONE WHO DOES NOT KNOW HOW TO ASK - you must open [the story] for him, as it is said: "And you shall tell your child on that day, 'Because of this the Lord acted for me when I came out of Egypt.'"

Blessed is He Who has Kept His Promise to Israel

This short prayer mentions God's promise to Abraham at the Covenant of the Parts that He would redeem the children of Israel from exile. This promise has carried the people of Israel through the ages, for in every generation there are those who rise up to destroy them. Though they might suffer setbacks and defeats, God will never abandon His people.

Baruch shomer havtachato

leyisra'el, baruch hu.

Shehakkadosh baruch hu

chishav et-hakkeitz, la'asot kemo

she'amar le'avraham avinu bivrit

bein habbetarim, shenne'emar:

vayyomer le'avram, yadoa' teida

ki-ger yihyeh zar'acha be'eretz

lo lahem, va'avadum ve'innu

otam arba mei'ot shanah. Vegam

et-haggoy asher ya'avodu dan

anochi ve'acharei-chein yeitze'u

birchush gadol.

בָּרוּךְ שׁוֹמֵר הַבְטָחָתוֹ

לְיִשְׂרָאֵל, בָּרוּךְ הוּא.

שֶׁהַקָּדוֹשׁ בָּרוּךְ הוּא

חִשַּׁב אֶת־הַקֵּץ, לַעֲשׂוֹת כְּמוֹ

שֶׁאָמַר לְאַבְרָהָם אָבִינוּ בִּבְרִית

בֵּין הַבְּתָרִים, שֶׁנֶּאֱמַר:

וַיֹּאמֶר לְאַבְרָם, יָדֹעַ תֵּדַע

כִּי־גֵר יִהְיֶה זַרְעֲךָ בְּאֶרֶץ

לֹא לָהֶם, וַעֲבָדוּם וְעִנּוּ

אֹתָם אַרְבַּע מֵאוֹת שָׁנָה. וְגַם

אֶת־הַגּוֹי אֲשֶׁר יַעֲבֹדוּ דָּן

אָנֹכִי וְאַחֲרֵי־כֵן יֵצְאוּ

בִּרְכֻשׁ גָּדוֹל.

Vehi she'amedah la'avoteinu

velanu. Shello echad bilvad

amad aleinu lechalloteinu, ella

shebbechol dor vador omedim

aleinu lechaloteinu, vehakkadosh

baruch hu matzileinu miyyadam.

וְהִיא שֶׁעָמְדָה לַאֲבוֹתֵינוּ

וְלָנוּ. שֶׁלֹּא אֶחָד בִּלְבַד

עָמַד עָלֵינוּ לְכַלּוֹתֵנוּ, אֶלָּא

שֶׁבְּכָל דּוֹר וָדוֹר עוֹמְדִים

עָלֵינוּ לְכַלּוֹתֵנוּ, וְהַקָּדוֹשׁ

בָּרוּךְ הוּא מַצִּילֵנוּ מִיָּדָם.

BLESSED IS THE ONE WHO HAS KEPT HIS PROMISE TO ISRAEL – blessed is He. For the Holy One calculated the end and fulfilled what He had spoken to our father Abraham in the Covenant between the Pieces. As it is said: "He said to Abram, 'Know that your descendants will be strangers in a land not their own, and they will be enslaved and oppressed for four hundred years; but know that I shall judge the nation that enslaves them, and then they will leave with great wealth.'"

AND THIS [promise] is what has stood by our ancestors and us; for it was not only one man who rose up to destroy us: in every single generation people rise up to destroy us – but the Holy One, Blessed Be He, saves us from their hands.

Pour Out Your Wrath and Pour Out Your Love

In this section of the *Haggadah*, we ask God to pour out His wrath on those who have persecuted the people of Israel throughout the centuries. In one manuscript from Worms, Germany, there was a unique addition to the *Haggadah* alongside Pour Out Your Wrath, called Pour Out Your Love. It is a prayer of gratitude for the righteous gentiles throughout history, who, rather than persecuting Jews, befriended them and protected them in times of danger. The prayer asks God to shower them with love.

Shefoch chamatecha el-haggoyim asher lo yeda'ucha ve'al-mamlachot asher beshimcha lo kara'u. Ki achal et-ya'akov ve'et-naveihu heishammu. Shefoch-aleihem za'amecha vacharon appecha yassigem. Tirdof be'af vetashmideim mittachat shemei adonai.

שְׁפֹךְ חֲמָתְךָ אֶל־הַגּוֹיִם
אֲשֶׁר לֹא יְדָעוּךָ וְעַל־
מַמְלָכוֹת אֲשֶׁר בְּשִׁמְךָ לֹא
קָרָאוּ. כִּי אָכַל אֶת־יַעֲקֹב וְאֶת־
נָוֵהוּ הֵשַׁמּוּ. שְׁפָךְ־
עֲלֵיהֶם זַעֲמֶךָ וַחֲרוֹן
אַפְּךָ יַשִּׂיגֵם. תִּרְדֹּף בְּאַף
וְתַשְׁמִידֵם מִתַּחַת שְׁמֵי
יְיָ.

POUR OUT Your rage upon the nations that do not know You, and on regimes that have not called upon Your name. For Jacob is devoured; they have laid his places waste. Pour out Your great anger upon them, and let Your blazing fury overtake them. Pursue them in Your fury and destroy them from under the heavens of the Lord.

Shefoch ahavatecha al haggoyim
asher yeda'ucha ve'al mamlachot
asher beshimcha kore'im biglal
chasadim sheheim osim im zera
ya'akov umeginim al ammecha
yisra'el mippenei ocheleihem,
yizku lir'ot betovat bechirecha
velismoach besimchat goyyecha.
(Psalms 106:5)

שְׁפֹךְ אֲהָבָתְךָ עַל הַגּוֹיִם
אֲשֶׁר יְדָעוּךָ, וְעַל מַמְלָכוֹת
אֲשֶׁר בְּשִׁמְךָ קוֹרְאִים. בִּגְלַל
חֲסָדִים שֶׁהֵם עוֹשִׂים עִם זֶרַע
יַעֲקֹב וּמְגִנִּים עַל עַמְּךָ
יִשְׂרָאֵל מִפְּנֵי אוֹכְלֵיהֶם,
יִזְכּוּ לִרְאוֹת בְּטוֹבַת בְּחִירֶךָ
וְלִשְׂמוֹחַ בְּשִׂמְחַת גּוֹיֶךָ.
(תהלים קו:ה)

POUR OUT Your love on the nations who know You, and on the kingdoms who call upon Your name. For they show loving-kindness to the seed of Jacob and they shield Your people Israel

from those who would devour them. May they see the good of Your chosen ones and rejoice in the gladness of Your nation. (Psalms 106:5)

Next Year in Jerusalem

The phrase "Next year in Jerusalem" is sung with great rejoicing at the end of *Yom Kippur* (Day of Atonement) in the synagogue and at the conclusion of the Passover *Seder*. By uttering these words, we express our hope and prayer that, although we have not yet seen the rebuilt city of Jerusalem in all its splendor and glory, we will be blessed to witness it in the year ahead.

Leshanah habba'ah birushalayim
habbenuyah

לְשָׁנָה הַבָּאָה בִּירוּשָׁלָיִם
הַבְּנוּיָה

Next year in rebuilt Jerusalem!

He is Majestic

As the Passover *seder* comes to a close, we call on God to rebuild the Temple in Jerusalem. Only when the Messiah comes and the Temple is rebuilt will the ultimate redemption be complete.

Addir hu yivneh veito bekarov. Bimheirah, bimheirah, beyameinu bekarov. El beneih, el beneih, beneih veitcha bekarov.

אַדִּיר הוּא יִבְנֶה בֵיתוֹ בְּקָרוֹב. בִּמְהֵרָה, בִּמְהֵרָה, בְּיָמֵינוּ בְּקָרוֹב. אֵל בְּנֵה, אֵל בְּנֵה, בְּנֵה בֵיתְךָ בְּקָרוֹב.

He is majestic, may He build His house soon, soon, speedily in our days. Build, O God, build, O God, build Your house soon.

Notes

Holocaust Remembrance Day

Y OM *HASHOAH*, HOLOCAUST Remembrance Day, is observed as a day of commemoration for the approximately six million Jews murdered in the Holocaust by the Nazis and their collaborators, as well as for the Jewish resistance during that period. It is customary to recite the following memorial prayer in memory of those who perished in the Holocaust.

El malei rachamim shochein
bammeromim, hamtzei menuchah
nechonah al kanfei hashechinah,
bema'alot kedoshim utehorim
kezohar harakia mazhirim et
kol hanneshamot shel sheishet
milyonei hayyehudim, chal'lei
hasho'ah, shennehergu,
shennishchatu, shennisrefu
veshennispu al kiddush
hashem, bidei hammeratzechim
haggermanim ve'ozereihem
mish'ar ha'ammim. Lachein ba'al
harachamim yastireim beseiter
kenafav le'olamim, veyitzror bitzror
hachayyim et nishmoteihem,
adonai hu nachalatam, began
eiden tehei menuchatam,
veya'emdu legoralam lekeitz
hayyamin, venomar amen.

אֵל מָלֵא רַחֲמִים שׁוֹכֵן
בַּמְּרוֹמִים, הַמְצֵא מְנוּחָה
נְכוֹנָה עַל כַּנְפֵי הַשְּׁכִינָה,
בְּמַעֲלוֹת קְדוֹשִׁים וּטְהוֹרִים
כְּזוֹהַר הָרָקִיעַ מַזְהִירִים אֶת
כָּל הַנְּשָׁמוֹת שֶׁל שֵׁשֶׁת
מִילְיוֹנֵי הַיְּהוּדִים, חַלְלֵי
הַשּׁוֹאָה, שֶׁנֶּהֶרְגוּ,
שֶׁנִּשְׁחֲטוּ, שֶׁנִּשְׂרְפוּ
וְשֶׁנִּסְפּוּ עַל קִדּוּשׁ
הַשֵּׁם, בִּידֵי הַמְרַצְּחִים
הַגֶּרְמָנִים וְעוֹזְרֵיהֶם
מִשְּׁאָר הָעַמִּים. לָכֵן בַּעַל
הָרַחֲמִים יַסְתִּירֵם בְּסֵתֶר
כְּנָפָיו לְעוֹלָמִים, וְיִצְרוֹר בִּצְרוֹר
הַחַיִּים אֶת נִשְׁמוֹתֵיהֶם,
ה׳ הוּא נַחֲלָתָם, בְּגַן
עֵדֶן תְּהֵא מְנוּחָתָם,
וְיַעַמְדוּ לְגוֹרָלָם לְקֵץ
הַיָּמִין, וְנֹאמַר אָמֵן.

Notes

Israel's Memorial Day

Y*OM HAZIKARON*, I*SRAEL'S* Memorial Day, is a solemn day dedicated to remembering the nation's fallen soldiers and those killed in terrorist attacks. It is a day of collective mourning and reflection, where the entire nation pauses to honor the sacrifice of its brave defenders. One of the most poignant moments of Yom Hazikaron is the sounding of a siren that echoes across the country. When the siren wails, everything comes to a standstill: traffic halts, workplaces fall silent, and people pause wherever they are, standing in solemn tribute. This profound moment symbolizes the unity and shared grief of the Israeli people, as they honor the memories of those who gave their lives for the country's security and freedom. It serves as a powerful reminder of the price of independence and the resilience of the Israeli spirit in the face of adversity.

Memorial Prayer for the Fallen

On Israel's Memorial Day, is customary to recite the following prayer for Israel's fallen soldiers and victims of terror:

El malei rachamim, shochein	אֵל מָלֵא רַחֲמִים, שׁוֹכֵן
bammeromim, hamtzei menuchah	בַּמְּרוֹמִים, הַמְצֵא מְנוּחָה
nechonah, al kanfei hashechinah,	נְכוֹנָה, עַל כַּנְפֵי הַשְּׁכִינָה,
bema'alot kedoshim, tehorim	בְּמַעֲלוֹת קְדוֹשִׁים, טְהוֹרִים
vegibbovrim, kezohar harakia'	וְגִבּוֹרִים, כְּזֹהַר הָרָקִיעַ
mazhirim, lenishmot chayyalei	מַזְהִירִים, לְנִשְׁמוֹת חַיָּלֵי
tzeva haganah leyisra'el	צְבָא הֲגָנָה לְיִשְׂרָאֵל
velochamei hammachtarot	וְלוֹחֲמֵי הַמַּחְתָּרוֹת
shennafelu bemilchamot yisra'el,	שֶׁנָּפְלוּ בְּמִלְחֲמוֹת יִשְׂרָאֵל,

vechol hallochamim bema'archot	וְכָל הַלוֹחֲמִים בְּמַעַרְכוֹת
ha'am shecheirefu nafsham lamut	הָעָם שֶׁחֵרְפוּ נַפְשָׁם לָמוּת
al kedushat hasheim, uve'ezrat	עַל קְדֻשַּׁת הַשֵּׁם, וּבְעֶזְרַת
elohei ma'archot yisra'el hevi'u	אֱלֹהֵי מַעַרְכוֹת יִשְׂרָאֵל הֵבִיאוּ
litkumat ha'ummah vehammedinah	לִתְקוּמַת הָאֻמָּה וְהַמְּדִינָה
velig'ullat ha'aretz ve'ir ha'elohim,	וְלִגְאֻלַּת הָאָרֶץ וְעִיר הָאֱלֹהִים,
vechol eilleh shennirtzechu	וְכָל אֵלֶּה שֶׁנִּרְצְחוּ
ba'aretz umichutzah lah bidei	בָּאָרֶץ וּמִחוּצָה לָהּ בִּידֵי
hammeratzechim me'irgunei	הַמְרַצְּחִים מֵאִרְגּוּנֵי
hatteiror. Lachein ba'al harachamim	הַטֵּרוֹר. לָכֵן בַּעַל הָרַחֲמִים
yastireim beseiter kenafav	יַסְתִּירֵם בְּסֵתֶר כְּנָפָיו
le'olamim, veyitzror bitzror	לְעוֹלָמִים, וְיִצְרוֹר בִּצְרוֹר
hachayyim et nishmatam. Adonai	הַחַיִּים אֶת נִשְׁמָתָם. יְיָ
hu nachalatam, began eiden	הוּא נַחֲלָתָם, בְּגַן עֵדֶן
(tehei) menuchatam, veyanuchu	(תְּהֵא) מְנוּחָתָם, וְיָנוּחוּ
beshalom al mishkavam,	בְּשָׁלוֹם עַל מִשְׁכָּבָם,
veya'amdu legoralam lekeitz	וְיַעַמְדוּ לְגוֹרָלָם לְקֵץ
hayyamin, venomar amen.	הַיָּמִין, וְנֹאמַר אָמֵן.

O God, full of mercy, who dwells on high, grant proper rest on the wings of the Divine Presence, in the heights of the holy and pure, who shine like the radiance of the sky, to the souls of the soldiers of the Israel Defense Forces and the underground fighters who fell in the wars of Israel, and all the fighters in the battles of the nation who sacrificed their lives for the sanctification of the Name, and with the help of the God of Israel's battles, brought about the rebirth of the nation and the state and the redemption of the land and the city of God, and all those who were murdered in the land and outside of it by the murderers of the terrorist organizations. Therefore, Master of Mercy, shelter them in the shadow of Your wings for eternity, and bind their souls in the bond of life. The Lord is their heritage. May they rest in peace in the Garden of Eden, and may they lie in peace on their resting places, and let us say, Amen.

Israel's Independence Day

Y*OM HAATZMAUT*, I*SRAEL'S* Independence Day, celebrates the Israeli Declaration of Independence on May 14, 1948, corresponding to the 5th day of the Hebrew month of *Iyar*. This historic declaration restored Jewish sovereignty to the land of Israel after 2,000 years, marking a significant milestone in Jewish history and a pivotal step on the path to redemption.

Psalm 107

The moment Israel's solemn Memorial Day ends, its joyous Independence Day begins, a proximity that adds profound meaning to both days. The realization that our independence is built on the dedication of those who fell gives us the strength to endure the sorrow of *Yom HaZikaron* (Memorial Day). Simultaneously, understanding the heavy price paid encourages us not only to appreciate the joy of *Yom Ha'atzmaut* (Independence Day), but also to strive to use our independence wisely and to never take it for granted.

This contrast between sorrow and joy during a time of redemption is reflected in Psalm 107, which is customarily recited before the evening prayers on *Yom Ha'atzmaut* (Independence Day).

Hodu ladonai ki-tov ki le'olam	הֹדוּ לַיהוָה כִּי־טוֹב כִּי לְעוֹלָם
chasdo. Yomru ge'ulei adonai	חַסְדּוֹ: יֹאמְרוּ גְּאוּלֵי יְהוָה
asher ge'alam miyyad-tzar.	אֲשֶׁר גְּאָלָם מִיַּד־צָר:
Umei'aratzot kibbetzam	וּמֵאֲרָצוֹת קִבְּצָם

mimmizrach umimma'arav   מִמִּזְרָח וּמִמַּעֲרָב

mitzafon umiyyam. Ta'u   מִצָּפוֹן וּמִיָּם: תָּעוּ

vammidbar bishimon darech   בַמִּדְבָּר בִּישִׁימוֹן דָּרֶךְ

ir moshav lo matza'u. Re'eivim   עִיר מוֹשָׁב לֹא מָצָאוּ: רְעֵבִים

gam-tzemei'im nafsham bahem   גַּם־צְמֵאִים נַפְשָׁם בָּהֶם

tit'attaf. Vayyitz'aku el-adonai   תִּתְעַטָּף: וַיִּצְעֲקוּ אֶל־יְהֹוָה

batzar lahem mimmetzukoteihem   בַּצַּר לָהֶם מִמְּצוּקוֹתֵיהֶם

yatzileim. Vayyadricheim   יַצִּילֵם: וַיַּדְרִיכֵם

bederech yesharah lalechet el-ir   בְּדֶרֶךְ יְשָׁרָה לָלֶכֶת אֶל־עִיר

moshav. yodu ladonai chasdo   מוֹשָׁב: יוֹדוּ לַיהֹוָה חַסְדּוֹ

venifle'otav livnei adam. Ki-hisbia'   וְנִפְלְאוֹתָיו לִבְנֵי אָדָם: כִּי־הִשְׂבִּיעַ

nefesh shokeikah venefesh   נֶפֶשׁ שֹׁקֵקָה וְנֶפֶשׁ

re'eivah millei-tov. Yoshevei   רְעֵבָה מִלֵּא־טוֹב: יֹשְׁבֵי

choshech vetzalmavet asirei   חֹשֶׁךְ וְצַלְמָוֶת אֲסִירֵי

ani uvarzel. Ki-himru imrei-el   עֳנִי וּבַרְזֶל: כִּי־הִמְרוּ אִמְרֵי־אֵל

va'atzat elyon na'atzu. Vayyachna   וַעֲצַת עֶלְיוֹן נָאָצוּ: וַיַּכְנַע

be'amal libbam kashelu ve'ein   בֶּעָמָל לִבָּם כָּשְׁלוּ וְאֵין

ozeir. Vayyiz'aku el-adonai   עֹזֵר: וַיִּזְעֲקוּ אֶל־יְהֹוָה בַּצַּר

batzar lahem mimmetzukoteihem   לָהֶם מִמְּצֻקוֹתֵיהֶם

yoshi'eim. Yotzi'eim mechoshech   יוֹשִׁיעֵם: יוֹצִיאֵם מֵחֹשֶׁךְ

vetzalmavet umoseroteihem   וְצַלְמָוֶת וּמוֹסְרוֹתֵיהֶם

yenatteik. yodu ladonai chasdo   יְנַתֵּק: יוֹדוּ לַיהֹוָה חַסְדּוֹ

venifle'otav livnei adam. Ki-shibbar   וְנִפְלְאוֹתָיו לִבְנֵי אָדָם: כִּי־שִׁבַּר

daltot nechoshet uverichei varzel   דַּלְתוֹת נְחֹשֶׁת וּבְרִיחֵי בַרְזֶל

giddei'a. Evilim midderech pish'am   גִּדֵּעַ: אֱוִלִים מִדֶּרֶךְ פִּשְׁעָם

ume'avonoteihem yit'annu.   וּמֵעֲוֹנֹתֵיהֶם יִתְעַנּוּ:

Kol-ochel teta'eiv nafsham   כָּל־אֹכֶל תְּתַעֵב נַפְשָׁם

vayyaggi'u ad-sha'arei-mavet.   וַיַּגִּיעוּ עַד־שַׁעֲרֵי־מָוֶת:

Vayyiz'aku el-adonai batzar lahem   וַיִּזְעֲקוּ אֶל־יְהֹוָה בַּצַּר לָהֶם

mimmetzukoteihem yoshi'eim.   מִמְּצֻקוֹתֵיהֶם יוֹשִׁיעֵם:

Yishlach devaro veyirpa'eim   יִשְׁלַח דְּבָרוֹ וְיִרְפָּאֵם

vimalleit mishechitotam. yodu   וִימַלֵּט מִשְּׁחִיתוֹתָם: יוֹדוּ

ladonai chasdo venifle'otav livnei   לַיהֹוָה חַסְדּוֹ וְנִפְלְאוֹתָיו לִבְנֵי

adam. Veyizbechu zivchei todah	אָדָם: וְיִזְבְּחוּ זִבְחֵי תוֹדָה
visapperu ma'asav berinnah.	וִיסַפְּרוּ מַעֲשָׂיו בְּרִנָּה:
Yoredei hayyam ba'oniyyot osei	יוֹרְדֵי הַיָּם בָּאֳנִיּוֹת עֹשֵׂי
melachah bemayim rabbim.	מְלָאכָה בְּמַיִם רַבִּים:
heimmah ra'u ma'asei adonai	הֵמָּה רָאוּ מַעֲשֵׂי יְהוָה
venifle'otav bimtzulah. Vayyomer	וְנִפְלְאוֹתָיו בִּמְצוּלָה: וַיֹּאמֶר
vayya'ameid ruach se'arah	וַיַּעֲמֵד רוּחַ סְעָרָה
vatteromeim gallav. Ya'alu	וַתְּרוֹמֵם גַּלָּיו: יַעֲלוּ
shamayim yeiredu tehomot	שָׁמַיִם יֵרְדוּ תְהוֹמוֹת
nafsham bera'ah titmogag.	נַפְשָׁם בְּרָעָה תִתְמוֹגָג:
Yachoggu veyanu'u kashikkor	יָחוֹגּוּ וְיָנוּעוּ כַּשִּׁכּוֹר
vechol-chochmatam titballa.	וְכָל־חָכְמָתָם תִּתְבַּלָּע:
Vayyitz'aku el-adonai batzar	וַיִּצְעֲקוּ אֶל־יְהוָה בַּצַּר
lahem umimmetzukoteihem	לָהֶם וּמִמְּצוּקֹתֵיהֶם
yotzi'em. Yakeim se'arah	יוֹצִיאֵם: יָקֵם סְעָרָה
lidmamah vayyecheshu galleihem.	לִדְמָמָה וַיֶּחֱשׁוּ גַּלֵּיהֶם:
Vayyismechu chi-yishtoku	וַיִּשְׂמְחוּ כִי־יִשְׁתֹּקוּ
vayyancheim el-mechoz cheftzam.	וַיַּנְחֵם אֶל־מְחוֹז חֶפְצָם:
yodu ladonai chasdo venifle'otav	יוֹדוּ לַיהוָה חַסְדּוֹ וְנִפְלְאוֹתָיו
livnei adam. Viromemuhu	לִבְנֵי אָדָם: וִירוֹמְמוּהוּ
bikhal-am uvemoshav zekeinim	בִּקְהַל־עָם וּבְמוֹשַׁב זְקֵנִים
yehalluhu. Yaseim neharot	יְהַלְלוּהוּ: יָשֵׂם נְהָרוֹת
lemidbar umotza'ei mayim	לְמִדְבָּר וּמֹצָאֵי מַיִם
letzimma'on. eretz peri limleichah	לְצִמָּאוֹן: אֶרֶץ פְּרִי לִמְלֵחָה
meira'at yoshevei vah. Yaseim	מֵרָעַת יֹשְׁבֵי בָהּ: יָשֵׂם
midbar la'agam-mayim ve'eretz	מִדְבָּר לַאֲגַם־מַיִם וְאֶרֶץ
tziyyah lemotza'ei mayim.	צִיָּה לְמֹצָאֵי מָיִם:
Vayyoshev sham re'eivim	וַיּוֹשֶׁב שָׁם רְעֵבִים
va'ychonenu ir moshav.	וַיְכוֹנְנוּ עִיר מוֹשָׁב:
Vayyizre'u sadot vayyitte'u	וַיִּזְרְעוּ שָׂדוֹת וַיִּטְּעוּ
cheramim vayya'asu peri tevu'ah.	כְרָמִים וַיַּעֲשׂוּ פְּרִי תְבוּאָה:
Va'yvarecheim vayyirbu me'od	וַיְבָרְכֵם וַיִּרְבּוּ מְאֹד
uvehemtam lo yam'it. Vayyim'atu	וּבְהֶמְתָּם לֹא יַמְעִיט: וַיִּמְעֲטוּ

vayyashochu mei'otzer ra'ah

veyagon. Shofeich buz al-nedivim

vayyat'eim betohu lo-darech.

Va'ysaggeiv evyon mei'oni

vayyasem katzon mishpachot.

Yir'u yesharim veyismachu vechol-

avlah kafetzah piha. Mi-chacham

veyishmor-eilleh veyitbonenu

chasdei adonai.

וַיָּשֹׁחוּ מֵעֹצֶר רָעָה

וְיָגוֹן: שֹׁפֵךְ בּוּז עַל־נְדִיבִים

וַיַּתְעֵם בְּתֹהוּ לֹא־דָרֶךְ:

וַיְשַׂגֵּב אֶבְיוֹן מֵעוֹנִי

וַיָּשֶׂם כַּצֹּאן מִשְׁפָּחוֹת:

יִרְאוּ יְשָׁרִים וְיִשְׂמָחוּ וְכָל־

עַוְלָה קָפְצָה פִּיהָ: מִי־חָכָם

וְיִשְׁמָר־אֵלֶּה וְיִתְבּוֹנְנוּ

חַסְדֵי יְהֹוָה:

"Praise the Lord, for He is good; His steadfast love is eternal!" Thus let the redeemed of the Lord say, those He redeemed from adversity, whom He gathered in from the lands, from east and west, from the north and from the sea. Some lost their way in the wilderness, in the wasteland; they found no settled place. Hungry and thirsty, their spirit failed. In their adversity they cried to the Lord, and He rescued them from their troubles. He showed them a direct way to reach a settled place. Let them praise the Lord for His steadfast love, His wondrous deeds for mankind; for He has satisfied the thirsty, filled the hungry with all good things. Some lived in deepest darkness, bound in cruel irons, because they defied the word of God, spurned the counsel of the Most High. He humbled their hearts through suffering; they stumbled with no one to help. In their adversity they cried to the Lord, and He rescued them from their troubles. He brought them out of deepest darkness, broke their bonds asunder. Let them praise the Lord for His steadfast love, His wondrous deeds for mankind; for He shattered gates of bronze, He broke their iron bars. There were fools who suffered for their sinful way, and for their iniquities. All food was loathsome to them; they reached the gates of death. In their adversity they cried to the Lord and He saved them from their troubles. He gave an order and healed them; He delivered them from the pits. Let them praise the Lord for His steadfast love, His wondrous deeds for mankind. Let them offer thanksgiving sacrifices, and tell His deeds

in joyful song. Others go down to the sea in ships, ply their trade in the mighty waters; they have seen the works of the Lord and His wonders in the deep. By His word He raised a storm wind that made the waves surge. Mounting up to the heaven, plunging down to the depths, disgorging in their misery, they reeled and staggered like a drunken man, all their skill to no avail. In their adversity they cried to the Lord, and He saved them from their troubles. He reduced the storm to a whisper; the waves were stilled. They rejoiced when all was quiet, and He brought them to the port they desired. Let them praise the Lord for His steadfast love, His wondrous deeds for mankind. Let them exalt Him in the congregation of the people, acclaim Him in the assembly of the elders. He turns the rivers into a wilderness, springs of water into thirsty land, fruitful land into a salt marsh, because of the wickedness of its inhabitants. He turns the wilderness into pools, parched land into springs of water. There He settles the hungry; they build a place to settle in. They sow fields and plant vineyards that yield a fruitful harvest. He blesses them and they increase greatly; and He does not let their cattle decrease, after they had been few and crushed by oppression, misery, and sorrow. He pours contempt on great men and makes them lose their way in trackless deserts; but the needy He secures from suffering, and increases their families like flocks. The upright see it and rejoice; the mouth of all wrongdoers is stopped. The wise man will take note of these things; he will consider the steadfast love of the Lord.

Psalm 126

Psalm 126 describes the miraculous return of the people of Israel to the land of Israel, likening it to a dream come true. It also highlights the recognition, both by Israel and the nations of the world, that God has done great things for the nation of Israel. This psalm is recited at the end of the evening prayers on *Yom Haatzmaut* (Independence Day).

Shir hamma'alot beshuv adonai et

shivat tziyyon hayinu kecholemim:

Az yimmalei sechok pinu

uleshoneinu rinnah az yomru

vaggoyim higdil adonai la'asot

im elleh: Higdil adonai la'asot

immanu hayinu semeichim:

Shuvah adonai et sheviteinu

ka'afikim bannegev: Hazzore'im

bedim'ah berinnah yiktzoru:

Haloch yeilech uvachoh nosei

meshech hazzara bo yavo

verinnah nosei alummotav:

שִׁיר הַמַּעֲלוֹת בְּשׁוּב יְהוָה אֶת

שִׁיבַת צִיּוֹן הָיִינוּ כְּחֹלְמִים:

אָז יִמָּלֵא שְׂחוֹק פִּינוּ

וּלְשׁוֹנֵנוּ רִנָּה אָז יֹאמְרוּ

בַגּוֹיִם הִגְדִּיל יְהוָה לַעֲשׂוֹת

עִם אֵלֶּה: הִגְדִּיל יְהוָה לַעֲשׂוֹת

עִמָּנוּ הָיִינוּ שְׂמֵחִים:

שׁוּבָה יְהוָה אֶת שְׁבִיתֵנוּ

כַּאֲפִיקִים בַּנֶּגֶב: הַזֹּרְעִים

בְּדִמְעָה בְּרִנָּה יִקְצֹרוּ:

הָלוֹךְ יֵלֵךְ וּבָכֹה נֹשֵׂא

מֶשֶׁךְ הַזָּרַע בֹּא יָבוֹא

בְרִנָּה נֹשֵׂא אֲלֻמֹּתָיו:

A song of ascents. When the Lord restores the fortunes of Zion —we see it as in a dream—our mouths shall be filled with laughter, our tongues, with songs of joy. Then shall they say among the nations, "The Lord has done great things for them!" The Lord will do great things for us and we shall rejoice. Restore our fortunes, O Lord, like watercourses in the Negeb. They who sow in tears shall reap with songs of joy. Though he goes along weeping, carrying the seed-bag, he shall come back with songs of joy, carrying his sheaves.

Hatikvah - The Hope

On Israel's Independence Day, it is customary to sing Israel's national anthem, known as *Hatikvah*, which means "The Hope." This poem reflects the 2,000-year-old yearning of the Jewish people to return to the land of Israel and to live on their land as a free nation.

Kol od balleivav penimah nefesh

כָּל עוֹד בַּלֵּבָב פְּנִימָה נֶפֶשׁ

yehudi homiyyah, ulefa'atei
mizrach kadimah, ayin letziyyon
tzofiyyah;

יְהוּדִי הוֹמִיָּה, וּלְפַאֲתֵי
מִזְרָח קָדִימָה, עַיִן לְצִיּוֹן
צוֹפִיָּה;

Od lo avedah tikvateinu, hattikvah
bat shenot alpayim, lihyot am
chofshi be'artzeinu, eretz tziyyon
virushalayim.

עוֹד לֹא אָבְדָה תִּקְוָתֵנוּ, הַתִּקְוָה
בַּת שְׁנוֹת אַלְפַּיִם, לִהְיוֹת עַם
חָפְשִׁי בְּאַרְצֵנוּ, אֶרֶץ צִיּוֹן
וִירוּשָׁלַיִם.

As long as in the heart, within
A Jewish soul still yearns
And onward, towards the ends of the east
An eye still yearns toward Zion

Our hope is not yet lost
The hope of two thousand years
To be a free people in our land
The land of Zion and Jerusalem

Notes

____

____

____

____

____

____

____

Lag Ba'Omer
(33rd Day of the Omer)

*L*AG *B*A*O*MER, THE 33rd day of the counting from Passover to *Shavuot* (Feast of Weeks), is celebrated as a minor Jewish holiday. During the weeks between Passover and *Shavuot* (Feast of Weeks), a plague struck the disciples of the great sage Rabbi Akiva due to their lack of respect for one another. Consequently, this period is observed as a time of mourning, with joyous activities restricted. The plague ended on *Lag BaOmer*, which is also the anniversary of the death of the great sage Rabbi Shimon bar Yochai, who instructed his students to mark the day of his passing with joy. For these reasons, *Lag BaOmer* is a joyous and festive day. It emphasizes the importance of loving and respecting one's fellow, a principle that Rabbi Akiva considered the most essential in the entire Bible, though his students failed to internalize that teaching. Therefore, it is customary to sing the following song on *Lag BaOmer*.

Amar rabbi akiva: ve'ahavta lerei'acha kamocha, zeh kelal gadol battorah.

אָמַר רַבִּי עֲקִיבָא: וְאָהַבְתָּ לְרֵעֲךָ כָּמוֹךָ, זֶה כְּלָל גָּדוֹל בַּתּוֹרָה.

Rabbi Akiva said: Love your neighbor as yourself (Leviticus 19:18); This is a very essential principle of the Torah.

Jerusalem Day

Y*OM* Y*ERUSHALAYIM*, J*ERUSALEM* Day, which falls on the 28th day of the Hebrew month of *Iyar*, celebrates the reunification of Jerusalem in 1967. Following the establishment of the State of Israel in 1948 and the end of the War of Independence in 1949, Israel only had sovereignty over West Jerusalem, while East Jerusalem, including the Old City and the Western Wall, was not under Israeli control. For the next 19 years, no Jew was permitted to pray at the Western Wall. Following the miraculous victory of the Six Day War in 1967, the Israel Defense Forces captured the ancient part of the city, marking the first time in two thousand years that all of Jerusalem was under Jewish control.

Here are three psalms that we include in our prayers on this special day, which commemorates the miracle of Jerusalem's reunification. The first psalm acknowledges God's sending redemption to His people, while the next two psalms focus on the significance and beauty of Jerusalem.

Psalm 111

Hallu-yah odeh adonai bechol-
leivav besod yesharim ve'eidah.
Gedolim ma'asei adonai derushim
lechol-cheftzeihem. Hod-vehadar
po'olo vetzidkato omedet la'ad.
zeicher asah lenifle'otav channun
verachum adonai. teref natan
lirei'av yizkor le'olam berito. koach

הַלְלוּ־יָהּ אוֹדֶה יְהֹוָה בְּכָל־
לֵבָב בְּסוֹד יְשָׁרִים וְעֵדָה:
גְּדֹלִים מַעֲשֵׂי יְהֹוָה דְּרוּשִׁים
לְכָל־חֶפְצֵיהֶם: הוֹד־וְהָדָר
פָּעֳלוֹ וְצִדְקָתוֹ עֹמֶדֶת לָעַד:
זֵכֶר עָשָׂה לְנִפְלְאוֹתָיו חַנּוּן
וְרַחוּם יְהֹוָה: טֶרֶף נָתַן
לִירֵאָיו יִזְכֹּר לְעוֹלָם בְּרִיתוֹ: כֹּחַ

ma'asav higgid le'ammo lateit מַעֲשָׂיו הִגִּיד לְעַמּוֹ לָתֵת

lahem nachalat goyim. Ma'asei לָהֶם נַחֲלַת גּוֹיִם: מַעֲשֵׂי

yadav emet umishpat ne'emanim יָדָיו אֱמֶת וּמִשְׁפָּט נֶאֱמָנִים

kol-pikkudav. Semuchim la'ad כָּל־פִּקּוּדָיו: סְמוּכִים לָעַד

le'olam asuyim be'emet veyashar. לְעוֹלָם עֲשׂוּיִם בֶּאֱמֶת וְיָשָׁר:

Pedut shalach le'ammo tzivvah- פְּדוּת שָׁלַח לְעַמּוֹ צִוָּה־

le'olam berito kadosh venora לְעוֹלָם בְּרִיתוֹ קָדוֹשׁ וְנוֹרָא

shemo. Reishit chochmah yir'at שְׁמוֹ: רֵאשִׁית חָכְמָה יִרְאַת

adonai seichel tov lechol-oseihem יְהֹוָה שֵׂכֶל טוֹב לְכָל־עֹשֵׂיהֶם

tehillato omedet la'ad. תְּהִלָּתוֹ עֹמֶדֶת לָעַד:

Hallelujah. I praise the Lord with all my heart in the assembled congregation of the upright. The works of the Lord are great, within reach of all who desire them. His deeds are splendid and glorious; His beneficence is everlasting; He has won renown for His wonders. The Lord is gracious and compassionate; He gives food to those who fear Him; He is ever mindful of His covenant. He revealed to His people His powerful works, in giving them the heritage of nations. His handiwork is truth and justice; all His precepts are enduring, well-founded for all eternity, wrought of truth and equity. He sent redemption to His people; He ordained His covenant for all time; His name is holy and awesome. The beginning of wisdom is the fear of the Lord; all who practice it gain sound understanding. Praise of Him is everlasting.

Psalm 125

Shir hamma'alot habbotechim שִׁיר הַמַּעֲלוֹת הַבֹּטְחִים

badonai kehar-tziyyon lo-yimmot בַּיהֹוָה כְּהַר־צִיּוֹן לֹא־יִמּוֹט

le'olam yeisheiv. Yerushalayim לְעוֹלָם יֵשֵׁב: יְרוּשָׁלַיִם

harim saviv lah va'adonai saviv הָרִים סָבִיב לָהּ וַיהֹוָה סָבִיב

le'ammo mei'attah ve'ad-olam. לְעַמּוֹ מֵעַתָּה וְעַד־עוֹלָם:

Ki lo yanuach sheivet haresha
al goral hatzaddikim lema'an lo-
yishlechu hatzaddikim be'avlatah
yedeihem. Heitivah adonai
lattovim velisharim belibbotam.
Vehammattim akalkallotam
yolicheim adonai et-po'alei
ha'aven shalom al-yisra'el.

כִּי לֹא יָנוּחַ שֵׁבֶט הָרֶשַׁע
עַל גּוֹרַל הַצַּדִּיקִים לְמַעַן לֹא־
יִשְׁלְחוּ הַצַּדִּיקִים בְּעַוְלָתָה
יְדֵיהֶם: הֵיטִיבָה יְהֹוָה
לַטּוֹבִים וְלִישָׁרִים בְּלִבּוֹתָם:
וְהַמַּטִּים עֲקַלְקַלּוֹתָם
יוֹלִיכֵם יְהֹוָה אֶת־פֹּעֲלֵי
הָאָוֶן שָׁלוֹם עַל־יִשְׂרָאֵל:

*A song of ascents. Those who trust in the Lord are like Mount Zion
that cannot be moved, enduring forever. Jerusalem, hills enfold it,
and the Lord enfolds His people now and forever. The scepter of
the wicked shall never rest upon the land allotted to the righteous,
that the righteous not set their hand to wrongdoing. Do good, O
Lord, to the good, to the upright in heart. But those who in their
crookedness act corruptly, let the Lord make them go the way of
evildoers. May it be well with Israel!*

Psalm 122

Shir hamma'alot ledavid samachti
be'omerim li beit adonai
neileich. Omedot hayu ragleinu
bish'arayich yerushalayim.
Yerushalayim habbenuyah ke'ir
shechubberah-lah yachdav.
Shesham alu shevatim shivtei-
yah eidut leyisra'el lehodot
lesheim adonai. Ki shammah
yashevu chis'ot lemishpat kis'ot
leveit david. Sha'alu shelom
yerushalayim yishlayu ohavayich.

שִׁיר הַמַּעֲלוֹת לְדָוִד שָׂמַחְתִּי
בְּאֹמְרִים לִי בֵּית יְהֹוָה
נֵלֵךְ: עֹמְדוֹת הָיוּ רַגְלֵינוּ
בִּשְׁעָרַיִךְ יְרוּשָׁלָם:
יְרוּשָׁלַם הַבְּנוּיָה כְּעִיר
שֶׁחֻבְּרָה־לָּה יַחְדָּו:
שֶׁשָּׁם עָלוּ שְׁבָטִים שִׁבְטֵי־
יָהּ עֵדוּת לְיִשְׂרָאֵל לְהֹדוֹת
לְשֵׁם יְהֹוָה: כִּי שָׁמָּה
יָשְׁבוּ כִסְאוֹת לְמִשְׁפָּט כִּסְאוֹת
לְבֵית דָּוִד: שַׁאֲלוּ שְׁלוֹם
יְרוּשָׁלָם יִשְׁלָיוּ אֹהֲבָיִךְ:

Yehi-shalom becheilech shalvah
be'armenotayich. Lema'an achai
verei'ai adabberah-na shalom
bach. Lema'an beit-adonai
eloheinu avakshah tov lach.

יְהִי־שָׁלוֹם בְּחֵילֵךְ שַׁלְוָה
בְּאַרְמְנוֹתָיִךְ: לְמַעַן אַחַי
וְרֵעָי אֲדַבְּרָה־נָּא שָׁלוֹם
בָּךְ: לְמַעַן בֵּית־יְהֹוָה
אֱלֹהֵינוּ אֲבַקְשָׁה טוֹב לָךְ:

A song of ascents. Of David. I rejoiced when they said to me, "We are going to the House of the Lord." Our feet stood inside your gates, O Jerusalem, Jerusalem built up, a city knit together, to which tribes would make pilgrimage, the tribes of the Lord, —as was enjoined upon Israel— to praise the name of the Lord. There the thrones of judgment stood, thrones of the house of David. Pray for the well-being of Jerusalem; "May those who love you be at peace. May there be well-being within your ramparts, peace in your citadels." For the sake of my kin and friends, I pray for your well-being; for the sake of the house of the Lord our God, I seek your good.

Notes

____

____

____

____

____

____

____

Shavuot (Feast of Weeks)

THE HOLIDAY OF *Shavuot*, also known as the Feast of Weeks or Pentecost, commemorates the giving of the Torah on Mount Sinai.

Ten Commandments

On *Shavuot* morning, we publicly read the Ten Commandments aloud as a community. The sages have said that hearing the Ten Commandments on *Shavuot* is akin to standing at Mount Sinai and hearing them directly from God Himself.

Anochi adonai elohecha asher hotzeiticha mei'eretz mitzrayim mibbeit avadim:

אָנֹכִי יְהֹוָה אֱלֹהֶיךָ אֲשֶׁר הוֹצֵאתִיךָ מֵאֶרֶץ מִצְרַיִם מִבֵּית עֲבָדִים׃

Lo yihyeh lecha elohim acheirim al-pana'y:

לֹא־יִהְיֶה־לְךָ אֱלֹהִים אֲחֵרִים עַל־פָּנָי׃

Lo ta'aseh lecha fesel vechol temunah asher bashamayim mimma'al va'asher ba'aretz mitachat va'asher bamayim mitachat la'aretz:

לֹא־תַעֲשֶׂה־לְךָ פֶסֶל וְכָל־תְּמוּנָה אֲשֶׁר בַּשָּׁמַיִם מִמַּעַל וַאֲשֶׁר בָּאָרֶץ מִתַּחַת וַאֲשֶׁר בַּמַּיִם מִתַּחַת לָאָרֶץ׃

Lo tishtachaveh lahem velo to'ovdeim ki anochi adonai elohecha el kanna pokeid avon avot al-banim al-shilleishim ve'al-ribbei'im lesone'ai:

לֹא־תִשְׁתַּחֲוֶה לָהֶם וְלֹא תָעָבְדֵם כִּי אָנֹכִי יְהֹוָה אֱלֹהֶיךָ אֵל קַנָּא פֹּקֵד עֲוֺן אָבֹת עַל־בָּנִים עַל־שִׁלֵּשִׁים וְעַל־רִבֵּעִים לְשֹׂנְאָי׃

Ve'oseh chesed la'alafim le'ohavai uleshomerei mitzvotai:	וְעֹשֶׂה חֶסֶד לַאֲלָפִים לְאֹהֲבַי וּלְשֹׁמְרֵי מִצְוֹתָי:
Lo tissa et-sheim-adonai elohecha lashav ki lo yenakkeh adonai eit asher-yissa et-shemo lashav:	לֹא תִשָּׂא אֶת־שֵׁם־יְהוָה אֱלֹהֶיךָ לַשָּׁוְא כִּי לֹא יְנַקֶּה יְהוָה אֵת אֲשֶׁר־יִשָּׂא אֶת־שְׁמוֹ לַשָּׁוְא:
Zachor et-yom hashabbat lekaddesho:	זָכוֹר אֶת־יוֹם הַשַּׁבָּת לְקַדְּשׁוֹ:
Sheishet yamim ta'avod ve'asita kol-melachtecha:	שֵׁשֶׁת יָמִים תַּעֲבֹד וְעָשִׂיתָ כָּל־מְלַאכְתֶּךָ:
Veyom hashevi'i shabbat ladonai elohecha lo-ta'aseh chol-melachah attah uvincha uvittecha avdecha va'amatecha uvehemtecha vegeirecha asher bish'arecha:	וְיוֹם הַשְּׁבִיעִי שַׁבָּת לַיהוָה אֱלֹהֶיךָ לֹא־תַעֲשֶׂה כָל־מְלָאכָה אַתָּה וּבִנְךָ וּבִתֶּךָ עַבְדְּךָ וַאֲמָתֶךָ וּבְהֶמְתֶּךָ וְגֵרְךָ אֲשֶׁר בִּשְׁעָרֶיךָ:
Ki sheishet-yamim asah adonai et-hashamayim ve'et-ha'aretz et-hayyam ve'et-kol-asher-bam vayyanach bayyom hashevi'i al-kein beirach adonai et-yom hashabbat vaykaddesheihu:	כִּי שֵׁשֶׁת־יָמִים עָשָׂה יְהוָה אֶת־הַשָּׁמַיִם וְאֶת־הָאָרֶץ אֶת־הַיָּם וְאֶת־כָּל־אֲשֶׁר־בָּם וַיָּנַח בַּיּוֹם הַשְּׁבִיעִי עַל־כֵּן בֵּרַךְ יְהוָה אֶת־יוֹם הַשַּׁבָּת וַיְקַדְּשֵׁהוּ:
Kabbeid et-avicha ve'et-immecha lema'an ya'arichun yamecha al ha'adamah asher-adonai elohecha notein lach:	כַּבֵּד אֶת־אָבִיךָ וְאֶת־אִמֶּךָ לְמַעַן יַאֲרִכוּן יָמֶיךָ עַל הָאֲדָמָה אֲשֶׁר־יְהוָה אֱלֹהֶיךָ נֹתֵן לָךְ:
Lo tirtzach: Lo tin'af: Lo tignov:	לֹא תִרְצָח: לֹא תִנְאָף: לֹא תִגְנֹב:

Lo-ta'aneh verei'acha eid shaker:

לֹא־תַעֲנֶה בְרֵעֲךָ עֵד שָׁקֶר׃

Lo tachmod beit rei'echa

לֹא תַחְמֹד בֵּית רֵעֶךָ

lo-tachmod eishet rei'echa

לֹא־תַחְמֹד אֵשֶׁת רֵעֶךָ

ve'avdo va'amato veshoro

וְעַבְדּוֹ וַאֲמָתוֹ וְשׁוֹרוֹ

vachamoro vechol asher

וַחֲמֹרוֹ וְכֹל אֲשֶׁר

lerei'echa.

לְרֵעֶךָ׃

I the Lord am your God who brought you out of the land of Egypt, the house of bondage:

You shall have no other gods besides Me.

You shall not make for yourself a sculptured image, or any likeness of what is in the heavens above, or on the earth below, or in the waters under the earth.

You shall not bow down to them or serve them. For I, the Lord, your God am an impassioned God, visiting the guilt of the parents upon the children, upon the third and upon the fourth generations of those who reject Me.

but showing kindness to the thousandth generation of those who love Me and keep My commandments.

You shall not swear falsely by the name of the Lord, your God; for the Lord will not clear one who swears falsely by God's name.

Remember the sabbath day and keep it holy.

Six days you shall labor and do all your work,

but the seventh day is a sabbath of the Lord, your God: you shall not do any work—you, your son or daughter, your male or female slave, or your cattle, or the stranger who is within your settlements.

For in six days the Lord made heaven and earth and sea—and all that is in them—and then rested on the seventh day; therefore the Lord blessed the sabbath day and hallowed it.

Honor your father and your mother, that you may long endure on the land that the Lord, your God is assigning to you.

You shall not murder. You shall not commit adultery. You shall not steal. You shall not bear false witness against your neighbor.

You shall not covet your neighbor's house: you shall not covet your neighbor's wife, or male or female slave, or ox or ass, or anything that is your neighbor's.

Prayer to Recite Before Studying God's Word

Yehi ratzon millefanecha adonai	יְהִי רָצוֹן מִלְּפָנֶיךָ ה'
eloheinu veilohei avoteinu, shello	אֱלֹהֵינוּ וֵאלֹהֵי אֲבֹתֵינוּ, שֶׁלֹּא
ye'era devar takkalah al yadi,	יֶאֱרַע דְּבַר תַּקָּלָה עַל יָדִי,
velo ekkasheil bidvar halachah,	וְלֹא אֶכָּשֵׁל בִּדְבַר הֲלָכָה,
veyismechu vi chaveirai, shello	וְיִשְׂמְחוּ בִי חֲבֵרַי, שֶׁלֹּא
omar al tamei tahor velo al tahor	אֹמַר עַל טָמֵא טָהוֹר וְלֹא עַל טָהוֹר
tamei, velo al muttar asur velo	טָמֵא, וְלֹא עַל מֻתָּר אָסוּר וְלֹא
al asur muttar, velo yikkashelu	עַל אָסוּר מֻתָּר, וְלֹא יִכָּשְׁלוּ
chaveirai bidvar halachah	חֲבֵרַי בִּדְבַר הֲלָכָה
ve'esmach bahem. Ki adonai	וְאֶשְׂמַח בָּהֶם. כִּי יְיָ
yittein chochmah mippiv da'at	יִתֵּן חָכְמָה מִפִּיו דַּעַת
utevunah. Gal einai ve'abbitah	וּתְבוּנָה. גַּל עֵינַי וְאַבִּיטָה
nifla'ot mittoratecha.	נִכְלָאֹת מִתּוֹרָתֶךָ.

May it be Your will, Lord our God and God of our ancestors, that no mishap come about through me, and may I not stumble in matters of law, and may my colleagues rejoice in me. May I not declare impure what is pure or pure what is impure; may I not declare permitted what is forbidden or forbidden what is permitted. May my colleagues not stumble in matters of law, and may I rejoice in them. For the Lord grants wisdom; from His mouth comes knowledge and understanding. Open my eyes, so that I may see the wonders of Your Torah.

Notes

The Three Weeks of Mourning for the Temple

FOR THREE WEEKS every summer, from the 17th of Tammuz, which commemorates the breach of Jerusalem's walls, to the 9th of Av, the day the Temple was burned, we mourn the destruction of the Temple in Jerusalem. During this period, it is customary to recite Psalm 137, which reminds us of the destruction of Jerusalem and the exile, before the Grace After Meals.

Al naharot bavel sham yashavnu	עַל נַהֲרוֹת בָּבֶל שָׁם יָשַׁבְנוּ
gam-bachinu bezochreinu et-	גַּם־בָּכִינוּ בְּזָכְרֵנוּ אֶת־
tziyyon: Al-aravim betochah talinu	צִיּוֹן: עַל־עֲרָבִים בְּתוֹכָהּ תָּלִינוּ
kinnoroteinu: Ki sham she'eilunu	כִּנֹּרוֹתֵינוּ: כִּי שָׁם שְׁאֵלוּנוּ
shoveinu divrei-shir vetolaleinu	שׁוֹבֵינוּ דִּבְרֵי־שִׁיר וְתוֹלָלֵינוּ
simchah shiru lanu mishir tziyyon:	שִׂמְחָה שִׁירוּ לָנוּ מִשִּׁיר צִיּוֹן:
Eich nashir et-shir-adonai al	אֵיךְ נָשִׁיר אֶת־שִׁיר־יְהוָה עַל
admat neichar: Im-eshkacheich	אַדְמַת נֵכָר: אִם־אֶשְׁכָּחֵךְ
yerushalayim tishkach yemini:	יְרוּשָׁלָ͏ִם תִּשְׁכַּח יְמִינִי:
Tidbak-leshoni lechikki im-lo	תִּדְבַּק־לְשׁוֹנִי לְחִכִּי אִם־לֹא
ezkereichi im-lo a'aleh et-	אֶזְכְּרֵכִי אִם־לֹא אַעֲלֶה אֶת־
yerushalayim al rosh simchati:	יְרוּשָׁלַ͏ִם עַל רֹאשׁ שִׂמְחָתִי:
Zechor adonai livnei edom et	זְכֹר יְהוָה לִבְנֵי אֱדוֹם אֵת
yom yerushalayim ha'omerim aru	יוֹם יְרוּשָׁלָ͏ִם הָאֹמְרִים עָרוּ
aru ad hayyesod bah: Bat-bavel	עָרוּ עַד הַיְסוֹד בָּהּ: בַּת־בָּבֶל
hashedudah ashrei sheyshalleim-	הַשְּׁדוּדָה אַשְׁרֵי שֶׁיְשַׁלֶּם־
lach et-gemuleich sheggamalt	לָךְ אֶת־גְּמוּלֵךְ שֶׁגָּמַלְתְּ
lanu: Ashrei sheyyocheiz	לָנוּ: אַשְׁרֵי שֶׁיֹּאחֵז
venippeitz et-olalayich el-hassala.	וְנִפֵּץ אֶת־עֹלָלַיִךְ אֶל־הַסָּלַע:

By the rivers of Babylon, there we sat, sat and wept, as we thought of Zion. There on the poplars we hung up our lyres, for our captors asked us there for songs, our tormentors, for amusement: "Sing us one of the songs of Zion." How can we sing a song of the Lord on alien soil? If I forget you, O Jerusalem, let my right hand wither; let my tongue stick to my palate if I cease to think of you, if I do not keep Jerusalem in memory even at my happiest hour. Remember, O Lord, against the Edomites the day of Jerusalem's fall; how they cried, "Strip her, strip her to her very foundations!" Fair Babylon, you predator, a blessing on him who repays you in kind what you have inflicted on us; a blessing on him who seizes your babies and dashes them against the rocks!

Notes

Ninth of Av

THE 9TH OF Av is the saddest day on the Jewish calendar due to many devastating events that occurred on this date, most famously the destruction of the Temple in Jerusalem. One of the ways we mourn is by reciting *kinnot*, poems of lament. While most kinnot focus on the loss of the Temple, later additions commemorate events like the First Crusade, when crusaders destroyed many Jewish communities on their way to the Holy Land, the burning of the Talmud by King Louis IX of France in 1242, the Inquisition and expulsion of the Jews from Spain in 1492, and the Holocaust. Some kinnot also express a longing to return from exile to the Promised Land, such as the *kinna* included below.

Will You not Seek the Remnant of Your Flock?

Tziyyon, halo tish'ali lishlom	צִיּוֹן, הֲלֹא תִשְׁאֲלִי לִשְׁלוֹם
asirayich, doreshei shelomeich	אֲסִירַיִךְ, דּוֹרְשֵׁי שְׁלוֹמֵךְ
veheim yeter adarayich:	וְהֵם יֶתֶר עֲדָרָיִךְ:
miyyam umizrach umitzafon	מִיָּם וּמִזְרָח וּמִצָּפוֹן
veteiman shelom rachok vekarov	וְתֵימָן שְׁלוֹם רָחוֹק וְקָרוֹב
se'i mikkol avarayich:	שְׂאִי מִכֹּל עֲבָרָיִךְ:
ushelom asir tikvah, notein	וּשְׁלוֹם אֲסִיר תַּאֲוָה, נוֹתֵן
dema'av ketal chermon venichsaf	דְּמָעָיו כְּטַל חֶרְמוֹן וְנִכְסַף
leridtam al hararayich:	לְרִדְתָּם עַל הֲרָרָיִךְ:
livkot enuteich ani tannim, ve'eit	לִבְכּוֹת עֱנוּתֵךְ אֲנִי תַנִּים, וְעֵת

echelom shivat shevuteich ani
chinnor leshirayich:

אֶחֱלֹם שִׁיבַת שְׁבוּתֵךְ אֲנִי
כִּנּוֹר לְשִׁירָיִךְ:

libbi leveit el velifni'el me'od
yehemeh ulemachanayim vechol
pig'ei tehorayich.

לִבִּי לְבֵית אֵל וְלִפְנִיאֵל מְאֹד
יֶהֱמֶה וּלְמַחֲנַיִם וְכֹל
פִּגְעֵי טְהוֹרָיִךְ,

sham hashechinah shechunah
lach, vehayyotzereich patach
lemul sha'arei shachak
she'arayich.

שָׁם הַשְּׁכִינָה שְׁכֵנָה
לָךְ, וְהַיּוֹצְרֵךְ פָּתַח
לְמוּל שַׁעֲרֵי שַׁחַק
שְׁעָרָיִךְ,

uchevod adonai levad hayah
me'oreich, ve'ein shemesh
vesahar vechochavim me'irayich.

וּכְבוֹד אֲדֹנָי לְבַד הָיָה
מְאוֹרֵךְ, וְאֵין שֶׁמֶשׁ
וְסַהַר וְכוֹכָבִים מְאִירָיִךְ.

Evchar lenafshi lehishtappeich
bemakom asher ruach elohim
shefuchah al bechirayich.

אֶבְחַר לְנַפְשִׁי לְהִשְׁתַּפֵּךְ
בְּמָקוֹם אֲשֶׁר רוּחַ אֱלֹהִים
שְׁפוּכָה עַל בְּחִירָיִךְ.

At beit meluchah ve'at kissei
adonai, ve'eich yashevu avadim
alei chis'ot gevirayich?

אַתְּ בֵּית מְלוּכָה וְאַתְּ כִּסֵּא
אֲדֹנָי, וְאֵיךְ יָשְׁבוּ עֲבָדִים
עֲלֵי כִסְאוֹת גְּבִירָיִךְ?

Mi yitteneini meshoteit
bammekomot asher niglu elohim
lechozayich vetzirayich!

מִי יִתְּנֵנִי מְשׁוֹטֵט
בַּמְּקוֹמוֹת אֲשֶׁר נִגְלוּ אֱלֹהִים
לְחוֹזַיִךְ וְצִירָיִךְ!

Mi ya'aseh li chenafayim ve'archik
nedod, anid levitrei levavi bein
betarayich!

מִי יַעֲשֶׂה לִי כְנָפַיִם וְאַרְחִיק
נְדוֹד, אָנִיד לְבִתְרֵי לְבָבִי בֵּין
בְּתָרָיִךְ!

Eppol le'appai alei artzeich

אֶפֹּל לְאַפַּי עֲלֵי אַרְצֵךְ

ve'ertzeh avanayich me'od
va'achonein et-afarayich,

וְאֶרְצֶה אֲבָנַיִךְ מְאֹד
וַאֲחֹנֵן אֶת-עֲפָרָיִךְ,

af ki ve'amedi alei kivrot avotai
ve'eshtomeim bechevron alei
mivchar kevarayich!

אַף כִּי בְעָמְדִי עֲלֵי קִבְרוֹת אֲבֹתַי
וְאֶשְׁתּוֹמֵם בְּחֶבְרוֹן עֲלֵי
מִבְחַר קְבָרָיִךְ!

E'vor beya'reich vecharmilleich
ve'e'mod begil'adeich
ve'eshtomamah el har avarayich,

אֶעְבֹר בְּיַעְרֵךְ וְכַרְמְלֵךְ
וְאֶעְמֹד בְּגִלְעָדֵךְ
וְאֶשְׁתּוֹמָמָה אֶל הַר עֲבָרָיִךְ,

har ha'avarim vehor hahar, asher
sham shenei orim gedolim
me'irayich umorayich.

הַר הָעֲבָרִים וְהֹר הָהָר, אֲשֶׁר
שָׁם שְׁנֵי אוֹרִים גְּדוֹלִים
מְאִירַיִךְ וּמוֹרָיִךְ.

Chayyei neshamot – avir artzeich,
umimmar deror avkat afareich,
venofet tzuf –neharayich!

חַיֵּי נְשָׁמוֹת ־ אֲוִיר אַרְצֵךְ,
וּמִמָּר דְּרוֹר אַבְקַת עֲפָרֵךְ,
וְנֹפֶת צוּף ־ נְהָרָיִךְ!

Yin'am lenafshi haloch arom
veyacheif, alei charevot
shemamah asher hayu devirayich,

יִנְעַם לְנַפְשִׁי הֲלֹךְ עָרֹם
וְיָחֵף, עֲלֵי חָרְבוֹת
שְׁמָמָה אֲשֶׁר הָיוּ דְבִירָיִךְ,

bimkom aroneich asher nignaz,
uvimkom keruvayich asher
shachenu chadrei chadarayich!

בִּמְקוֹם אֲרוֹנֵךְ אֲשֶׁר נִגְנַז,
וּבִמְקוֹם כְּרוּבַיִךְ אֲשֶׁר
שָׁכְנוּ חַדְרֵי חֲדָרָיִךְ!

Agoz ve'ashlich pe'eir nizri
ve'ekkov zeman, chilleil be'eretz
temei'ah et-nezirayich–

אָגֹז וְאַשְׁלִיךְ פְּאֵר נִזְרִי
וְאֶקֹּב זְמָן, חִלֵּל בְּאֶרֶץ
טְמֵאָה אֶת-נְזִירָיִךְ־

eich ye'erav li achol ushetot be'eit
echezeh, ki yischavu hakkelavim

אֵיךְ יֶעֱרַב לִי אֲכֹל וּשְׁתוֹת בְּעֵת
אֶחֱזֶה, כִּי יִסְחֲבוּ הַכְּלָבִים

et-kefirayich?   אֶת-כְּפִירָיִךְ?

O eich me'or yom yehi matok   אוֹ אֵיךְ מְאוֹר יוֹם יְהִי מָתוֹק
le'einai be'od er'eh befi orevim   לְעֵינַי בְּעוֹד אֶרְאֶה בְּפִי עֹרְבִים
pigrei nesharayich?   פִּגְרֵי נְשָׁרָיִךְ?

Kos hayyegonim, le'at! Harpi   כּוֹס הַיְגוֹנִים, לְאַט! הַרְפִּי
me'at, ki chevar male'u chesalai   מְעַט, כִּי כְבָר מָלְאוּ כְסָלַי
venafshi mammerorayich.   וְנַפְשִׁי מַמְּרוֹרָיִךְ.

Eit ezkerah oholah – eshteh   עֵת אֶזְכְּרָה אָהֳלָה ⁻ אֶשְׁתֶּה
chamateich, ve'ezkor oholivah –   חֲמָתֵךְ, וְאֶזְכֹּר אָהֳלִיבָה ⁻
ve'emtzeh et-shemarayich!   וְאֶמְצֶה אֶת-שְׁמָרָיִךְ!

Tziyyon kelilat yofi, ahvah vechein   צִיּוֹן כְּלִילַת יָפִי, אַהֲבָה וְחֵן
tiksheri mei'az, uvach niksheru   תִּקְשְׁרִי מֵאָז, וּבָךְ נִקְשְׁרוּ
nafshot chaveirayich–   נַפְשׁוֹת חֲבֵרָיִךְ⁻

heim hassemeichim leshalvateich   הֵם הַשְּׂמֵחִים לְשַׁלְוָתֵךְ
vehakko'avim al shomamuteich   וְהַכּוֹאֲבִים עַל שׁוֹמֲמוּתֵךְ
uvochim al shevarayich.   וּבוֹכִים עַל שְׁבָרָיִךְ.

Mibbor shevi sho'afim negdeich   מִבּוֹר שְׁבִי שׁוֹאֲפִים נֶגְדֵּךְ
umishtachavim ish mimmekomo   וּמִשְׁתַּחֲוִים אִישׁ מִמְּקוֹמוֹ
elei nochach she'arayich,   אֱלֵי נֹכַח שְׁעָרָיִךְ,

edrei hamoneich, asher galu,   עֶדְרֵי הֲמוֹנֵךְ, אֲשֶׁר גָּלוּ
vehitpazzeru meihar legiv'ah, velo   וְהִתְפַּזְּרוּ מֵהַר לְגִבְעָה וְלֹא
shachechu gedeirayich,   שָׁכְחוּ גְדֵרָיִךְ,

hammachazikim beshulayich   הַמַּחֲזִיקִים בְּשׁוּלַיִךְ
umit'ammetzim la'lot vele'echoz   וּמִתְאַמְּצִים לַעֲלוֹת וְלֶאֱחֹז
besansinnei temarayich.   בְּסַנְסִנֵּי תְמָרָיִךְ.

Shin'ar ufatros haya'archuch
begodlam, ve'im hevlam
yedammu letummayich
ve'urayich?

שִׁנְעָר וּפַתְרוֹס הֲיַעַרְכוּךְ
בְּגָדְלָם, וְאִם הֶבְלָם
יְדַמּוּ לְתָמַּיִךְ
וְאוּרַיִךְ?

El mi yedammu meshichayich
ve'el mi nevi'ayich ve'el mi
leviyayich vesharayich?

אֶל מִי יְדַמּוּ מְשִׁיחַיִךְ
וְאֶל מִי נְבִיאַיִךְ וְאֶל מִי
לְוִיַּךְ וְשָׁרָיִךְ?

Yishneh veyachlof kelil kol-
mamlechot ha'elil. Chaseneich
le'olam, ledor vador nezarayich.

יִשְׁנֶה וְיַחְלֹף כְּלִיל כָּל־
מַמְלְכוֹת הָאֱלִיל.חָסְנֵךְ
לְעוֹלָם, לְדוֹר וָדוֹר נְזָרָיִךְ.

Ivach lemoshav elohayich,
ve'ashrei enosh yivchar yekareiv
veyishkon bachatzeirayich!

אִוָּךְ לְמוֹשָׁב אֱלֹהַיִךְ,
וְאַשְׁרֵי אֱנוֹשׁ יִבְחַר יְקָרֵב
וְיִשְׁכֹּן בַּחֲצֵרָיִךְ!

Ashrei mechakkeh veyaggia'
veyir'eh alot oreich veyibbake'u
alav shecharayich,

אַשְׁרֵי מְחַכֶּה וְיַגִּיעַ
וְיִרְאֶה עֲלוֹת אוֹרֵךְ וְיִבָּקְעוּ
עָלָיו שְׁחָרָיִךְ,

lir'ot betovat bechirayich vela'loz
besimchateich beshuveich elei
kadmat ne'urayich!

לִרְאוֹת בְּטוֹבַת בְּחִירַיִךְ וְלַעְלֹז
בְּשִׂמְחָתֵךְ בְּשׁוּבֵךְ אֱלֵי
קַדְמַת נְעוּרָיִךְ!

*O Zion, will you not ask about the welfare of your prisoners, who
seek your welfare and are the remnant of your flock?*

*From the west, east, north, and south, the welfare of those far and
near, inquire from your every side.*

And the welfare of the prisoner who is still full of hope, who sheds tears like the dew of Hermon and yearns for them to fall upon your mountains.

To weep for your suffering, I am a jackal, and when I dream of your return, I am a harp for your songs.

My heart yearns for Bethel and for Peniel it greatly years, and for Mahanaim and all the places of your pure ones.

There the Shechinah dwelled for you, and your creator opened your gates facing the heavens.

And the glory of the Lord alone was your light, and no sun, moon, or stars gave you illumination. I would choose to pour out my soul in a place where the spirit of God is poured upon your chosen ones.

You are a royal palace and God's Throne of Glory, how have slaves sat upon the thrones of your nobles?

If only I could wander in the places where God was revealed to your seers and messengers?

Who will make me wings so I can fly far away, I would cause my shattered heart to wander among your shattered ruins.

I would fall upon my face on your land and be cherish your stones and find favor in your dust.

Even while standing by the graves of my ancestors, I behold in wonder in Hebron your choice burial sites.

I will pass through your forests and Carmel, and stand in your Gilead, amazed at your Mount Abarim.

Mount Abarim and Mount Hor, the resting places of your two great lights (Moses and Aaron) who illuminated your path and guided you.

The breath of life for our souls is the air of your land, the powder of your dust is finer than flowing myrrh and your river is like the honeycomb's drippings.

It will be pleasant for my soul to walk naked and barefoot on the desolate ruins that were once your sanctuaries, in the place of your Ark, which was was later hidden and where your cherubs dwelled in your innermost chambers.

I will clip and throw away my glorious crown, and curse the time when your Nazirites were defiled in the land of Babylon.

How could I find pleasure in eating and drinking when I see the dogs dragging your young lions?

Or how could the light of day be sweet to my eyes when I see the ravens devouring the flesh of your corpses?

O cup of sorrows, slow down, give me some respite, for my thoughts and my soul are already filled from your bitterness.

When I remember Oholah, I will drink your wine, and when I recall Oholibah, and I drain your dregs!

O Zion, crowned with beauty, braided with love and grace since ancient times, in you are bound the souls of your companions.

They rejoice in your peace, grieve over your desolation, and weep for your devestation.

From the pit of captivity, they yearn for you and bow, each in his place, towards your gates.

The flocks of your multitudes, who have gone into exile and been scattered from mountain to hill ,have not forgotten your fences, they hold onto your hems and strive to climb and grasp the branches of your date palms.

Can Shinar and Pathros compare with you despite their greatness, and can their vanity and worthless deities resembles your Urim v'Tummim (part of the High Priest's breastplate)?

To whom can your anointed ones compared, and to whom your prophets, your Levites, and your singers?

The crown of all idolatrous kingdoms will fade and change. Your strength is forever; your crown endures for generations.

Your dwelling is the abode of your God, and fortunate is the man who chooses to draw near and dwell in your courts!

Fortunate is he who waits and arrives, and sees the dawn of your light break upon him, to see the good of your chosen ones and to rejoice in your joy, as you return to the former days of your youth.

Console the Mourners

The following paragraph is added to the afternoon *Amida* prayer on the Ninth of Av. In it, we ask God to console those who mourn over Zion and Jerusalem. The ultimate consolation will come when the Temple is rebuilt and Jerusalem returns to her former glory.

<table>
<tr><td>

Nacheim adonai eloheinu et
aveilei tziyyon ve'et aveilei
yerushalayim. Ve'et ha'ir
ha'aveilah vehachareivah
vehabbezuyah vehashomeimah.
Ha'aveilah mibbeli vaneha.
Vehachareivah mimme'onoteha.
Vehabbezuyah mikkevodah.
Vehashomeimah mei'ein
yosheiv. Vehi yoshevet veroshah
chafui ke'ishah akarah shello
yaladah. Va'yevale'uha ligyonot.
Veyirashuha ovedei fesilim.
Vayattilo et ammecha yisra'el
lecharev. Vayyahargu vezadon
chasidei elyon. Al kein tziyyon
bemar tivkeh. Virushalayim tittein
kolah. Libbi libbi al chal'leihem.
Mei'ai mei'ai al chal'leihem. Ki
attah adonai ba'eish hitzattah.
Uva'eish attah atid livnotah.
Ka'amur va'ani ehyeh lah ne'um
adonai chomat eish saviv
ulechavod ehyeh betochah:
baruch attah adonai menacheim
tziyyon uvoneih yerushalayim.

</td><td dir="rtl">

נַחֵם יְהֹוָה אֱלֹהֵינוּ אֶת
אֲבֵלֵי צִיּוֹן וְאֶת אֲבֵלֵי
יְרוּשָׁלָיִם. וְאֶת הָעִיר
הָאֲבֵלָה וְהַחֲרֵבָה
וְהַבְּזוּיָה וְהַשּׁוֹמֵמָה.
הָאֲבֵלָה מִבְּלִי בָנֶיהָ.
וְהַחֲרֵבָה מִמְּעוֹנוֹתֶיהָ.
וְהַבְּזוּיָה מִכְּבוֹדָהּ.
וְהַשּׁוֹמֵמָה מֵאֵין
יוֹשֵׁב. וְהִיא יוֹשֶׁבֶת וְרֹאשָׁהּ
חָפוּי כְּאִשָּׁה עֲקָרָה שֶׁלֹּא
יָלָדָה. וַיְבַלְעוּהָ לִגְיוֹנוֹת.
וַיִּירָשׁוּהָ עוֹבְדֵי פְסִילִים.
וַיַּטִּילוּ אֶת עַמְּךָ יִשְׂרָאֵל
לֶחָרֶב. וַיַּהַרְגוּ בְזָדוֹן
חֲסִידֵי עֶלְיוֹן. עַל כֵּן צִיּוֹן
בְּמַר תִּבְכֶּה. וִירוּשָׁלַיִם תִּתֵּן
קוֹלָהּ. לִבִּי לִבִּי עַל חַלְלֵיהֶם.
מֵעַי מֵעַי עַל חַלְלֵיהֶם. כִּי
אַתָּה יְהֹוָה בָּאֵשׁ הִצַּתָּהּ.
וּבָאֵשׁ אַתָּה עָתִיד לִבְנוֹתָהּ.
כָּאָמוּר וַאֲנִי אֶהְיֶה לָהּ נְאֻם
יְהֹוָה חוֹמַת אֵשׁ סָבִיב
וּלְכָבוֹד אֶהְיֶה בְתוֹכָהּ:
בָּרוּךְ אַתָּה יְהֹוָה מְנַחֵם
צִיּוֹן וּבוֹנֵה יְרוּשָׁלָיִם.

</td></tr>
</table>

O Lord, our God, console the mourners of Zion and the mourners of Jerusalem and the city that is in mourning and in ruins, despised and desolate. Mourning because she is bereft of her children, ruined of her dwellings, despised in contrast to her former glory, desolate without inhabitants, she sits alone with her head covered like a barren woman who never gave birth. Legions have devoured her, idolaters have deprived her of her inheritance; they have put Your people Israel to the sword and have wantonly murdered the pious ones of the Most High. Therefore, Zion weeps bitterly, and Jerusalem raises her voice, "My heart, my heart [grieves] for their slain, my innards, my innards, [ache] for their slain. For you, O Lord, set her afire, and with fire You will ultimately rebuild her, as it is said, "I will be to her, says the Lord, a wall of fire around [her], and I shall be for glory in her midst." Blessed are You, O Lord, Consoler of Zion and Builder of Jerusalem.

Notes

Rosh Hashana (Jewish New Year)

Rosh Hashana, the Jewish New Year, falls on the first day of the Hebrew month of *Tishrei* and begins a new year on the Hebrew calendar. The day is marked by fervent prayers, the blowing of the *shofar* (ram's horn) and festive holiday meals. *Rosh Hashana* is the first of the High Holidays, as well as the first day of the Ten Days of Repentance.

Psalm 24

On Rosh Hashanah night, we recite Psalm 24. In this psalm, King David asks, "Who can ascend the mountain of the Lord and stand in His holy place?" and then answers, "One who has clean hands and a pure heart, who has not borne My soul in vain, and has not sworn deceitfully." According to biblical commentator Amos Hakham, this means that to merit standing in God's presence, one's actions, thoughts, and speech must all be pure. Therefore, we must strive to purify and perfect all aspects of our being and our interactions with others to draw closer to the Almighty. This idea is particularly relevant to the High Holidays, when we seek to cleanse ourselves and draw nearer to the Divine.

Ledavid mizmor ladonai ha'aretz	לְדָוִד מִזְמוֹר לַיהוָה הָאָרֶץ
umelo'ah teiveil veyoshvei vah:	וּמְלוֹאָהּ תֵּבֵל וְיֹשְׁבֵי
ki hu al yammim yesadah ve'al	בָהּ: כִּי הוּא עַל יַמִּים יְסָדָהּ
neharot yechoneneha: mi ya'aleh	וְעַל נְהָרוֹת יְכוֹנְנֶהָ: מִי
vehar adonai umi yakum bimkom	יַעֲלֶה בְהַר יְהוָה וּמִי יָקוּם
kodsho: neki chappayim uvar	בִּמְקוֹם קָדְשׁוֹ: נְקִי כַפַּיִם
leivav asher lo nasa lashav nafshi	וּבַר לֵבָב אֲשֶׁר לֹא נָשָׂא לַשָּׁוְא

velo nishba lemirmah:

yissa verachah mei'eit adonai

utzedakah mei'elohei yish'o: zeh

dor doreshav mevakshei fanecha

ya'akov selah: se'u she'arim

rasheichem vehinnase'u pitchei

olam veyavo melech hakkavod:

mi zeh melech hakkavod

adonai izzuz vegibbor adonai

gibbor milchamah: se'u she'arim

rasheichem use'u pitchei olam

veyavo melech hakkavod: mi hu

zeh melech hakkavod adonai

tzeva'ot hu melech hakkavod

selah:

A psalm of David: the earth is the Lord's and the fullness thereof, the inhabited world and those who dwell in it. For He founded it upon the seas, and established it upon rivers. Who may ascend the mountain of the Lord, and who may stand in the place of His holiness? The clean of hands and the pure of heart, who has not borne My soul in vain, and has not sworn deceitfully. He will bear the Lord's blessing and righteousness from the God of his deliverance. This is the generation of those who seek Him, the seekers of Your Presence, [God of] Jacob, Selah. Lift up your heads, gates, and be uplifted [you] entrance ways to eternity, so that the King of Glory may enter. Who is this King of Glory? The Lord, strong and mighty; the Lord, the Mighty One in battle. Lift up your heads, gates, and lift, entrance ways to eternity, so that the King of Glory may enter. Who is He, this King of Glory? The Lord of hosts, He is the King of Glory, Selah.

Let Us Speak of the Awesome Holiness of this Day

The following moving prayer, one of the high moments of the high holiday prayers, is recited on both Rosh Hashanah (Jewish New Year) and Yom Kippur (Day of Atonement), when we sit in judgment before our Creator. It vividly describes the awe and solemnity of the Day of Judgment in stirring and poignant language. The prayer contrasts the fleeting nature of human life with God's eternal reign, reminding worshippers of their mortality and the enduring sovereignty of God.

Unetanneh tokef kedushat	וּנְתַנֶּה תֹּקֶף קְדֻשַּׁת
hayyom ki hu nora ve'ayom uvo	הַיּוֹם כִּי הוּא נוֹרָא וְאָיֹם וּבוֹ
tinnasei malchutecha veyikkon	תִּנָּשֵׂא מַלְכוּתֶךָ וְיִכּוֹן
bechesed kis'echa veteisheiv alav	בְּחֶסֶד כִּסְאֶךָ וְתֵשֵׁב עָלָיו
be'emet	בֶּאֱמֶת

Emet ki attah hu dayyan	אֱמֶת כִּי אַתָּה הוּא דַיָּן
umochiach veyodeia'	וּמוֹכִיחַ וְיוֹדֵעַ
va'eid vechoteiv vechoteim	וָעֵד וְכוֹתֵב וְחוֹתֵם
vesofer umoneh vetizkor kol	וְסוֹפֵר וּמוֹנֶה וְתִזְכֹּר כָּל
hannishkachot vetiftach et seifer	הַנִּשְׁכָּחוֹת וְתִפְתַּח אֶת סֵפֶר
hazzichronot umei'eilav yikkarie	הַזִּכְרוֹנוֹת וּמֵאֵלָיו יִקָּרֵא
vechotam yad kol adam bo	וְחוֹתָם יַד כָּל אָדָם בּוֹ

Uveshofar gadol yittaka vekol	וּבְשׁוֹפָר גָּדוֹל יִתָּקַע וְקוֹל
demamah dakkah yishama	דְּמָמָה דַקָּה יִשָּׁמַע
umal'achim yeichafeizun vechil	וּמַלְאָכִים יֵחָפֵזוּן וְחִיל
ure'adah yocheizun veyomru	וּרְעָדָה יֹאחֵזוּן וְיֹאמְרוּ
hinneih yom haddin lifkod al	הִנֵּה יוֹם הַדִּין לִפְקֹד עַל
tzeva marom baddin ki lo yizku	צְבָא מָרוֹם בַּדִּין כִּי לֹא יִזְכּוּ
be'einecha baddin vechol ba'ei	בְּעֵינֶיךָ בַּדִּין וְכָל בָּאֵי

olam ya'avrun lefanecha kivnei
maron kevakkarat ro'eh edro
ma'avir tzono tachat shivto kein
ta'avir vetispor vetimneh vetifkod
nefesh kol chai vetachtoch kitzvah
lechol beriyyah vetichtov et gezar
dinam.

עוֹלָם יַעַבְרוּן לְפָנֶיךָ כִּבְנֵי
מָרוֹן כְּבַקָּרַת רוֹעֶה עֶדְרוֹ
מַעֲבִיר צֹאנוֹ תַּחַת שִׁבְטוֹ כֵּן
תַּעֲבִיר וְתִסְפֹּר וְתִמְנֶה וְתִפְקֹד
נֶפֶשׁ כָּל חָי וְתַחְתֹּךְ קִצְבָה
לְכָל בְּרִיָּה וְתִכְתֹּב אֶת גְּזַר
דִּינָם

Berosh hashanah yikkateivun,
uveyom tzom kippur
yeichateimun. Kammah ya'avrun,
vechammah yibbarei'un, mi
yichyeh, umi yamut, mi vekitzo,
umi lo bekitzo, mi vammayim,
umi va'eish, mi vacherev, umi
vachayyah, mi vara'av, umi
vatzama, mi vara'ash, umi
vammaggeifah, mi vachanikah,
umi vassekilah, mi yanuach, umi
yanua', mi yishakeit, umi yetoreif,
mi yishalev, umi yityassar, mi
ya'ani, umi ya'ashir, mi yushpal,
umi yarum. Uteshuvah utefillah
utzedakah ma'avirin et roa'
haggezeirah.

בְּרֹאשׁ הַשָּׁנָה יִכָּתֵבוּן,
וּבְיוֹם צוֹם כִּפּוּר
יֵחָתֵמוּן. כַּמָּה יַעַבְרוּן,
וְכַמָּה יִבָּרֵאוּן, מִי
יִחְיֶה, וּמִי יָמוּת, מִי בְקִצּוֹ,
וּמִי לֹא בְקִצּוֹ, מִי בַמַּיִם,
וּמִי בָאֵשׁ, מִי בַחֶרֶב, וּמִי
בַחַיָּה, מִי בָרָעָב, וּמִי
בַצָּמָא, מִי בָרַעַשׁ, וּמִי
בַמַּגֵּפָה, מִי בַחֲנִיקָה,
וּמִי בַסְּקִילָה, מִי יָנוּחַ, וּמִי
יָנוּעַ, מִי יִשָּׁקֵט, וּמִי יִטָּרֵף,
מִי יִשָּׁלֵו, וּמִי יִתְיַסָּר, מִי
יֵעָנִי, וּמִי יַעֲשִׁיר, מִי יֻשְׁפַּל,
וּמִי יָרוּם. וּתְשׁוּבָה וּתְפִלָּה
וּצְדָקָה מַעֲבִירִין אֶת רֹעַ
הַגְּזֵרָה.

Ki keshimcha kein tehillatecha,
kasheh lich'os venoach lirtzot, ki
lo tachpotz bemot hammeit, ki
im beshuvo middarko vechayah,
ve'ad yom moto techakkeh lo, im
yashuv miyyad tekabbelo. emet ki
attah hu yotzeram veyodei'a

כִּי כְּשִׁמְךָ כֵּן תְּהִלָּתֶךָ,
קָשֶׁה לִכְעוֹס וְנוֹחַ לִרְצוֹת, כִּי
לֹא תַחְפֹּץ בְּמוֹת הַמֵּת, כִּי
אִם בְּשׁוּבוֹ מִדַּרְכּוֹ וְחָיָה,
וְעַד יוֹם מוֹתוֹ תְּחַכֶּה לּוֹ, אִם
יָשׁוּב מִיַּד תְּקַבְּלוֹ. אֱמֶת
כִּי אַתָּה הוּא יוֹצְרָם וְיוֹדֵעַ

yitzram, ki heim basar vadam.

יִצְרָם, כִּי הֵם בָּשָׂר וָדָם.

Adam yesodo mei'afar vesofo
le'afar. Benafsho yavi lachmo.
Mashul kecheres hannishbar,
kechatzir yaveish, uchetzitz novel,
ketzeil oveir, uche'anan kalah,
ucheruach noshavet, uche'avak
porei'ach, vechachalom ya'uf.
Ve'attah hu melech el chai
vekayyam.

אָדָם יְסוֹדוֹ מֵעָפָר וְסוֹפוֹ
לֶעָפָר. בְּנַפְשׁוֹ יָבִיא לַחְמוֹ.
מָשׁוּל כְּחֶרֶס הַנִּשְׁבָּר,
כְּחָצִיר יָבֵשׁ, וּכְצִיץ נוֹבֵל,
כְּצֵל עוֹבֵר, וּכְעָנָן כָּלָה,
וּכְרוּחַ נוֹשָׁבֶת, וּכְאָבָק
פּוֹרֵחַ, וְכַחֲלוֹם יָעוּף.
וְאַתָּה הוּא מֶלֶךְ אֵל חַי
וְקַיָּם.

We lend power to the holiness of this day. For it is tremendous and awe filled, and on it Your kingship will be exalted, Your throne will be established in loving-kindness, and You will sit on that throne in truth.

It is true that You are the one who judges, and reproves, who knows all, and bears witness, who inscribes, and seals, who reckons and enumerates. You remember all that is forgotten. You open the book of records, and from it, all shall be read. In it lies each person's insignia.

And with a great shofar it is sounded, and a thin silent voice shall be heard. And the angels shall be alarmed, and dread and fear shall seize them as they proclaim: behold! the Day of Judgment on which the hosts of heaven shall be judged, for they too shall not be judged blameless by You, and all creatures shall parade before You as a herd of sheep. As a shepherd herds his flock, directing his sheep to pass under his staff, so too You shall pass, count, and record the souls of all living, and decree a limit to each persons days, and inscribe their final judgment.

On Rosh Hashanah (Jewish New Year) it is inscribed, and on Yom Kippur (Day of Atonement) it is sealed - how many shall pass away and how many shall be born, who shall live and who shall die, who in good time, and who by an untimely death, who by water and who by fire, who by sword and who by wild beast, who by famine and who by thirst, who by earthquake and who by plague, who by strangulation and who by lapidation, who shall have rest and who wander, who shall be at peace and who pursued, who shall be serene and who tormented, who shall become impoverished and who wealthy, who shall be debased, and who exalted. But repentance, prayer and righteousness avert the severity of the decree.

For Your praise is just as your name. You are slow to anger and quick to be appeased. For You do not desire the death of the condemned, rather, that they turn from their path and live and you wait for them until the day of their death, and if they repent, you receive them immediately. It is true - [For] You are their Creator and You understand their inclination, for they are but flesh and blood.

We come from dust, and return to dust. We labour by our lives for bread, we are like broken shards, like dry grass, and like a withered flower; like a passing shadow and a vanishing cloud, like a breeze that passes, like dust that scatters, like a fleeting dream. But You are the King who lives eternal.

Psalm 130

Psalm 130 is recited every day from *Rosh Hashanah* (Jewish New Year) through *Yom Kippur* (Day of Atonement), during the Ten Days of Repentance. These ten days focus on repenting for our sins and seeking God's forgiveness, making this psalm particularly fitting as it asks God to redeem

Shir hamma'alot mimma'amakkim keraticha adonai: Adonai shim'ah vekoli tihyenah oznecha kashuvot lekol tachanunai: Im-avonot tishmor-yah adonai mi ya'amod: Ki-immecha hasselichah lema'an tivvarei: Kivviti adonai kivvetah nafshi velidvaro hochaleti: Nafshi ladonai mishomerim labboker shomerim labboker: Yacheil yisra'el el-adonai ki-im-adonai hachesed veharbeih immo fedut: Vehu yifdeh et-yisra'el mikkol avonotav.

שִׁיר הַמַּעֲלוֹת מִמַּעֲמַקִּים קְרָאתִיךָ יְהוָה: אֲדֹנָי שִׁמְעָה בְקוֹלִי תִּהְיֶינָה אָזְנֶיךָ קַשֻּׁבוֹת לְקוֹל תַּחֲנוּנָי: אִם־עֲוֹנוֹת תִּשְׁמָר־יָהּ אֲדֹנָי מִי יַעֲמֹד: כִּי־עִמְּךָ הַסְּלִיחָה לְמַעַן תִּוָּרֵא: קִוִּיתִי יְהוָה קִוְּתָה נַפְשִׁי וְלִדְבָרוֹ הוֹחָלְתִּי: נַפְשִׁי לַאדֹנָי מִשֹּׁמְרִים לַבֹּקֶר שֹׁמְרִים לַבֹּקֶר: יַחֵל יִשְׂרָאֵל אֶל־יְהוָה כִּי־עִם־יְהוָה הַחֶסֶד וְהַרְבֵּה עִמּוֹ פְדוּת: וְהוּא יִפְדֶּה אֶת־יִשְׂרָאֵל מִכֹּל עֲוֹנֹתָיו:

A song of ascents. Out of the depths I call You, O Lord. O Lord, listen to my cry; let Your ears be attentive to my plea for mercy. If You keep account of sins, O Lord, Lord, who will survive? Yours is the power to forgive so that You may be held in awe. I look to the Lord; I look to Him; I await His word. I am more eager for the Lord than watchmen for the morning, watchmen for the morning. O Israel, wait for the Lord; for with the Lord is steadfast love and great power to redeem. It is He who will redeem Israel from all their iniquities.

Psalm 27

Psalm 27 is recited at the conclusion of morning and evening prayers from the first day of the Hebrew month of *Elul* through the High Holidays and *Sukkot* (Feast of Tabernacles). It acknowledges God's light, salvation and protection, themes particularly relevant for the High Holiday and Sukkot season. Rabbi Jonathan Sacks describes it as beautifully capturing the quiet confidence of faith, making it ideal for times of judgment and reminding us that God shelters us from harm.

Ledavid adonai ori veyish'i mimmi	לְדָוִד יְהֹוָה אוֹרִי וְיִשְׁעִי מִמִּי
ira adonai ma'oz chayyai mimmi	אִירָא יְהֹוָה מָעוֹז חַיַּי מִמִּי
efchad: bikrov alai merei'im	אֶפְחָד: בִּקְרֹב עָלַי מְרֵעִים
le'echol et besari tzarai ve'oyevai	לֶאֱכֹל אֶת בְּשָׂרִי צָרַי וְאֹיְבַי
li heimmah chashelu venafalu: im	לִי הֵמָּה כָּשְׁלוּ וְנָפָלוּ: אִם
tachaneh alai machaneh lo yira	תַּחֲנֶה עָלַי מַחֲנֶה לֹא יִירָא
libbi im takum alai milchamah	לִבִּי אִם תָּקוּם עָלַי מִלְחָמָה
bezot ani voteach: achat sha'alti	בְּזֹאת אֲנִי בוֹטֵחַ: אַחַת שָׁאַלְתִּי
mei'eit adonai otah avakkeish	מֵאֵת יְהֹוָה אוֹתָהּ אֲבַקֵּשׁ
shivti beveit adonai kol yemei	שִׁבְתִּי בְּבֵית יְהֹוָה כָּל יְמֵי
chayyai lachazot beno'am	חַיַּי לַחֲזוֹת בְּנֹעַם
adonai ulevakkeir beheichalo:	יְהֹוָה וּלְבַקֵּר בְּהֵיכָלוֹ:
ki yitzpeneini besukkoh beyom	כִּי יִצְפְּנֵנִי בְּסֻכֹּה בְּיוֹם
ra'ah yastireini beseiter oholo	רָעָה יַסְתִּרֵנִי בְּסֵתֶר אָהֳלוֹ
betzur yeromemeini: ve'attah	בְּצוּר יְרוֹמְמֵנִי: וְעַתָּה
yarum roshi al oyevai sevivotai	יָרוּם רֹאשִׁי עַל אֹיְבַי סְבִיבוֹתַי
ve'ezbechah ve'oholo zivchei	וְאֶזְבְּחָה בְאָהֳלוֹ זִבְחֵי
teru'ah ashirah va'azammerah	תְרוּעָה אָשִׁירָה וַאֲזַמְּרָה
ladonai: shema adonai koli ekra	לַיהֹוָה: שְׁמַע יְהֹוָה קוֹלִי אֶקְרָא
vechanneini va'aneini: lecha amar	וְחָנֵּנִי וַעֲנֵנִי: לְךָ
libbi bakkeshu fanai et	אָמַר לִבִּי בַּקְּשׁוּ פָנָי אֶת

panecha adonai avakkeish: al   אֵל אֲבַקֵּשׁ: יְהֹוָה פָּנֶיךָ

tasteir panecha mimmenni al tat   תַּט אַל מִמֶּנִּי פָּנֶיךָ תַּסְתֵּר

be'af avdecha ezrati hayita al   אַל הָיִיתָ עֶזְרָתִי עַבְדֶּךָ בְּאַף

tittesheini ve'al ta'azveini elohei   אֱלֹהֵי תַּעַזְבֵנִי וְאַל תִּטְּשֵׁנִי

yish'i: ki avi ve'immi azavuni   עֲזָבוּנִי וְאִמִּי אָבִי כִּי יִשְׁעִי:

va'donai ya'asfeini: horeini adonai   יְהֹוָה הוֹרֵנִי יַאַסְפֵנִי: וַיהֹוָה

darkecha unecheini be'orach   בְּאֹרַח וּנְחֵנִי דַּרְכֶּךָ

mishor lema'an shorerai: al   אַל שׁוֹרְרָי: לְמַעַן מִישׁוֹר

titteneini benefesh tzarai ki kamu   קָמוּ כִּי צָרָי בְּנֶפֶשׁ תִּתְּנֵנִי

vi edei sheker vifei'ach chamas: חָמָס: וִיפֵחַ שֶׁקֶר עֵדֵי בִי

lulei he'emanti lir'ot betuv adonai   יְהֹוָה בְּטוּב לִרְאוֹת הֶאֱמַנְתִּי לוּלֵא

be'eretz chayyim: kavveh el   אֶל קַוֵּה חַיִּים: בְּאֶרֶץ

adonai chazak veya'ameitz   וְיַאֲמֵץ חֲזַק יְהֹוָה

libbecha vekavveih el adonai: יְהֹוָה: אֶל וְקַוֵּה לִבֶּךָ

By David: the Lord is my light and my salvation, whom shall I fear? the Lord is the strength of my life, of whom shall I be afraid? When evildoers approach me to devour my flesh— my tormentors and my foes they stumble and fall. If an army should encamp against me, my heart would not fear; if war were to rise against me, in this I trust. One thing I request of the Lord, [only] that shall I seek, that I may dwell in the House of the Lord all the days of my life, to behold the pleasantness of the Lord, and to meditate in His Sanctuary. For He will hide me in His Tabernacle on the day of distress, He will conceal me in the shelter of His Tent, upon a rock He will lift me. And now my head is raised high above my enemies around me; and I will offer in His Tent, sacrifices accompanied by trumpets of joy; I will sing and chant to the Lord. O Lord, hear my voice when I call; be gracious to me and answer me. Of You, my heart has said, Seek My Presence; Your Presence, O Lord I will seek. Conceal not Your Presence from me, do not turn away Your servant in anger. You have been my help; neither cast me off nor abandon me, God of my deliverance. When my father and mother abandon me, the

Lord will gather me up. O Lord, teach me Your way, and lead me in the path of uprightness, because of my watchers. Do not deliver me to the will of my tormentors, for false witnesses have risen against me, who breathe violence. Had I not believed that I would see the goodness of the Lord in the land of living. Hope to the Lord, be strong and He will give you courage; and hope to the Lord.

Notes

Yom Kippur (Day of Atonement)

Yom Kippur, THE Day of Atonement, is the holiest day of the Jewish year. On this day, we fast, pray, and repent for our sins, seeking God's forgiveness and atonement. In our striving for spiritual purity, we resemble angels: we abstain from physical pleasures such as eating, drinking, and marital relations, and we don white garments, symbolizing purity and repentance. We spend the day immersed in prayer and reflection, standing before God in humility and reverence, as the heavenly beings do. This resemblance to angels underscores our yearning to transcend our earthly limitations and connect with God on this holiest day of the year.

Our Father, Our King

This unique and moving prayer was first recited by the great Jewish sage Rabbi Akiva. The Talmud relates that during a terrible drought, one of the sages known as Rabbi Eliezer declared a fast day and recited 24 different blessings, but his prayers were not answered. Rabbi Akiva then stepped forward and exclaimed, "Our Father, our King, we have no king except You. Our Father, our King, for Your sake have mercy on us," and it immediately began to rain.

Our Father, Our King perfectly encapsulates our relationship with God: we are both His children and His subjects. As our Father, He loves and forgives us, but as our King, He sets rules to guide us. This dual relationship also means that as our Father, God desires to help us, and as our King, He has the power to resolve any issue we face.

Avinu malkeinu chatanu lefanecha:	אָבִינוּ מַלְכֵּנוּ חָטָאנוּ לְפָנֶיךָ:
Avinu malkeinu ein lanu melech ella attah:	אָבִינוּ מַלְכֵּנוּ אֵין לָנוּ מֶלֶךְ אֶלָּא אָתָּה:
Avinu malkeinu aseih immanu lema'an shemecha:	אָבִינוּ מַלְכֵּנוּ עֲשֵׂה עִמָּנוּ לְמַעַן שְׁמֶךָ:
Avinu malkeinu chaddeish aleinu shanah tovah:	אָבִינוּ מַלְכֵּנוּ חַדֵּשׁ עָלֵינוּ שָׁנָה טוֹבָה:
Avinu malkeinu battel mei'aleinu kol gezeirot kashot:	אָבִינוּ מַלְכֵּנוּ בַּטֵּל מֵעָלֵינוּ כָּל גְּזֵרוֹת קָשׁוֹת:
Avinu malkeinu batteil machshevot sone'einu:	אָבִינוּ מַלְכֵּנוּ בַּטֵּל מַחְשְׁבוֹת שׂוֹנְאֵינוּ:
Avinu malkeinu hafeir atzat oyeveinu:	אָבִינוּ מַלְכֵּנוּ הָפֵר עֲצַת אוֹיְבֵינוּ:
Avinu malkeinu kalleih kol tzar umastin mei'aleinu:	אָבִינוּ מַלְכֵּנוּ כַּלֵּה כָּל צַר וּמַשְׂטִין מֵעָלֵינוּ:
Avinu malkeinu setom piyyot mastineinu umekatrigeinu:	אָבִינוּ מַלְכֵּנוּ סְתוֹם פִּיּוֹת מַשְׂטִינֵנוּ וּמְקַטְרִיגֵנוּ:
Avinu malkeinu kalleih dever vecherev vera'av ushevi umashchit ve'avon mibbenei veritecha:	אָבִינוּ מַלְכֵּנוּ כַּלֵּה דֶּבֶר וְחֶרֶב וְרָעָב וּשְׁבִי וּמַשְׁחִית וְעָוֹן מִבְּנֵי בְרִיתֶךָ:
Avinu malkeinu mena maggeifah minnachalatecha:	אָבִינוּ מַלְכֵּנוּ מְנַע מַגֵּפָה מִנַּחֲלָתֶךָ:

Avinu malkeinu selach umechal
lechol avonoteinu:

אָבִינוּ מַלְכֵּנוּ סְלַח וּמְחַל
לְכָל עֲוֺנוֹתֵינוּ:

Avinu malkeinu mecheih
veha'aveir pesha'einu
vechattoteinu minneged einecha:

אָבִינוּ מַלְכֵּנוּ מְחֵה
וְהַעֲבֵר פְּשָׁעֵינוּ
וְחַטֹּאתֵינוּ מִנֶּגֶד עֵינֶיךָ:

Avinu malkeinu mechok
berachamecha harabbim kol
shitrei chovoteinu:

אָבִינוּ מַלְכֵּנוּ מְחוֹק
בְּרַחֲמֶיךָ הָרַבִּים כָּל
שִׁטְרֵי חוֹבוֹתֵינוּ:

Avinu malkeinu hachazireinu
bitshuvah sheleimah lefanecha:

אָבִינוּ מַלְכֵּנוּ הַחֲזִירֵנוּ
בִּתְשׁוּבָה שְׁלֵמָה לְפָנֶיךָ:

Avinu malkeinu shelach refu'ah
sheleimah lecholei ammecha:

אָבִינוּ מַלְכֵּנוּ שְׁלַח רְפוּאָה
שְׁלֵמָה לְחוֹלֵי עַמֶּךָ:

Avinu malkeinu kera roa' gezar
dineinu:

אָבִינוּ מַלְכֵּנוּ קְרַע רֹעַ גְּזַר
דִּינֵנוּ:

Avinu malkeinu zachereinu
bezikkaron tov lefanecha:

אָבִינוּ מַלְכֵּנוּ זָכְרֵנוּ
בְּזִכָּרוֹן טוֹב לְפָנֶיךָ:

Avinu malkeinu kateveinu beseifer
chayyim tovim:

אָבִינוּ מַלְכֵּנוּ כָּתְבֵנוּ בְּסֵפֶר
חַיִּים טוֹבִים:

Avinu malkeinu kateveinu beseifer
ge'ullah vishu'ah:

אָבִינוּ מַלְכֵּנוּ כָּתְבֵנוּ בְּסֵפֶר
גְּאֻלָּה וִישׁוּעָה:

Avinu malkeinu kateveinu beseifer
parnasah vechalkalah:

אָבִינוּ מַלְכֵּנוּ כָּתְבֵנוּ בְּסֵפֶר
פַּרְנָסָה וְכַלְכָּלָה:

Avinu malkeinu kateveinu beseifer

אָבִינוּ מַלְכֵּנוּ כָּתְבֵנוּ בְּסֵפֶר

zechuyyot:	זְכֻיּוֹת:
Avinu malkeinu kateveinu beseifer selichah umechilah:	אָבִינוּ מַלְכֵּנוּ כָּתְבֵנוּ בְּסֵפֶר סְלִיחָה וּמְחִילָה:
Avinu malkeinu hatzmach lanu yeshu'ah bekarov:	אָבִינוּ מַלְכֵּנוּ הַצְמַח לָנוּ יְשׁוּעָה בְּקָרוֹב:
Avinu malkeinu hareim keren yisra'el ammecha:	אָבִינוּ מַלְכֵּנוּ הָרֵם קֶרֶן יִשְׂרָאֵל עַמֶּךָ:
Avinu malkeinu hareim keren meshichecha:	אָבִינוּ מַלְכֵּנוּ הָרֵם קֶרֶן מְשִׁיחֶךָ:
Avinu malkeinu mallei yadeinu mibbirchotecha:	אָבִינוּ מַלְכֵּנוּ מַלֵּא יָדֵינוּ מִבִּרְכוֹתֶיךָ:
Avinu malkeinu mallei asameinu sava:	אָבִינוּ מַלְכֵּנוּ מַלֵּא אֲסָמֵינוּ שָׂבָע:
Avinu malkeinu shema koleinu chus veracheim aleinu:	אָבִינוּ מַלְכֵּנוּ שְׁמַע קוֹלֵנוּ חוּס וְרַחֵם עָלֵינוּ:
Avinu malkeinu kabbeil berachamim uveratzon et tefillatenu:	אָבִינוּ מַלְכֵּנוּ קַבֵּל בְּרַחֲמִים וּבְרָצוֹן אֶת תְּפִלָּתֵנוּ:
Avinu malkeinu petach sha'arei shamayim litfillateinu:	אָבִינוּ מַלְכֵּנוּ פְּתַח שַׁעֲרֵי שָׁמַיִם לִתְפִלָּתֵנוּ:
Avinu malkeinu zachor ki afar anachenu:	אָבִינוּ מַלְכֵּנוּ זָכוֹר כִּי עָפָר אֲנָחְנוּ:

Avinu malkeinu na al teshiveinu reikam millefanecha:

אָבִינוּ מַלְכֵּנוּ נָא אַל תְּשִׁיבֵנוּ רֵיקָם מִלְּפָנֶיךָ:

Avinu malkeinu tehei hasha'ah hazzot she'at rachamim ve'eit ratzon millefanecha:

אָבִינוּ מַלְכֵּנוּ תְּהֵא הַשָּׁעָה הַזֹּאת שְׁעַת רַחֲמִים וְעֵת רָצוֹן מִלְּפָנֶיךָ:

Avinu malkeinu chamol aleinu ve'al olaleinu vetappeinu:

אָבִינוּ מַלְכֵּנוּ חֲמוֹל עָלֵינוּ וְעַל עוֹלָלֵינוּ וְטַפֵּנוּ:

Avinu malkeinu aseih lema'an harugim al sheim kodshecha:

אָבִינוּ מַלְכֵּנוּ עֲשֵׂה לְמַעַן הֲרוּגִים עַל שֵׁם קָדְשֶׁךָ:

Avinu malkeinu aseih lema'an tevuchim al yichudecha:

אָבִינוּ מַלְכֵּנוּ עֲשֵׂה לְמַעַן טְבוּחִים עַל יִחוּדֶךָ:

Avinu malkeinu aseih lema'an ba'ei va'eish uvammayim al kiddush shemecha:

אָבִינוּ מַלְכֵּנוּ עֲשֵׂה לְמַעַן בָּאֵי בָאֵשׁ וּבַמַּיִם עַל קִדּוּשׁ שְׁמֶךָ:

Avinu malkeinu nekom nikmat dam avadecha hashafuch:

אָבִינוּ מַלְכֵּנוּ נְקוֹם נִקְמַת דַּם עֲבָדֶיךָ הַשָּׁפוּךְ:

Avinu malkeinu aseih lema'ancha im lo lema'aneinu:

אָבִינוּ מַלְכֵּנוּ עֲשֵׂה לְמַעַנְךָ אִם לֹא לְמַעֲנֵנוּ:

Avinu malkeinu aseih lema'ancha vehoshi'einu:

אָבִינוּ מַלְכֵּנוּ עֲשֵׂה לְמַעַנְךָ וְהוֹשִׁיעֵנוּ:

Avinu malkeinu aseih lema'an rachamecha harabbim:

אָבִינוּ מַלְכֵּנוּ עֲשֵׂה לְמַעַן רַחֲמֶיךָ הָרַבִּים:

Avinu malkeinu aseih lema'an

אָבִינוּ מַלְכֵּנוּ עֲשֵׂה לְמַעַן

shimcha haggadol haggibbor

vehannora shennikra aleinu:

שִׁמְךָ הַגָּדוֹל הַגִּבּוֹר

וְהַנּוֹרָא שֶׁנִּקְרָא עָלֵינוּ:

Avinu malkeinu chonneinu

va'aneinu ki ein banu ma'asim

aseih immanu tzedakah vachesed

vehoshi'einu:

אָבִינוּ מַלְכֵּנוּ חָנֵּנוּ

וַעֲנֵנוּ כִּי אֵין בָּנוּ מַעֲשִׂים

עֲשֵׂה עִמָּנוּ צְדָקָה וָחֶסֶד

וְהוֹשִׁיעֵנוּ:

Our Father, our King! we have sinned before You.

Our Father our King! we have no King except You.

Our Father, our King! deal with us [kindly] for the sake of Your Name.

Our Father, our King! renew for us a good year.

Our Father, our King! annul all harsh decrees concerning us.

Our Father, our King! annul the designs of those who hate us.

Our Father, our King! thwart the plans of our enemies.

Our Father, our King! rid us of every oppressor and adversary.

Our Father, our King! close the mouths of our adversaries and our accusers.

Our Father, our King! remove pestilence, sword, famine, captivity, destruction and [the burden of] iniquity from the members of Your covenant.

Our Father, our King! withhold the plague from Your inheritance.

Our Father, our King! forgive and pardon all our iniquities.

Our Father, our King! blot out and remove our transgressions and sins from before Your eyes.

Our Father ,our King !erase in Your abundant mercy all records of our liabilities.

Our Father, our King! bring us back in wholehearted repentance before You.

Our Father, our King! send complete healing to the sick among Your people.

Our Father, our King! tear up the evil [parts] of our sentence.

Our Father, our King! remember us favorably before You.

Our Father, our King! inscribe us in the Book of Good Life.

Our Father, our King! inscribe us in the Book of Redemption and Deliverance.

Our Father, our King! inscribe us in the Book of Maintenance and Sustenance.

Our Father, our King! inscribe us in the Book of Merits.

Our Father, our King! inscribe us in the Book of Pardon and Forgiveness.

Our Father, our King! cause deliverance to spring forth for us soon.

Our Father, our King! raise up the might of Israel Your people.

Our Father, our King! raise up the might of Your anointed.

Our Father, our King! fill our hands with Your blessings.

Our Father, our King! fill our storehouses with abundance.

Our Father, our King! hear our voice, spare us and have compassion upon us.

Our Father, our King! accept our prayer with compassion and favor.

Our Father, our King! open the gates of heaven to our prayer.

Our Father, our King! remember, that we are dust.

Our Father, our King! please do not turn us away empty-handed from You.

Our Father, our King! let this hour be an hour of compassion and a time of favor before You.

Our Father, our King! have compassion upon us, and upon our children and infants.

Our Father, our King! do it for the sake of those who were slain for Your Holy Name.

Our Father, our King! do it for the sake of those who were slaughtered for [proclaiming] Your Unity.

Our Father, our King! do it for the sake of those who went through fire and water for the sanctification of Your Name.

Our Father, our King! avenge the spilled blood of Your servants.

Our Father, our King! do it for Your sake if not for ours.

Our Father ,our King !do it for Your sake and deliver us.

Our Father, our King! do it for the sake of Your great mercy.

Our Father, our King! do it for the sake of Your great, mighty, and awesome Name which is proclaimed upon us.

Our Father, our King! favor us and answer us for we have no accomplishments; deal with us charitably and kindly and deliver us.

Confession Prayer

Viduy, the Confession Prayer, is one of the central prayers of *Yom Kippur*. As we stand before God in judgment, we openly acknowledge our sins before God and seek His forgiveness. Confession is an essential part of the repentance process, as it says in Numbers 5:7 "he shall confess the wrong that he has done."

When reciting *Viduy* we stand humbly, our bodies bowed, as we acknowledge and confess each sin. With every confession, we express deep regret and firmly resolve to turn away from these missteps, shedding the burdens of past transgressions and embarking on a path of spiritual purification and renewal.

Eloheinu veilohei avoteinu tavo	אֱלֹהֵינוּ וֵאלֹהֵי אֲבוֹתֵינוּ
lefanecha tefillateinu, ve'al	תָּבֹא לְפָנֶיךָ תְּפִלָּתֵנוּ, וְאַל־
tit'allam mittechinnateinu she'ein	תִּתְעַלַּם מִתְּחִנָּתֵנוּ שֶׁאֵין
anu azzei fanim ukeshei oref	אָנוּ עַזֵּי פָנִים וּקְשֵׁי עֹרֶף
lomar lefanecha adonai eloheinu	לוֹמַר לְפָנֶיךָ יְהֹוָה אֱלֹהֵינוּ
veilohei avoteinu tzaddikim	וֵאלֹהֵי אֲבוֹתֵינוּ צַדִּיקִים
anachnu velo chatanu aval	אֲנַחְנוּ וְלֹא חָטָאנוּ אֲבָל
anachnu va'avoteinu chatanu:	אֲנַחְנוּ וַאֲבוֹתֵינוּ חָטָאנוּ:

Ashamnu .Bagadnu .Gazalnu.	אָשַׁמְנוּ. בָּגַדְנוּ. גָּזַלְנוּ.
Dibbarnu dofi. He'evinu.	דִּבַּרְנוּ דֹפִי. הֶעֱוִינוּ.
Vehirsha'nu. zadnu. Chamasnu.	וְהִרְשַׁעְנוּ. זַדְנוּ. חָמַסְנוּ.
Tafalnu sheker. Ya'atznu ra.	טָפַלְנוּ שֶׁקֶר. יָעַצְנוּ רָע.
Kizzavnu. latznu. Maradnu.	כִּזַּבְנוּ. לַצְנוּ. מָרַדְנוּ.
Ni'atznu. Sararnu. Avinu. Pasha'nu.	נִאַצְנוּ. סָרַרְנוּ. עָוִינוּ. פָּשַׁעְנוּ.
Tzararnu. Kishinu oref. Rasha'nu.	צָרַרְנוּ. קִשִּׁינוּ עֹרֶף. רָשַׁעְנוּ.
Shichatnu. Ti'avnu. Ta'inu.	שִׁחַתְנוּ. תִּעַבְנוּ. תָּעִינוּ.
Ti'ta'enu:	תִּעְתָּעְנוּ:

Sarnu mimmitzvotecha	סַרְנוּ מִמִּצְוֹתֶיךָ
umimmishpatecha hattovim velo	וּמִמִּשְׁפָּטֶיךָ הַטּוֹבִים וְלֹא
shavah lanu. Ve'attah tzaddik al	שָׁוָה לָנוּ. וְאַתָּה צַדִּיק עַל
kol habba aleinu. Ki emet asita	כָּל הַבָּא עָלֵינוּ. כִּי אֱמֶת עָשִׂיתָ
va'anachnu hirsha'enu:	וַאֲנַחְנוּ הִרְשָׁעְנוּ:

El erech appayim attah. Uva'al	אֵל אֶרֶךְ־אַפַּיִם אַתָּה. וּבַעַל
harachamim nikreita. Vederech	הָרַחֲמִים נִקְרֵאתָ. וְדֶרֶךְ
teshuvah horeita: gedullat	תְּשׁוּבָה הוֹרֵיתָ: גְּדֻלַּת
rachamecha vachasadecha.	רַחֲמֶיךָ וַחֲסָדֶיךָ.
Tizkor hayyom uvechol yom	תִּזְכֹּר הַיּוֹם וּבְכָל־יוֹם
lezera yedidecha: teifen eileinu	לְזֶרַע יְדִידֶיךָ: תֵּפֶן אֵלֵינוּ
berachamim. Ki attah hu ba'al	בְּרַחֲמִים. כִּי אַתָּה הוּא בַּעַל
harachamim: betachanun uvitfillah	הָרַחֲמִים: בְּתַחֲנוּן וּבִתְפִלָּה

panecha nekaddeim. Kehoda'ta   פָּנֶיךָ נְקַדֵּם. כְּהוֹדַעְתָּ

le'anav mikkedem: mecharon   לֶעָנָיו מִקֶּדֶם: מֵחֲרוֹן

appecha shuv. Kemo betorat'cha   אַפְּךָ שׁוּב. כְּמוֹ בְּתוֹרָתְךָ

katuv: uvetzeil kenafecha   כָּתוּב: וּבְצֵל כְּנָפֶיךָ

necheseh venitlonan. Keyom   נֶחֱסֶה וְנִתְלוֹנָן. כְּיוֹם

vayeired adonai be'anan: ta'avor   וַיֵּרֶד יְהֹוָה בֶּעָנָן: תַּעֲבֹר

al pesha vetimcheh asham.   עַל־פֶּשַׁע וְתִמְחֶה אָשָׁם.

Keyom vaayyityatzeiv immo sham: כְּיוֹם וַיִּתְיַצֵּב עִמּוֹ שָׁם:

ta'azin shav'ateinu vetakshiv   תַּאֲזִין שַׁוְעָתֵנוּ וְתַקְשִׁיב מֶנּוּ

menu ma'amar. Keyom vayyikra   מַאֲמָר. כְּיוֹם וַיִּקְרָא בְשֵׁם

vesheim adonai, vesham ne'emar: יְהֹוָה, וְשָׁם נֶאֱמַר:

Vayya'avor adonai al panav   וַיַּעֲבֹר יְהֹוָה עַל פָּנָיו

vayyikra: וַיִּקְרָא:

Adonai adonai el rachum   יְהֹוָה יְהֹוָה אֵל רַחוּם

vechannun erech appayim verav   וְחַנּוּן אֶרֶךְ אַפַּיִם וְרַב־

chesed ve'emet: notzeir chesed   חֶסֶד וֶאֱמֶת: נֹצֵר חֶסֶד

la'alafim nosei avon vafesha   לָאֲלָפִים נֹשֵׂא עָוֹן וָפֶשַׁע

vechatta'ah venakkeh: וְחַטָּאָה וְנַקֵּה:

Vesalachta la'avoneinu   וְסָלַחְתָּ לַעֲוֹנֵנוּ

ulechattateinu unechaltanu: וּלְחַטָּאתֵנוּ וּנְחַלְתָּנוּ:

selach lanu avinu ki chatanu.   סְלַח־לָנוּ אָבִינוּ כִּי־חָטָאנוּ.

Mechal lanu malkeinu ki fasha'nu: מְחַל־לָנוּ מַלְכֵּנוּ כִּי־פָשָׁעְנוּ:

ki attah adonai tov vesallach verav   כִּי־אַתָּה אֲדֹנָי טוֹב וְסַלָּח וְרַב־

chesed lechol kore'echa: חֶסֶד לְכָל־קוֹרְאֶיךָ:

Our God and God of our fathers, let our prayer come before you and do not ignore our supplication. For we are not so brazen-faced and stiff-necked to say to you, Lord, our God, and God of our fathers, We are righteous and have not sinned. But, indeed, we and our fathers have sinned.

We have trespassed against God and man, and we are devastated by our guilt; We have betrayed God and man, we have been ungrateful for the good done to us; We have stolen; We have slandered. We have caused others to sin; We have caused others to commit sins for which they are called wicked; We have sinned with malicious intent; We have forcibly taken other's possessions even though we paid for them; We have added falsehood upon falsehood; we have joined with evil individuals or groups. We have given harmful advice; We have deceived; We have mocked; We have rebelled against God and His Bible; We have caused God to be angry with us; We have turned away from God's Bible; We have sinned deliberately; We have been negligent in our performance of the commandments; We have caused our friends grief; We have been stiff-necked, refusing to admit that the cause of our suffering is our own sins. We have committed sins for which we are called evil, such as raising a hand to hit someone. We have committed sins which are the result of moral corruption; We have committed sins which the Bible refers to as abominations; We have gone astray; We have led others astray.

We have turned away from Your commandments and from Your good laws, and we have gained nothing from it. And You are the Righteous One in all punishment that has come upon us; for You have acted truthfully and we have acted wickedly.

You are Almighty, slow to anger, Lord of Mercy You are called, and the way of repentance You have taught us. The greatness of Your mercy and kindness, remember this day and every day for the descendants of Your loved ones. Turn to us with compassion for You are the Lord of Mercy. With supplication and prayer we approach Your Presence, as You made known to Moses, the modest one of old. From Your fierce anger turn, as it is written in Your Bible: In the shadow of Your wings, may we be sheltered and lodged, as on the day of which it is said: When the Lord descended in the cloud. Remove our transgression, and blot out our iniquity, as on the day of which it is said: And He stood with him there. Give ear to our cry and listen to our speech, as on the day of which it is said: And He proclaimed in the Name, Lord, and there it is said:

And the Lord passed before Moses and proclaimed:

Lord, Lord, Almighty, Merciful, Gracious, Slow to Anger, and Abundant in Kindness and Truth. Keeper of kindness for thousands of generations, Endurer of iniquity and transgression, and sin, and Acquitter of those who repent.

And pardon our iniquity and our sin, and take us for Your inheritance. Pardon us, our Father, for we have sinned, forgive us, our King, for we have transgressed. For You, my Master, are good and forgiving, and abounding in kindness to all who call upon You.

Notes

Sukkot (Feast of Tabernacles)

Sukkot, the Feast of Tabernacles, is a seven-day holi-day during which we leave our permanent homes and dwell in temporary huts called *sukkot*. This practice commemorates the huts the people of Israel lived in while traveling through the desert and the divine clouds of glory that accompanied and protected them on their journey.

Inviting "Guests"

Each day of the *Sukkot* festival, we symbolically invite one of seven special guests into our *sukkot*. These guests, the "founding fathers" of the people of Israel, are Abraham, Isaac, Jacob, Moses, Aaron, Joseph, and David. Below is the text we recite to invite them to join us in our temporary homes.

Azamin lis'udati ushepizin ila'in	אֲזַמִין לִסְעוּדָתִי אוּשְׁפִיזִין עִילָאִין
avraham yitzchak ya'akov mosheh	אַבְרָהָם יִצְחָק יַעֲקב משֶׁה
aharon yosef vedavid:	אַהֲרן יוֹסֵף וְדָוִד:

On the first day say:	בַּיּוֹם הָרִאשׁוֹן אוֹמֵר:
bematei minach avraham ushepizi	בְּמָטֵי מִינָךְ אַבְרָהָם אוּשְׁפִיזִי
ila'i deyatvei immi ve'immach kol	עִילָאִי דְיַתְבֵי עִמִי וְעִמָךְ כָּל
ushepizei ila'i yitzchak ya'akov	אוּשְׁפִיזֵי עִילָאִי יִצְחָק יַעֲקב
mosheh aharon yosef vedavid:	משֶׁה אַהֲרן יוֹסֵף וְדָוִד:

On the second day say:	בַּיּוֹם הַשֵׁנִי אוֹמֵר:
bematei minach yitzchak ushepizi	בְּמָטֵי מִינָךְ יִצְחָק אוּשְׁפִיזִי

ila'i deyatvei immi ve'immach kol
ushepizei ila'i avraham ya'akov
mosheh aharon yosef vedavid:

עִילָאִי דְּיַתְבֵי עִמִּי וְעִמָּךְ כָּל
אוּשְׁפִּיזֵי עִילָאִי אַבְרָהָם יַעֲקֹב
מֹשֶׁה אַהֲרֹן יוֹסֵף וְדָוִד:

On the third day say:
bematei minach ya'akov ushepizi
ila'i deyatvei immi ve'immach kol
ushepizei ila'i avraham yitzchak
mosheh aharon yosef vedavid:

בְּיוֹם הַשְּׁלִישִׁי אוֹמֵר:
בְּמָטֵי מִינָךְ יַעֲקֹב אוּשְׁפִּיזֵי
עִילָאִי דְּיַתְבֵי עִמִּי וְעִמָּךְ כָּל
אוּשְׁפִּיזֵי עִילָאִי אַבְרָהָם יִצְחָק
מֹשֶׁה אַהֲרֹן יוֹסֵף וְדָוִד:

On the fourth day say:
bematei minach mosheh ushepizi
ila'i deyatvei immi ve'immach kol
ushepizei ila'i avraham yitzchak
ya'akov aharon yosef vedavid:

בְּיוֹם הָרְבִיעִי אוֹמֵר:
בְּמָטֵי מִינָךְ מֹשֶׁה אוּשְׁפִּיזֵי
עִילָאִי דְּיַתְבֵי עִמִּי וְעִמָּךְ כָּל
אוּשְׁפִּיזֵי עִילָאִי אַבְרָהָם יִצְחָק
יַעֲקֹב אַהֲרֹן יוֹסֵף וְדָוִד:

On the fifth day say:
bematei minach aharon ushepizi
ila'i deyatvei immi ve'immach kol
ushepizei ila'i avraham yitzchak
ya'akov mosheh yosef vedavid:

בְּיוֹם הַחֲמִישִׁי אוֹמֵר:
בְּמָטֵי מִינָךְ אַהֲרֹן אוּשְׁפִּיזֵי
עִילָאִי דְּיַתְבֵי עִמִּי וְעִמָּךְ כָּל
אוּשְׁפִּיזֵי עִילָאִי אַבְרָהָם יִצְחָק
יַעֲקֹב מֹשֶׁה יוֹסֵף וְדָוִד:

On the sixth day say:
bematei minach yosef ushepizi
ila'i deyatvei immi ve'immach kol
ushepizei ila'i avraham yitzchak
ya'akov mosheh aharon vedavid:

בְּיוֹם הַשִּׁשִּׁי אוֹמֵר:
בְּמָטֵי מִינָךְ יוֹסֵף אוּשְׁפִּיזֵי
עִילָאִי דְּיַתְבֵי עִמִּי וְעִמָּךְ כָּל
אוּשְׁפִּיזֵי עִילָאִי אַבְרָהָם יִצְחָק
יַעֲקֹב מֹשֶׁה אַהֲרֹן וְדָוִד:

On the seventh day say:
bematei minach david ushepizi
ila'i deyatvei immi ve'immach kol
ushepizei ila'i avraham yitzchak
ya'akov mosheh aharon veyosef:

בְּיוֹם הַשְּׁבִיעִי אוֹמֵר:
בְּמָטֵי מִינָךְ דָּוִד אוּשְׁפִּיזֵי
עִילָאִי דְּיַתְבֵי עִמִּי וְעִמָּךְ כָּל
אוּשְׁפִּיזֵי עִילָאִי אַבְרָהָם יִצְחָק
יַעֲקֹב מֹשֶׁה אַהֲרֹן וְיוֹסֵף:

I am inviting to my meal the lofty guests, Abraham, Isaac, Jacob, Moses, Aaron, Joseph and David.

On the first day, one says:
If you please, Abraham, my lofty guest, may all of the exalted guests - Isaac, Jacob, Moses, Aaron, Joseph and David - sit with me and you.

On the second day, one says:
If you please, Isaac, my lofty guest, let all of the exalted guests - Abraham, Jacob, Moses, Aaron, Joseph and David - sit with me and with you.

On the third day, one says:
If you please, Jacob, my lofty guest, may all of the exalted guests - Abraham, Isaac, Moses, Aaron, Joseph and David - sit with me and you.

On the fourth day, one says:
If you please, Moses, my lofty guest, may all of the exalted guests - Abraham, Isaac, Jacob, Aaron, Joseph and David - sit with me and you.

On the fifth day, one says:
If you please, Aaron, my lofty guest, may all of the exalted guests - Abraham, Isaac, Jacob, Moses, Joseph and David - sit with me and you.

On the sixth day, one says:
If you please, Joseph, my lofty guest, may all of the exalted guests - Abraham, Isaac, Jacob, Moses, Aaron, and David - sit with me and you.

On the seventh day, one says:

*If you please, David, my lofty guest, may all of the exalted guests -
Abraham, Isaac, Jacob, Moses, Aaron and Joseph - sit with me and
you.*

Salvation Prayer

Hoshanot, derived from the words "*hosha na*," meaning
"bring us salvation, please," are special prayers recited
each day of the *Sukkot* festival while holding the four spe-
cies. During *Sukkot*, we pray for rain, hoping that God will
provide ample rainfall throughout the year and particularly
during Israel's winter rainy season. This period also marks
the end of the time granted for forgiveness. For one final
week, we ask God to cleanse us from our sins and save us
from our adversaries.

Included here are the opening lines and the concluding
paragraph of the *Hoshanot* prayers.

Hosha na lema'ancha eloheinu   הוֹשַׁע נָא לְמַעַנְךָ אֱלֹהֵינוּ
hosha na: הוֹשַׁע נָא:

Hosha na lema'ancha bore'enu   הוֹשַׁע נָא לְמַעַנְךָ בּוֹרְאֵנוּ
hosha na: הוֹשַׁע נָא:

Hosha na lema'ancha go'alenu   הוֹשַׁע נָא לְמַעַנְךָ גּוֹאֲלֵנוּ
hosha na: הוֹשַׁע נָא:

Hosha na lema'ancha doreshenu   הוֹשַׁע נָא לְמַעַנְךָ דּוֹרְשֵׁנוּ
hosha na: הוֹשַׁע נָא:

Please save, for Your sake, our God, please save!

Please save ,for Your sake, our Creator, please save!

Please save, for Your sake, our Redeemer, please save!

Please save, for Your sake, our Attender, please save!

Hoshi'ah et ammecha uvareich et
nachalatecha ure'eim venasse'eim
ad ha'olam: veyihyu devarai eilleh
asher hitchannanti lifnei adonai
kerovim el adonai eloheinu
yomam vala'yelah la'asot mishpat
avdo umishpat ammo yisra'el
devar yom beyomo: lema'an da'at
kol ammei ha'aretz ki adonai hu
ha'elohim ein od:

הוֹשִׁיעָה אֶת עַמֶּךָ וּבָרֵךְ אֶת
נַחֲלָתֶךָ וּרְעֵם וְנַשְּׂאֵם
עַד הָעוֹלָם: וְיִהְיוּ דְבָרַי אֵלֶּה
אֲשֶׁר הִתְחַנַּנְתִּי לִפְנֵי יְיָ
קְרוֹבִים אֶל יְיָ אֱלֹהֵינוּ
יוֹמָם וָלַיְלָה לַעֲשׂוֹת מִשְׁפַּט
עַבְדּוֹ וּמִשְׁפַּט עַמּוֹ יִשְׂרָאֵל
דְּבַר יוֹם בְּיוֹמוֹ: לְמַעַן דַּעַת
כָּל עַמֵּי הָאָרֶץ כִּי יְיָ הוּא
הָאֱלֹהִים אֵין עוֹד:

*Deliver and bless Your people; tend them and sustain them forever
(Psalms 28:9). And may these words of mine, which I have offered
in supplication before the Lord, be close to the Lord our God day
and night, that He may provide for His servant and for His people
Israel, according to each day's needs. In order that all the peoples
of the earth may know that the Lord alone is God, there is no other
(I Kings 8:59-60).*

Prayer to say when leaving the Sukkah

When we leave the *sukkah* for the last time and move back
into our permanent homes, we say the following prayer.
According to the sages, in the time of the Messiah, God
will prepare a *sukkah* for the righteous from the skin of
the Leviathan, and that whoever fulfills the command to
dwell in the *sukkah* properly will merit to sit in this special

יְהִי רָצוֹן מִלְּפָנֶיךָ ה׳   לִוְיָתָן.

Yehi ratzon millefanecha adonai

אֱלֹהֵינוּ וֵאלֹהֵי אֲבוֹתֵינוּ
כְּשֵׁם שֶׁקִּיַּמְתִּי וְיָשַׁבְתִּי
בְּסֻכָּה זוֹ כֵּן אֶזְכֶּה לְשָׁנָה
הַבָּאָה לֵישֵׁב בְּסֻכָּה שֶׁל

eloheinu veilohei avoteinu kesheim shekiyyamti veyashavti besukkah zu kein ezkeh leshanah habba'ah leishev besukkah shel livyatan.

May it be Your will in front of You, Lord, our God and God of our fathers - in the same way that I have fulfilled [the commandment] and dwelt in this sukkah, so may I merit next year to dwell in the sukkah (made from the skin) of the Leviathan.

Notes

____

____

____

____

____

Chanukah (Hanukkah)

CHANUKAH IS AN eight-day holiday that celebrates the victory of the Jews over their Syrian-Greek oppressors, the rededication of the Temple following that victory, and the miracle in which a small flask of oil, enough to last one night, burned in Temple menorah for eight straight days. We celebrate the holiday by lighting candles on each of the eight Chanukah nights.

We Thank You for the Miracles

The following words of thanks are added to the silent *Amida* prayer and the Grace After Meals on Chanukah. We thank God for the salvation and miracles He performed for our forefathers during the time of Chanukah.

Al hannissim ve'al happurkan	עַל הַנִּסִּים וְעַל הַפֻּרְקָן
ve'al haggevurot ve'al hatteshu'ot	וְעַל הַגְּבוּרוֹת וְעַל הַתְּשׁוּעוֹת
ve'al hammilchamot she'asita	וְעַל הַמִּלְחָמוֹת שֶׁעָשִׂיתָ
la'avoteinu bayyamim haheim	לַאֲבוֹתֵינוּ בַּיָּמִים הָהֵם
bazzeman hazzeh:	בַּזְּמַן הַזֶּה:
Bimei mattityahu ben yochanan	בִּימֵי מַתִּתְיָהוּ בֶּן יוֹחָנָן
kohein gadol chashmona'i	כֹּהֵן גָּדוֹל חַשְׁמוֹנָאִי
uvanav keshe'amedah	וּבָנָיו כְּשֶׁעָמְדָה
malchut yavan haresha'ah al-	מַלְכוּת יָוָן הָרְשָׁעָה עַל־
ammecha yisra'el lehashkicham	עַמְּךָ יִשְׂרָאֵל לְהַשְׁכִּיחָם
toratecha uleha'aviram	תּוֹרָתֶךָ וּלְהַעֲבִירָם
mechukkei retzonecha, ve'attah	מֵחֻקֵּי רְצוֹנֶךָ, וְאַתָּה
berachamecha harabbim amadta	בְּרַחֲמֶיךָ הָרַבִּים עָמַדְתָּ

lahem be'eit tzaratam ravta et-	לָהֶם בְּעֵת צָרָתָם רַבְתָּ אֶת־
rivam danta et-dinam nakamta	רִיבָם דַּנְתָּ אֶת־דִּינָם נָקַמְתָּ
et-nikmatam masarta gibborim	אֶת־נִקְמָתָם מָסַרְתָּ גִבּוֹרִים
beyad challashim verabbim	בְּיַד חַלָּשִׁים וְרַבִּים
beyad me'attim utemei'im	בְּיַד מְעַטִּים וּטְמֵאִים
beyad tehorim uresha'im beyad	בְּיַד טְהוֹרִים וּרְשָׁעִים בְּיַד
tzaddikim vezeidim beyad osekei	צַדִּיקִים וְזֵדִים בְּיַד עוֹסְקֵי
toratecha, ulecha asita sheim	תוֹרָתֶךָ וּלְךָ עָשִׂיתָ שֵׁם
gadol vekadosh be'olamecha	גָּדוֹל וְקָדוֹשׁ בְּעוֹלָמֶךָ
ule'ammecha yisra'el asita	וּלְעַמְּךָ יִשְׂרָאֵל עָשִׂיתָ
teshu'ah gedolah ufurkan	תְּשׁוּעָה גְדוֹלָה וּפֻרְקָן
kehayyom hazzeh ve'achar-kein	כְּהַיּוֹם הַזֶּה וְאַחַר־כֵּן
ba'u vanecha lidvir beitecha	בָּאוּ בָנֶיךָ לִדְבִיר בֵּיתֶךָ
ufinnu et-heichalecha vetiharu	וּפִנּוּ אֶת־הֵיכָלֶךָ וְטִהֲרוּ
et-mikdashecha vehidliku neirot	אֶת־מִקְדָּשֶׁךָ וְהִדְלִיקוּ נֵרוֹת
bechatzrot kodshecha vekave'u	בְּחַצְרוֹת קָדְשֶׁךָ וְקָבְעוּ
shemonat yemei chanukkah	שְׁמוֹנַת יְמֵי חֲנֻכָּה
eillu lehodot ulehallel leshimcha	אֵלּוּ לְהוֹדוֹת וּלְהַלֵּל לְשִׁמְךָ
haggadol.	הַגָּדוֹל.

[We thank You] for the miracles, for the redemption, for the mighty deeds, for the deliverances and for the wars that You performed for our fathers in those days at this season.

In the days of Mattathias, son of Johanan the High Priest, the Hasmonean and his sons, when the evil Greek kingdom rose up against Your people Israel to make them forget Your Torah and to turn them away from the statutes of Your will— You, in Your abundant mercy, stood by them in their time of distress, You defended their cause, You judged their grievances, You avenged them. You delivered the mighty into the hands of the weak, many into the hands of the few, defiled people into the hands of the undefiled, the wicked into the hands of the righteous, and insolent [sinners] into the hands of diligent students of Your Torah. And You made Yourself a great and sanctified name in Your world. And for Your people, Israel, You performed a great deliverance and redemption unto this very day. Afterwards, Your sons entered the Holy of Holies of Your Abode, cleaned Your Temple, purified Your Sanctuary, and kindled lights in the Courtyards of Your Sanctuary, and designated these eight days of Chanukah to thank and praise Your great Name.

Psalm 30

It is customary to recite Psalm 30, a song for the dedication of the Temple, at the end of the morning prayers on each of the eight days of Chanukah, to celebrate the rededication of the Temple on Chanukah. The psalm also expresses David's gratitude to the Almighty for sparing him from his enemies, for healing him and for delivering him from the grave, a gratitude shared by the Maccabees, who miraculously defeated the vaunted Greek army to liberate the people of Israel.

Mizmor shir-chanukkat habbayit	מִזְמוֹר שִׁיר־חֲנֻכַּת הַבַּיִת
ledavid. Aromimcha adonai ki	לְדָוִד: אֲרוֹמִמְךָ יְהֹוָה כִּי
dillitani velo-simmachta oyevai	דִלִּיתָנִי וְלֹא־שִׂמַּחְתָּ אֹיְבַי
li. Adonai elohai shivva'ti eilecha	לִי: יְהֹוָה אֱלֹהָי שִׁוַּעְתִּי אֵלֶיךָ
vattirpa'eini. Adonai he'elita min-	וַתִּרְפָּאֵנִי: יְהֹוָה הֶעֱלִיתָ מִן־
she'ol nafshi chiyyitani miyyordi-	שְׁאוֹל נַפְשִׁי חִיִּיתַנִי מִיָּרְדִי־
vor. Zammeru ladonai chasidav	בוֹר: זַמְּרוּ לַיהֹוָה חֲסִידָיו
vehodu lezeicher kodsho. Ki rega	וְהוֹדוּ לְזֵכֶר קָדְשׁוֹ: כִּי
be'appo chayyim birtzono ba'erev	רֶגַע בְּאַפּוֹ חַיִּים בִּרְצוֹנוֹ
yalin bechi velabboker rinnah.	בָּעֶרֶב יָלִין בֶּכִי וְלַבֹּקֶר
Va'ani amarti veshalvi bal-emmot	רִנָּה: וַאֲנִי אָמַרְתִּי בְשַׁלְוִי
le'olam. Adonai	בַּל־אֶמּוֹט לְעוֹלָם: יְהֹוָה

birtzonecha he'emadtah leharri- בִּרְצוֹנְךָ הֶעֱמַדְתָּה לְהַרְרִי־
oz histarta fanecha hayiti nivhal. עֹז הִסְתַּרְתָּ פָנֶיךָ הָיִיתִי נִבְהָל:
Eilecha adonai ekra ve'el-adonai אֵלֶיךָ יְהוָה אֶקְרָא וְאֶל־אֲדֹנָי
etchannan. Mah-betza bedami אֶתְחַנָּן: מַה־בֶּצַע בְּדָמִי
beridti el-shachat hayodecha בְּרִדְתִּי אֶל־שָׁחַת הֲיוֹדְךָ
afar hayaggid amittecha. עָפָר הֲיַגִּיד אֲמִתֶּךָ:
Shema-adonai vechonneini שְׁמַע־יְהוָה וְחָנֵּנִי
adonai heyeih-ozeir li. Hafachta יְהוָה הֱיֵה־עֹזֵר לִי: הָפַכְתָּ
mispedi lemachol li pittachta מִסְפְּדִי לְמָחוֹל לִי פִּתַּחְתָּ
sakki vatte'azzereini simchah. שַׂקִּי וַתְּאַזְּרֵנִי שִׂמְחָה:
Lema'an yezammercha chavod לְמַעַן יְזַמֶּרְךָ כָבוֹד
velo yiddom adonai elohai le'olam וְלֹא יִדֹּם יְהוָה אֱלֹהַי לְעוֹלָם
odekka. אוֹדֶךָ:

A psalm of David. A song for the dedication of the House. I extol You, O Lord, for You have lifted me up, and not let my enemies rejoice over me. O Lord, my God, I cried out to You, and You healed me. O Lord, You brought me up from Sheol, preserved me from going down into the Pit. O you faithful of the Lord, sing to Him, and praise His holy name. For He is angry but a moment, and when He is pleased there is life. One may lie down weeping at nightfall; but at dawn there are shouts of joy. When I was untroubled, I thought, "I shall never be shaken," for You, O Lord, when You were pleased, made [me] firm as a mighty mountain. When You hid Your face, I was terrified. I called to You, O Lord; to my Lord I made appeal, "What is to be gained from my death, from my descent into the Pit? Can dust praise You? Can it declare Your faithfulness? Hear, O Lord, and have mercy on me; O Lord, be my help!" You turned my lament into dancing, you undid my sackcloth and girded me with joy, that [my] whole being might sing hymns to You endlessly; O Lord my God, I will praise You forever.

Mighty Stronghold of My Salvation

This poem is sung every night of Chanukah after lighting the Chanukah candles. It recounts how God has saved the people of Israel from many different oppressors and attempts at annihilation throughout history. It is a song of spiritual resistance, expressing Israel's confidence that it will ultimately triumph over the many antisemites throughout the generations who arrogantly and foolishly try to destroy God's people. It ends by calling on God to bring the final redemption. May we see that day soon!.

Ma'oz tzur yeshu'ati lecha na'eh
leshabbeach tikkon beit tefillati
vesham todah nezabbei'ach
le'eit tachin matbei'ach mitzar
hammenabbei'ach az egmor
beshir mizmor chanukkat
hammizbei'ach.

מָעוֹז צוּר יְשׁוּעָתִי לְךָ נָאֶה
לְשַׁבֵּחַ תִּכּוֹן בֵּית תְּפִלָּתִי
וְשָׁם תּוֹדָה נְזַבֵּחַ
לְעֵת תָּכִין מַטְבֵּחַ מִצָּר
הַמְנַבֵּחַ אָז אֶגְמֹר
בְּשִׁיר מִזְמוֹר חֲנֻכַּת
הַמִּזְבֵּחַ.

Ra'ot save'ah nafshi beyagon
kochi kilah chayyai meireru
vekoshi beshi'bud malchut eglah
uveyado haggedolah hotzi et
hassegullah cheil par'oh vechol
zar'o yaredu ke'even bimtzulah.

רָעוֹת שָׂבְעָה נַפְשִׁי בְּיָגוֹן
כֹּחִי כִּלָּה חַיַּי מֵרְרוּ
בְּקֹשִׁי בְּשִׁעְבּוּד מַלְכוּת עֶגְלָה
וּבְיָדוֹ הַגְּדוֹלָה הוֹצִיא אֶת
הַסְּגֻלָּה חֵיל פַּרְעֹה וְכָל
זַרְעוֹ יָרְדוּ כְּאֶבֶן בִּמְצוּלָה.

Devir kodsho hevi'ani vegam
sham lo shakat'ti uva nogeis
vehiglani ki zarim avad'ti veyein
ra'al masachti kim'at she'avarti
keitz bavel zerubbavel lekeitz
shiv'im nosha'ti.

דְּבִיר קָדְשׁוֹ הֱבִיאַנִי וְגַם
שָׁם לֹא שָׁקַטְתִּי וּבָא נוֹגֵשׂ
וְהִגְלַנִי כִּי זָרִים עָבַדְתִּי וְיֵין
רַעַל מָסַכְתִּי כִּמְעַט שֶׁעָבַרְתִּי
קֵץ בָּבֶל זְרֻבָּבֶל לְקֵץ
שִׁבְעִים נוֹשַׁעְתִּי.

Kerot komat berosh bikkeish   כָּרוֹת קוֹמַת בְּרוֹשׁ בִּקֵּשׁ

agagi ben hammedata venihyatah   אֲגָגִי בֶּן הַמְּדָתָא וְנִהְיָתָה

lo lefach ulemokeish vega'avato   לוֹ לְפַח וּלְמוֹקֵשׁ וְגַאֲוָתוֹ

nishbatah rosh yemini nisseita   נִשְׁבָּתָה רֹאשׁ יְמִינִי נִשֵּׂאתָ

ve'oyeiv shemo machita rov   וְאוֹיֵב שְׁמוֹ מָחִיתָ רֹב בָּנָיו

banav vekinyanav al ha'eitz talita.   וְקִנְיָנָיו עַל הָעֵץ תָּלִיתָ.

Yevanim nikbetzu alai azai   יְוָנִים נִקְבְּצוּ עָלַי אֲזַי

bimei chashmannim ufaretzu   בִּימֵי חַשְׁמַנִּים וּפָרְצוּ

chomot migdalai vetimme'u   חוֹמוֹת מִגְדָּלַי וְטִמְּאוּ

kol hashemanim uminnotar   כָּל הַשְּׁמָנִים וּמִנּוֹתַר

kankannim na'asah neis   קַנְקַנִּים נַעֲשָׂה נֵס

lashoshannim benei vinah yemei   לַשּׁוֹשַׁנִּים בְּנֵי בִינָה יְמֵי

shemonah kave'u shir urenanim.   שְׁמוֹנָה קָבְעוּ שִׁיר וּרְנָנִים.

Chasof zeroa' kodshecha vekareiv   חֲשׂוֹף זְרוֹעַ קָדְשֶׁךָ וְקָרֵב

keitz hayyeshu'ah nekom nikmat   קֵץ הַיְשׁוּעָה נְקֹם נִקְמַת

avadecha mei'ummah haresha'ah   עֲבָדֶיךָ מֵאֻמָּה הָרְשָׁעָה

ki arechah hasha'ah ve'ein keitz   כִּי אָרְכָה הַשָּׁעָה וְאֵין קֵץ

limei hara'ah decheih admon   לִימֵי הָרָעָה דְּחֵה אַדְמוֹן

betzeil tzalmon hakeim lanu ro'im   בְּצֵל צַלְמוֹן הָקֵם לָנוּ רוֹעִים

shiv'ah.   שִׁבְעָה.

O mighty rock of my salvation, to praise You is a delight. Restore my House of Prayer and there we will bring a thanksgiving offering. When You will have prepared the slaughter for the blaspheming foe, Then I shall complete with a song of hymn the dedication of the Altar.

My soul had been sated with troubles, my strength has been consumed with grief. They had embittered my life with hardship, with the calf-like kingdom's bondage. But with His great power, He brought forth the treasured ones, Pharaoh's army and all his offspring went down like a stone into the deep.

To the abode of His holiness He brought me. But there, too, I had no rest And an oppressor came and exiled me. For I had served aliens, And had drunk benumbing wine. Scarcely had I departed When at Babylon's end Zerubabel came. At the end of seventy years I was saved.

To sever the towering cypress sought the Aggagite, son of Hammedatha, But it became a snare and a stumbling block to him and his arrogance was stilled. The head of the Benjaminite You lifted and the enemy, his name You obliterated His numerous progeny - his possessions - on the gallows You hanged.

Greeks gathered against me then in Hasmonean days. They breached the walls of my towers and they defiled all the oils; And from the one remnant of the flasks a miracle was wrought for the roses. Men of insight - eight days established for song and jubilation

Bare Your holy arm and hasten the End for salvation - Avenge the vengeance of Your servants' blood from the wicked nation. For the triumph is too long delayed for us, and there is no end to days of evil, Repel the Red One in the nethermost shadow and establish for us the seven shepherds.

Notes

____

____

____

Tu B'Shevat (New Year for Trees)

THE 15TH DAY of the Hebrew month of Shevat, Tu B'Shevat, is known as the New Year for Trees. This special day marks the start of the season when the trees of Israel awaken from their winter slumber and begin a new cycle of fruit-bearing. It is customary to celebrate Tu B'Shevat by enjoying the fruits of the land of Israel.

Tu B'Shevat is a celebration of renewal. In Jewish literature, people are often compared to trees. Just as trees rejuvenate on this day, we are also encouraged to focus on self-renewal and strive to become the best versions of ourselves. Furthermore, the people of Israel are also likened to a tree. The prophet Isaiah portrays them as a winter tree, stripped of its leaves and seemingly lifeless, with only a bare stump remaining (Isaiah 6:13), a reference to the people of Israel in exile. Just as a tree springs back to life, so too will the people of Israel be reborn and experience redemption, making Tu B'Shevat, when trees begin to show signs of life, an auspicious day to pray for the redemption of Israel.

The following Tu B'Shevat prayer was adapted by Rabbi David Seidenberg:

Anna ha'el, ha'oseh vehayyotzeir	אָנָּא הָאֵל, הָעוֹשֶׂה וְהַיּוֹצֵר
vehabborei vehamma'atzil olamot	וְהַבּוֹרֵא וְהַמַּאֲצִיל עוֹלָמוֹת
elyonim ve'ilanin udesha'im	עֶלְיוֹנִים וְאִילָנִין וּדְשָׁאִים
min ha'adamah hitzmachta	מִן הָאֲדָמָה הִצְמַחְתָּ
bekomatam uvetzivyonam shel	בְּקוֹמָתָם וּבְצִבְיוֹנָם
ma'lah. Vezeh hayarei'ach	שֶׁל מַעְלָה. וְזֶה הַיָרֵחַ

techilat ma'asecha lehachnitam	תְּחִלַּת מַעֲשֶׂיךָ לְהַחְנִיטָם
ulechaddesham ki chein yimle'u	וּלְחַדְּשָׁם כִּי כֵן יִמְלְאוּ
yemei hachanutim lefeirot	יְמֵי הַחֲנוּטִים לְפֵירוֹת
ha'ilan ha'elyon, eitz hachayyim	הָאִילָן הָעֶלְיוֹן, עֵץ הַחַיִּים
asher betoch haggan. Vihi	אֲשֶׁר בְּתוֹךְ הַגָּן. וִיהִי
ratzon milfanecha adonai	רָצוֹן מִלְּפָנֶיךָ יְיָ
eloheinu veilohei avoteinu,	אֱלֹהֵינוּ וֵאלֹהֵי אֲבוֹתֵינוּ,
shebbechoach segullat achilat	שֶׁבְּכֹחַ סְגֻלַּת אֲכִילַת
happeirot shennochal unevareich	הַפֵּירוֹת שֶׁנֹּאכַל וּנְבָרֵךְ
aleihen attah va'asher nehaneh	עֲלֵיהֶן עַתָּה וַאֲשֶׁר נֶהֱנֶה
besod sharesheihen yit'oreir	בְּסוֹד שָׁרְשֵׁיהֶן יִתְעוֹרֵר
lehashpia' aleihen shefa	לְהַשְׁפִּיעַ עֲלֵיהֶן שֶׁפַע
ratzon berachah unedavah,	רָצוֹן בְּרָכָה וּנְדָבָה,
lehagdilam ulehatzmicham,	לְהַגְדִּילָם וּלְהַצְמִיחָם,
letovah velivrachah lechayyim	לְטוֹבָה וְלִבְרָכָה לְחַיִּים
tovim uleshalom. Veyashuv	טוֹבִים וּלְשָׁלוֹם. וְיָשׁוּב
attah hakol le'eitano harishon	עַתָּה הַכֹּל לְאֵיתָנוֹ הָרִאשׁוֹן
venir'atah hakeshet sas umitpa'eir	וְנִרְאָתָה הַקֶּשֶׁת שָׂשׂ וּמִתְפָּאֵר
begavonim. Vechol hannitzotzot	בְּגָווֹנִים. וְכָל הַנִּצוֹצוֹת
shennitpazzeru al yadeinu o al	שֶׁנִּתְפַּזְּרוּ עַל יָדֵינוּ אוֹ עַל
yedei avoteinu uve'avon adam	יְדֵי אֲבוֹתֵינוּ וּבְעֲוֹן אָדָם
harishon asher chata vefeirot	הָרִאשׁוֹן אֲשֶׁר חָטָא בְּפֵירוֹת
ha'ilan attah yashuvu lehitkalleil	הָאִילָן עַתָּה יָשׁוּבוּ לְהִתְכַּלֵּל
be'oz hadar eitz hachayim.	בְּעוֹז הֲדַר עֵץ הַחַיִּים.

O God, who makes, forms, creates, and emanates the highest worlds! You made the trees and grasses grow from the ground in the shape and pattern of these highest worlds. And this full moon is the beginning of Your work to renew and ripen the fruit trees, for so will be ripened the fruit of the highest tree, "the Tree of Life in the midst of the garden." May it be Your will, O Lord, our God, and the God of our ancestors, that our eating and blessing these fruits, and our meditating over their roots above, will strengthen the flow of love and blessing and free gift over the trees, to make them grow and bloom, for good life, for blessing and for peace. May the whole Creation return again to its original strength, and may the rainbow appear rejoicing and beautiful in its colors. And may all the sparks of divinity, scattered by our hands, or by the hands of our ancestors, or by the sin of the first human against the fruit of the tree, be restored and included in the majestic might of the Tree of Life.

Notes

Purim

THE HOLIDAY OF Purim celebrates the salvation of the Jewish people from a decree of annihilation by the evil Haman. It is observed by reading the Scroll of Esther, giving gifts of food to others, giving charity to the poor, and enjoying a festive meal.

Maimonides writes that the essence of Purim is to praise God and make it known that He is always near whenever we call out to Him (Deuteronomy 4:7). According to the sages, Esther's call for a three-day fast was actually a call for prayer, which led to the people's salvation. Purim demonstrates the power of prayer and is traditionally a particularly auspicious time to call out to God.

We Thank You for the Miracles

The following prayer is added to the silent *Amida* and the Grace After Meals on Purim. It thanks God for the salvation and miracles He performed for our forefathers during the time of Mordecai and Esther.

Al hannissim ve'al happurkan	עַל הַנִּסִּים וְעַל הַפֻּרְקָן
ve'al haggevurot ve'al hatteshu'ot	וְעַל הַגְּבוּרוֹת וְעַל הַתְּשׁוּעוֹת
ve'al hammilchamot she'asita	וְעַל הַמִּלְחָמוֹת שֶׁעָשִׂיתָ
la'avoteinu bayyamim haheim	לַאֲבוֹתֵינוּ בַּיָּמִים הָהֵם
bazzeman hazzeh:	בַּזְּמַן הַזֶּה:
Bimei moredechai ve'esteir	בִּימֵי מָרְדְּכַי וְאֶסְתֵּר
beshushan habbirah keshe'amad	בְּשׁוּשַׁן הַבִּירָה כְּשֶׁעָמַד

aleihem haman harasha bikkeish
lehashmid laharog ule'abbeid
et-kol-hayyehudim minna'ar
ve'ad-zakein taf venashim
beyom echad bishloshah asar
lechodesh sheneim-asar hu-
chodesh adar ushelalam lavoz:
ve'attah berachamecha harabbim
heifarta et-atzato vekilkalta et-
machashavto vahasheivota lo
gemulo berosho vetalu oto ve'et-
banav al-ha'etz.

עֲלֵיהֶם הָמָן הָרָשָׁע בִּקֵּשׁ
לְהַשְׁמִיד לַהֲרֹג וּלְאַבֵּד
אֶת־כָּל־הַיְּהוּדִים מִנַּעַר
וְעַד־זָקֵן טַף וְנָשִׁים
בְּיוֹם אֶחָד בִּשְׁלוֹשָׁה עָשָׂר
לְחֹדֶשׁ שְׁנֵים־עָשָׂר הוּא־
חֹדֶשׁ אֲדָר וּשְׁלָלָם לָבוֹז:
וְאַתָּה בְּרַחֲמֶיךָ הָרַבִּים
הֵפַרְתָּ אֶת־עֲצָתוֹ וְקִלְקַלְתָּ אֶת־
מַחֲשַׁבְתּוֹ וַהֲשֵׁבוֹתָ לּוֹ
גְּמוּלוֹ בְּרֹאשׁוֹ וְתָלוּ אוֹתוֹ וְאֶת־
בָּנָיו עַל־הָעֵץ.

[We thank You] for the miracles, for the redemption, for the mighty deeds, for the deliverances and for the wars that You performed for our fathers in those days at this season.

In the days of Mordecai and Esther in Shushan the Capital [of Persia], when the evil Haman rose up against them, he sought to destroy, to kill, and to annihilate all the Jews, young and old, infants and women, in one day, the thirteenth day of the twelfth month, which is the month of Adar, and to plunder their wealth— And You, in Your abundant mercy, annulled his counsel, frustrated his intention, and brought his evil plan upon his own head, and they hanged him and his sons upon the gallows.

Psalm 22

It is customary to recite Psalm 22 on Purim. According to the sages, Esther recited this prayer on her way to Ahasuerus' throne room. They also interpret the verses of this psalm as alluding to the events described in the Book of Esther. The psalm underscores the importance of having faith

לַמְנַצֵּחַ עַל־אַיֶּלֶת הַשַּׁחַר מִזְמוֹר לְדָוִד: אֵלִי אֵלִי לָמָה עֲזַבְתָּנִי רָחוֹק מִישׁוּעָתִי דִּבְרֵי שַׁאֲגָתִי: אֱלֹהַי אֶקְרָא יוֹמָם וְלֹא תַעֲנֶה וְלַיְלָה וְלֹא־דֻמִיָּה לִי: וְאַתָּה קָדוֹשׁ יוֹשֵׁב תְּהִלּוֹת יִשְׂרָאֵל: בְּךָ בָּטְחוּ אֲבֹתֵינוּ בָּטְחוּ וַתְּפַלְּטֵמוֹ: אֵלֶיךָ זָעֲקוּ וְנִמְלָטוּ בְּךָ בָטְחוּ וְלֹא־ בוֹשׁוּ: וְאָנֹכִי תוֹלַעַת וְלֹא־אִישׁ חֶרְפַּת אָדָם וּבְזוּי עָם: כָּל־רֹאַי יַלְעִגוּ לִי יַפְטִירוּ בְשָׂפָה יָנִיעוּ רֹאשׁ: גֹּל אֶל־יְהֹוָה יְפַלְּטֵהוּ יַצִּילֵהוּ כִּי חָפֵץ בּוֹ: כִּי־אַתָּה גֹחִי מִבָּטֶן מַבְטִיחִי עַל־ שְׁדֵי אִמִּי: עָלֶיךָ הָשְׁלַכְתִּי מֵרָחֶם מִבֶּטֶן אִמִּי אֵלִי אָתָּה: אַל־תִּרְחַק מִמֶּנִּי כִּי־צָרָה קְרוֹבָה כִּי־אֵין עוֹזֵר: סְבָבוּנִי פָּרִים רַבִּים אַבִּירֵי בָשָׁן כִּתְּרוּנִי: פָּצוּ עָלַי פִּיהֶם אַרְיֵה טֹרֵף וְשֹׁאֵג: כַּמַּיִם נִשְׁפַּכְתִּי וְהִתְפָּרְדוּ כָּל־ עַצְמוֹתָי הָיָה לִבִּי כַּדּוֹנָג נָמֵס בְּתוֹךְ

Lammenatzeach al-ayyelet hashachar mizmor ledavid. Eli eli lamah azavtani rachok mishu'ati divrei sha'agati. Elohai ekra yomam velo ta'aneh vela'yyelah velo-dumiyyah li. Ve'attah kadosh yosheiv tehillot yisra'el. Becha batechu avoteinu batechu vattefalleteimo. Eilecha za'aku venimlatu becha vatechu velo-voshu. Ve'anochi tola'at velo-ish cherpat adam uvezui am. Kol-ro'ai yal'igu li yaftiru vesafah yani'u rosh. Gol el-adonai yefalleteihu yatzileihu ki chafeitz bo. Ki-attah gochi mibbaten mavtichi al-shedei immi. Alecha hoshlachti meirachem mibbeten immi eli attah. Al-tirchak mimmenni ki-tzarah kerovah ki-ein ozer. Sevavuni parim rabbim abbirei vashan kitteruni. Patzu alai pihem aryeih toreif vesho'eig. Kammayim nishpachti vehitparedu kol-atzmotai hayah libbi kaddonag nameis betoch

mei'ai. Yaveish kacheres kochi
uleshoni mudbak malkochai
vela'afar-mavet tishpeteini. Ki
sevavuni kelavim adat merei'im
hikkifuni ka'ari yadai veraglai.
Asapper kol-atzmotai heimmah
yabbitu yir'u-vi. Yechalleku
vegadai lahem ve'al-levushi
yappilu goral. Ve'attah adonai
al-tirchak eyaluti le'ezrati chushah.
Hatzilah meicherev nafshi miyyad-
kelev yechidati. Hoshi'eini mippi
aryeh umikkarnei reimim anitani.
Asapperah shimcha le'echai
betoch kahal ahallekka. Yir'ei
adonai hal'luhu kol-zera ya'akov
kabbeduhu veguru mimmennu
kol-zera yisra'el. Ki lo-vazah velo
shikkatz enut ani velo-histir panav
mimmennu uveshavve'o eilav
shamei'a. Mei'ittecha tehillati
bekahal rav nedarai ashalleim
neged yerei'av. Yochlu anavim
veyisba'u yehal'lu adonai
doreshav yechi levavchem la'ad.
Yizkeru veyashuvu el-adonai
kol-afsei-aretz veyishtachavu
lefanecha kol-mishpechot goyim.
Ki ladonai hammeluchah umosheil
baggoyim. Achelu vayyishtachavu
kol-dishnei-eretz lefanav yichre'u
kol-yoredei afar venafsho lo
chiyyah. zera ya'avdennu

מֵעָי: יָבֵשׁ כַּחֶרֶשׂ כֹּחִי
וּלְשׁוֹנִי מֻדְבָּק מַלְקוֹחָי
וְלַעֲפַר־מָוֶת תִּשְׁפְּתֵנִי: כִּי
סְבָבוּנִי כְּלָבִים עֲדַת מְרֵעִים
הִקִּיפוּנִי כָּאֲרִי יָדַי וְרַגְלָי:
אֲסַפֵּר כָּל־עַצְמוֹתָי הֵמָּה
יַבִּיטוּ יִרְאוּ־בִי: יְחַלְּקוּ
בְגָדַי לָהֶם וְעַל־לְבוּשִׁי
יַפִּילוּ גוֹרָל: וְאַתָּה יְהוָה
אַל־תִּרְחָק אֱיָלוּתִי לְעֶזְרָתִי חוּשָׁה:
הַצִּילָה מֵחֶרֶב נַפְשִׁי מִיַּד־
כֶּלֶב יְחִידָתִי: הוֹשִׁיעֵנִי מִפִּי
אַרְיֵה וּמִקַּרְנֵי רֵמִים עֲנִיתָנִי:
אֲסַפְּרָה שִׁמְךָ לְאֶחָי
בְּתוֹךְ קָהָל אֲהַלְלֶךָּ: יִרְאֵי
יְהוָה הַלְלוּהוּ כָּל־זֶרַע יַעֲקֹב
כַּבְּדוּהוּ וְגוּרוּ מִמֶּנּוּ
כָּל־זֶרַע יִשְׂרָאֵל: כִּי לֹא־בָזָה
וְלֹא שִׁקַּץ עֱנוּת עָנִי וְלֹא־הִסְתִּיר
פָּנָיו מִמֶּנּוּ וּבְשַׁוְּעוֹ
אֵלָיו שָׁמֵעַ: מֵאִתְּךָ
תְהִלָּתִי בְּקָהָל רָב נְדָרַי
אֲשַׁלֵּם נֶגֶד יְרֵאָיו: יֹאכְלוּ
עֲנָוִים וְיִשְׂבָּעוּ יְהַלְלוּ יְהוָה
דֹּרְשָׁיו יְחִי לְבַבְכֶם לָעַד:
יִזְכְּרוּ וְיָשֻׁבוּ אֶל־יְהוָה
כָּל־אַפְסֵי־אָרֶץ וְיִשְׁתַּחֲווּ
לְפָנֶיךָ כָּל־מִשְׁפְּחוֹת גּוֹיִם:
כִּי לַיהוָה הַמְּלוּכָה וּמֹשֵׁל
בַּגּוֹיִם: אָכְלוּ וַיִּשְׁתַּחֲווּ
כָּל־דִּשְׁנֵי־אֶרֶץ לְפָנָיו יִכְרְעוּ
כָּל־יוֹרְדֵי עָפָר וְנַפְשׁוֹ
לֹא חִיָּה: זֶרַע יַעַבְדֶנּוּ

yesuppar ladonai laddor. Yavo'u
veyaggidu tzidkato le'am nolad ki
asah.

יְסֻפַּר לַאדֹנָי לַדּוֹר: יָבֹאוּ
וְיַגִּידוּ צִדְקָתוֹ לְעַם נוֹלָד כִּי
עָשָׂה:

For the leader; on ayyeleth ha-shahar. A psalm of David. My God, my God, why have You abandoned me; why so far from delivering me and from my anguished roaring? My God, I cry by day—You answer not; by night, and have no respite. But You are the Holy One, enthroned, the Praise of Israel. In You our fathers trusted; they trusted, and You rescued them. To You they cried out and they escaped; in You they trusted and were not disappointed. But I am a worm, less than human; scorned by men, despised by people. All who see me mock me; they curl their lips, they shake their heads. "Let him commit himself to the Lord; let Him rescue him, let Him save him, for He is pleased with him." You drew me from the womb, made me secure at my mother's breast. I became Your charge at birth; from my mother's womb You have been my God. Do not be far from me, for trouble is near, and there is none to help. Many bulls surround me, mighty ones of Bashan encircle me. They open their mouths at me like tearing, roaring lions. My life ebbs away: all my bones are disjointed; my heart is like wax, melting within me; my vigor dries up like a shard; my tongue cleaves to my palate; You commit me to the dust of death. Dogs surround me; a pack of evil ones closes in on me, like lions [they maul] my hands and feet. I take the count of all my bones while they look on and gloat. They divide my clothes among themselves, casting lots for my garments. But You, O Lord, be not far off; my strength, hasten to my aid. Save my life from the sword, my precious life from the clutches of a dog. Deliver me from a lion's mouth; from the horns of wild oxen rescue me. Then will I proclaim Your fame to my brethren, praise You in the congregation. You who fear the Lord, praise Him! All you offspring of Jacob, honor Him! Be in dread of Him, all you offspring of Israel! For He did not scorn, He did not

spurn the plea of the lowly; He did not hide His face from him;
when he cried out to Him, He listened. Because of You I offer praise
in the great congregation; I pay my vows in the presence of His
worshipers. Let the lowly eat and be satisfied; let all who seek the
Lord praise Him. Always be of good cheer! Let all the ends of the
earth pay heed and turn to the Lord, and the peoples of all nations
prostrate themselves before You; for kingship is the Lord's and
He rules the nations. All those in full vigor shall eat and prostrate
themselves; all those at death's door, whose spirits flag, shall bend
the knee before Him. Offspring shall serve Him; the Lord's fame
shall be proclaimed to the generation to come; they shall tell of His
beneficence to people yet to be born, for He has acted.

The Rose of Jacob

It is customary to recite the following paragraph after reading the Scroll of Esther. In the Song of Songs, the people of Israel are compared to a rose, and in this paragraph, they are referred to as the "Rose of Jacob." This brief passage reiterates the outcome of the Purim story, blessing its heroes and cursing its villains.

Shoshannat ya'akov tzahalah	שׁוֹשַׁנַּת יַעֲקֹב צָהֲלָה
vesameichah bir'otam yachad	וְשָׂמֵחָה בִּרְאוֹתָם יַחַד
techeilet moredechai teshu'atam	תְּכֵלֶת מָרְדְּכַי תְּשׁוּעָתָם
hayita lanetzach, tikvatam bechol	הָיִיתָ לָנֶצַח, תִּקְוָתָם בְּכָל
dor vador. Lehodia' shekkol	דּוֹר וָדוֹר. לְהוֹדִיעַ שֶׁכָּל
kovecha lo yeivoshu velo	קֹוֶיךָ לֹא יֵבֹשׁוּ וְלֹא
yikkalemu lanetzach kol hachosim	יִכָּלְמוּ לָנֶצַח כָּל הַחוֹסִים
bach. Arur haman asher bikeish	בָּךְ. אָרוּר הָמָן אֲשֶׁר בִּקֵּשׁ
l'abbedi baruch moredechai	לְאַבְּדִי בָּרוּךְ מָרְדְּכַי
hayyehudi. Arurah zeresh eishet	הַיְהוּדִי. אֲרוּרָה זֶרֶשׁ אֵשֶׁת

mafchidi beruchah ester ba'adi
vegam charvonah zachur lattov.

מַכְחִידִי בְּרוּכָה אֶסְתֵּר בַּעֲדִי
וְגַם חַרְבוֹנָה זָכוּר לַטּוֹב.

The rose of Jacob exulted and rejoiced when they saw Mordecai garbed in royal blue. You have always been their salvation, their hope in every generation. To make known that all who hope in You will not be shamed, nor will they be humiliated forever, all who trust in You. Cursed be Haman who sought to destroy me; blessed be Mordecai the Jew. Cursed be Zeresh, the wife of my terrorizer; blessed be Esther for [interceded] on my behalf. And may Charvonah also be remembered for good.

Notes

____

____

____

____

____

____

____

____

____

____

Sponsored by

Michele Burke

Trina Oshman

Israel Bible Plus

UNPACK THE BIBLE LIKE
NEVER BEFORE

Learn more at
israel365store.com